THE CAMPGROUNDS
OF
NEW YORK

A Guide to the

State Parks and

Public Campgrounds

Gary Hartman

THE CAMPGROUNDS OF NEW YORK
A Guide to the State Parks and Public Campgrounds

Copyright © 1997
by Gary Hartman
Third Edition 2002

ISBN 0-925168-49-1

Library of Congress Cataloging-in-Publication Data

Hartman, Gary, 1958-
 The Campgrounds of New York: a guide to the state parks and public campgrounds / by
Gary Hartman
 p.   cm.
 ISBN 0-925168-49-1 (alk. paper)
 1.   Camp sites, facilities, etc – New York (State) – Directories. 2. Camping – New York
(State) – Guidebooks. 3. New York (State) – Guidebooks. 1. Title.
 GV194.N7H37 1996
 796.54'025747-dc 20

96-14998
CIP

North Country Books, Inc
PUBLISHER – DISTRIBUTION
311 Turner Street
Utica, New York 13501

This guide is dedicated to my father-in-law

Robert Seils

for his love of camping and the outdoors

and

To my family

Barbara, Ben and Brian

for their support in making this book possible

Contents

Introduction

New York has camping facilities in 115 of its more than 200 state parks. Whether it is a weekend trip, a get-together with friends, or an annual family vacation, camping is a way to get away and enjoy the great outdoors.

The state parks and public campgrounds of New York offer a vast range of geographical landscapes, from lakeside beaches and rugged glens to the mountains of the Adirondacks and the Catskills. The variety of activities available range from playgrounds to bike trails, hiking nature trails to fishing, or canoeing a lake or river. Participating in a recreation program is also a popular activity for all ages.

The State Office of Parks, Recreation, and Historic Preservation operates the New York State Parks. The State Department of Environmental Conservation (DEC) operates the Public Campgrounds in the Adirondacks and Catskill Forest Preserves.

This guide was conceived in 1994 after several campgrounds began offering site-specific reservations. Our family visited and camped at a number of New York State Parks and desired to seek out new campgrounds within the state parks system. To help us choose a location and site prior to visiting, we wanted to see a map of the campground and park. The only means at that time for obtaining campground maps was either by visiting or writing the state park or public campground of choice. Today, the Internet has attempted to provide this information, but it is very time consuming to obtain the type of information for the state parks and public campground, which is provided in this guide. Also, it is not convenient while sitting around the campfire or picnic table discussing your next camping trip. It is my hope that you will find this guide helpful, easy to use, and comprehensive enough to help plan your next outing in any of New York's outstanding state parks and public campgrounds.

- Gary Hartman

Author's Note

Special thanks goes to Scott Krontilik and Andrew Moore, both of whom spent many hours between classes studying to create the campground maps for the first edition. Without their help, this book would not have been possible. Also, thanks to my wife, Barbara, for her support and input into the guide; Martin Webster, for his help with the layout and writing; and to Paul and Joan Hartman for the hours they spent proofreading.

The information contained in this guide is gathered from a variety of sources and is intended to provide the reader with useful facts that will help make every camping experience more informative and enjoyable. The New York State Office of Parks and Recreation, and the Department of Environmental Conservation agreed to provide current, accurate information for this guide. Also, thanks go to those people at the campgrounds who reviewed the summary and map pages. The author is not an agent of, nor does he represent the Office of Parks and Recreation or the Department of Environmental Conservation for the State of New York. The author is not responsible for the accuracy of the information herein and accepts no responsibility for any actions resulting from the contents of this guide.

How To Use This Guide

This guide has been designed to acquaint you with the campgrounds and state parks in New York *before you* visit them. Some of the campgrounds are very popular, while others are more secluded and less popular. Every effort has been made to give you all the available information for each state park and public campground; however, answers to specific questions may be obtained by calling or writing the particular state park, public campground, or regional office.

The State of New York has been separated into four map sections: Western, Northern, Southern, and Long Island. Each campground location is shown on these maps and has been assigned a map location number. Using the campground location number, you can easily look up the corresponding state park or public campground on the Campground Profile Chart. The profile chart summarizes the facilities and activities of each campground for quick and easy comparison. This chart also contains a letter symbol, which corresponds to the regional office. Addresses and phone numbers for the regional offices are listed for reference.

The Map Key shows the symbols used in the campground maps.

Each state park and public campground in this guide has a summary page and a campground map. They are listed in alphabetical order, which also corresponds to the numerical order in the profile chart. Almost all of the campgrounds have site-specific reservations, which can be made through the ReserveAmerica camping reservation system. The New York state map in the upper right hand corner of each summary page shows the map section, campground location number, and approximate location of the state park or public campground. Refer to the larger map sections for more exact locations.

An excellent resource for more specific location of the campground, nearby lakes and mountains, and other general information on things to do is "The New York State Atlas and Gazateer" by DeLorme. It can be found at most bookstores.

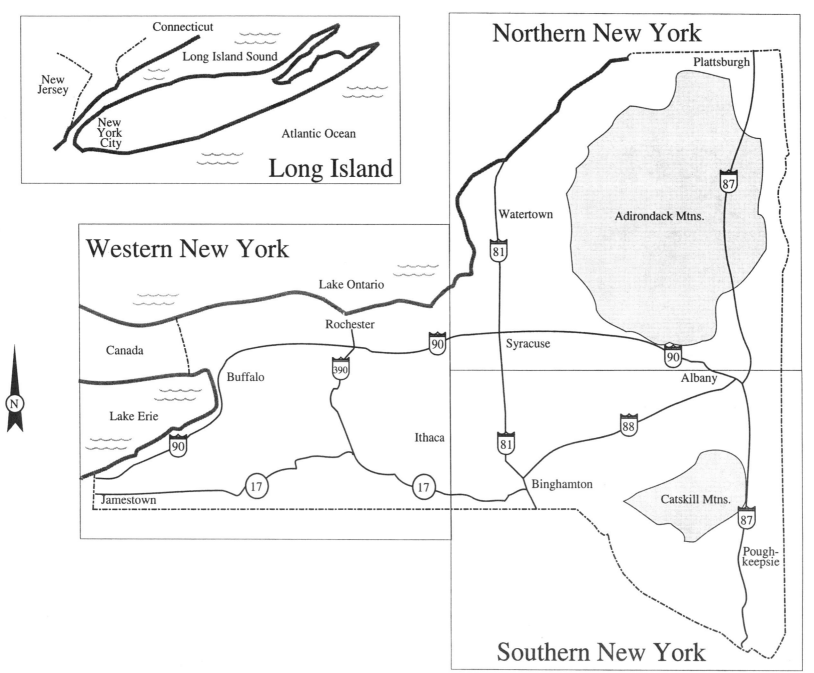

Connecticut

Long Island Sound

New Jersey

New York City

Atlantic Ocean

Long Island

Northern New York

Plattsburgh

Watertown

Adirondack Mtns.

87

81

Western New York

Lake Ontario

Canada

Rochester

Syracuse

Buffalo

390

90

90

Albany

Lake Erie

Ithaca

81

88

90

17

17

Binghamton

Catskill Mtns.

87

Jamestown

Pough-keepsie

N

Southern New York

See Long Island

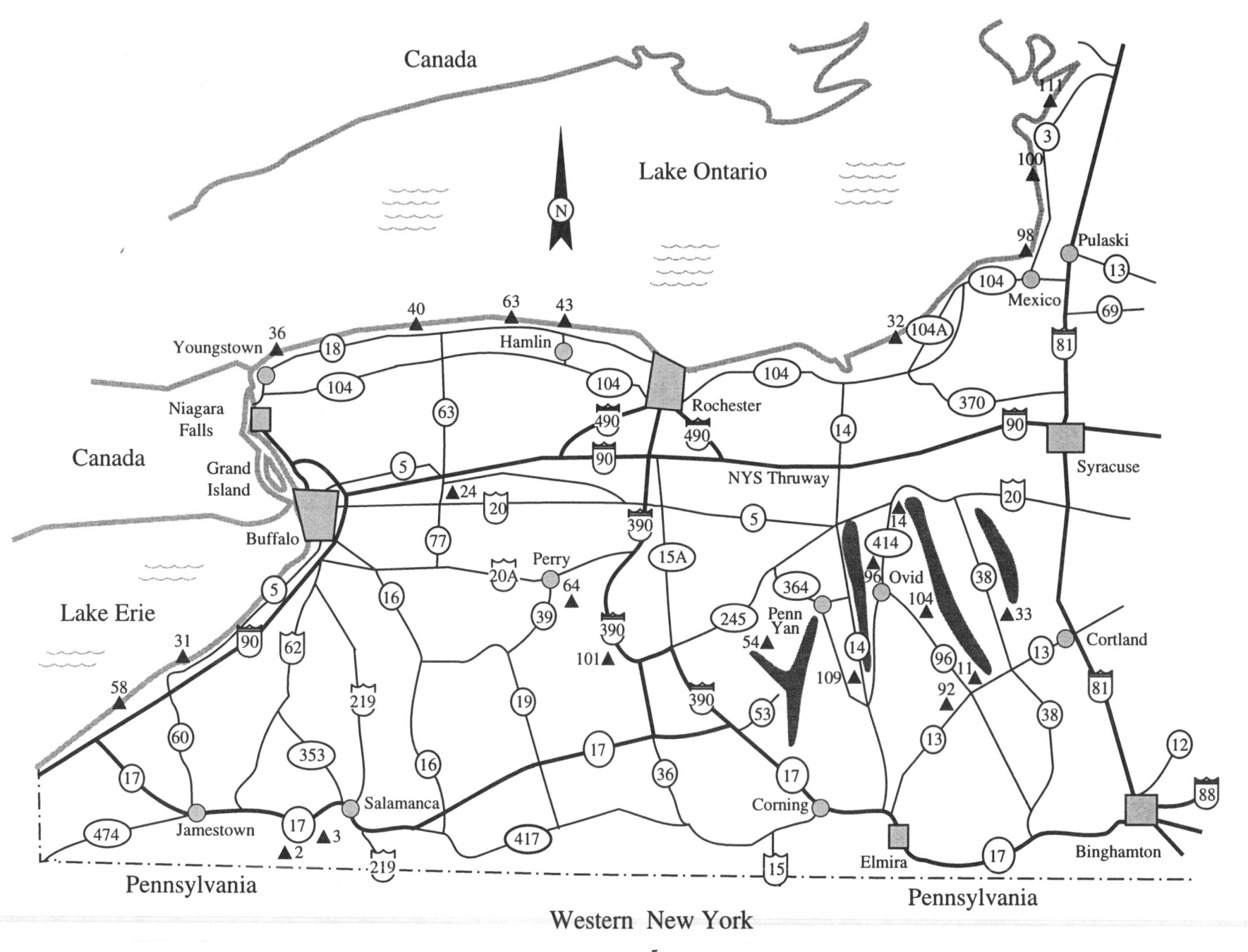

Western New York

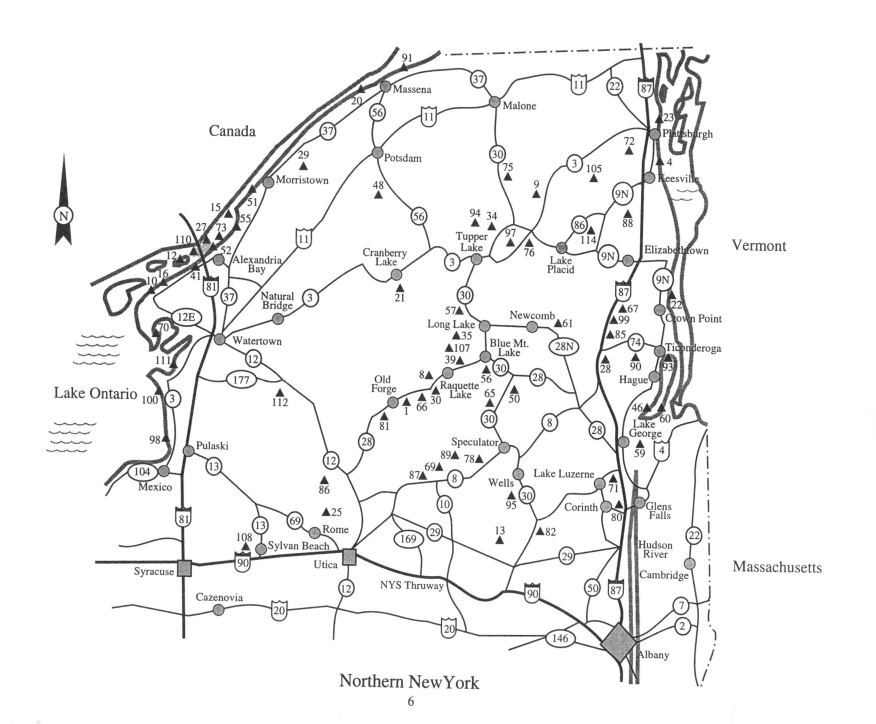

Northern New York

6

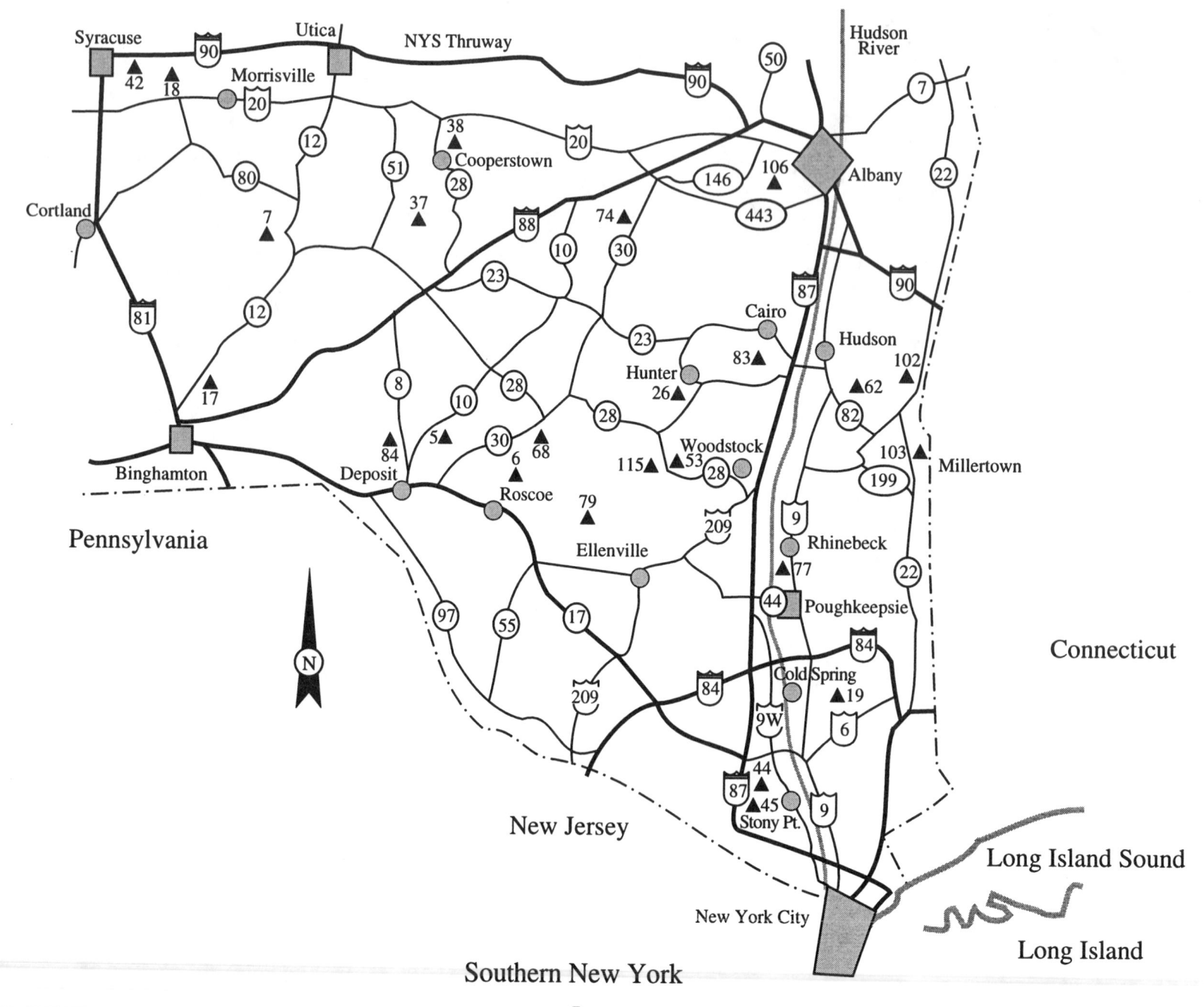

Southern New York

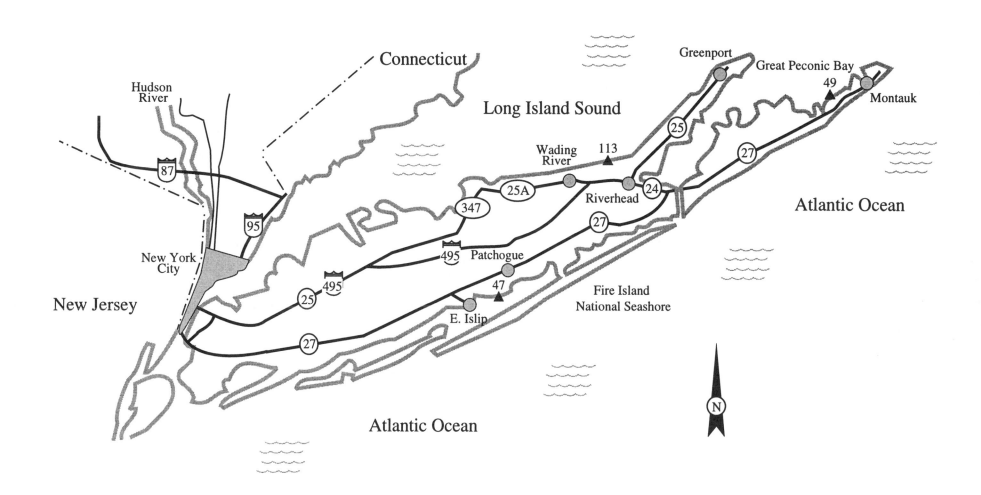

Long Island

8

Campground Profiles

State Map Location #	State Park or Public Campground	Map Region	Tent / Trailer Sites	Trailer Dump	Recycling	Cabins	Comfort Station-Flush Toilets	Pit / Vault / Solar Toilet	Showers	Potable/Drinking Water	Public Telephone	Pets Allowed	Handicapped Accessible	Picnic Area	Picnic Pavilion	Recreation Program	Hiking / Nature Trail	Exercise Course	Swimming / Beach	Swimming / Pool	Bath House	Fishing	Dock / Pier	Bicycling / Rollerblading	Ball Field / Soccer Field	Basketball Court	Horseshoe Pits	Playground	Tennis Courts	Volleyball Court	Golf Course	Hunting	Bridle Trails	Pond / Lake / Ocean	River / Stream / Creek	Boat Launch	Cartop Launch	Powerboats	Marina	Boat Rental	Cross Country Skiing	Ice Fishing	Ice Skating	Sledding Hills	Snowshoeing	Snowmobiling	Store / Concession	Regional Offices	Page Number
1	Alger Island	North	17					•		•		•		•			•		•			•	•						•						•				•										Q	23
2	Allegany: Quaker	West	164	•		•	•		•	•	•	•	•	•	•	•	•		•		•	•		•		•							•	•	•	•	•				•		•	•	•	•	•	A	27
3	Allegany: Red House	West	139	•		•	•		•	•		•	•	•	•	•	•		•		•	•		•		•	•	•	•	•			•	•	•	•	•				•	•		•	•	•	•	•	A	29
4	Ausable Point	North	120	•	•		•		•	•		•	•						•		•	•		•		•		•		•						•	•		•	•									P	31
5	Bear Spring Mountain	South	41	•	•			•		•	•	•	•		•			•		•		•	•	•						•	•	•	•	•						•	•								L	33
6	Beaverkill	South	107	•	•		•		•	•		•		•					•		•	•							•				•														K	35
7	Bowman Lake	South	210	•	•		•		•	•	•		•	•	•	•	•		•			•		•		•		•		•				•		•						•	•				•	•	B	37
8	Brown Tract Pond	North	90	•	•			•		•		•		•					•			•		•		•				•		•				•				•								M	41
9	Buck Pond	North	114	•	•			•	•	•	•	•		•					•		•	•		•		•		•	•	•				•														P	43
10	Burnham Point	North	49	•				•	•	•	•	•							•	•						•		•	•	•	•				•													J	45
11	Buttermilk Falls	West	45	•	•	•	•		•	•		•	•	•	•	•		•		•	•		•					•		•	•				•						•								C	47
12	Canoe Point	North	25		•	•	•			•		•	•	•					•	•			•		•		•		•		•				•				•									J	51
13	Caroga Lake	North	158	•			•	•	•	•	•	•	•	•	•		•	•	•	•			•					•		•																	N	53
14	Cayuga Lake	West	286	•		•	•		•	•	•	•	•					•		•	•		•			•		•		•				•				•	•	•		•		•		C	55
15	Cedar Island	North	18			•			•		•	•	•	•					•	•			•		•		•		•		•				•												J	57
16	Cedar Point	North	174	•	•		•		•	•	•	•	•						•	•	•		•	•		•		•		•				•	•	•	•	•	•							J	59
17	Chenango Valley	South	216	•		•	•		•	•	•	•	•	•	•	•	•		•		•	•		•			•		•	•				•	•					•	•	•	•		•	B	61
18	Chittenango Falls	South	22			•		•	•	•	•	•	•	•				•		•		•		•	•		•		•				•												B	65
19	Clarence Fahnestock	South	80			•		•	•		•	•	•	•	•	•		•		•		•		•				•	•	•		•		•		•	•	•	•	•	•		I	67
20	Coles Creek	North	235	•			•		•	•	•	•	•	•	•		•		•		•	•	•		•		•	•	•	•	•			•	J	71
21	Cranberry Lake	North	163	•	•		•		•	•	•	•	•		•	•		•		•	•	•	•		•		•	•	•			•	R	73
22	Crown Point Reservation	North	66	•	•		•		•	•	•	•	•						•	•	•	•		•		•	•		P	75
23	Cumberland Bay	North	207	•		•		•	•	•	•	•	•		•			•		•	•	•	•	•	•		•	•	J	77
24	Darien Lake	West	155	•			•		•	•	•	•	•	•		•		•		•	•	•	•	•	•	•	•	•		•	•		•	D	79
25	Delta Lake	North	101	•	•		•		•	•	•	•	•		•			•		•	•	•	•	•	•		•		•	•	•	•	•	•	•	•	B	83
26	Devil's Tombstone	South	24			•		•	•	•	•	•		•	•								•		•			•	L	85
27	Dewolf Point	North	14			•	•		•	•		•		•					•			•		•			•	•	•			•	J	87
28	Eagle Point	North	72	•	•			•	•	•	•	•		•					•		•	•		•		•		•	O	89
29	Eel Weir	North	34			•		•	•	•	•	•	•					•			•		•	•	•	J	91
30	Eighth Lake	North	111	•			•		•	•	•	•		•			•		•	•	•	•		•		•		•	•	M	93

State Map Location #	State Park or Public Campground	Map Region	Tent / Trailer Sites	Trailer Dump	Recycling	Cabins	Comfort Station-Flush Toilets	Pit / Vault / Solar Toilet	Showers	Potable/Drinking Water	Public Telephone	Pets Allowed	Handicapped Accessible	Picnic Area	Picnic Pavilion	Recreation Program	Hiking / Nature Trail	Exercise Course	Swimming / Beach	Swimming / Pool	Bath House	Fishing	Dock / Pier	Bicycling / Rollerblading	Ball Field / Soccer Field	Basketball Court	Horseshoe Pits	Playground	Tennis Courts	Volleyball Court	Golf Course	Hunting	Bridle Trails	Pond / Lake / Ocean	River / Stream / Creek	Boat Launch	Cartop Launch	Powerboats	Marina	Boat Rental	Cross Country Skiing	Ice Fishing	Ice Skating	Sledding Hills	Snowshoeing	Snowmobiling	Store / Concession	Regional Offices	Page Number
31	Evangola	West	122	•			•			•	•	•	•	•	•	•	•	•		•		•	•		•	•	•	•	•		•				•																93
32	Fair Haven Beach	West	185	•		•	•		•	•	•	•	•	•	•	•	•	•		•		•	•		•	•	•	•	•							•							•					•	•	F	95
33	Fillmore Glen	West	70	•		•	•		•	•		•	•	•	•	•	•	•		•	•	•	•					•				•		•		•		•	•	•	•	•	•		•	•	•	C	97
34	Fish Creek Pond	North	355	•	•		•		•	•	•	•	•	•	•		•		•		•			•		•	•			•						•				•						•		C	99
35	Forked Lake	North	77					•		•				•			•		•		•			•					•						•		•		•									P	101
36	Four Mile Creek	West	278	•			•			•		•	•	•	•			•		•					•					•		•		•		•										M	103
37	Gilbert Lake	South	221	•		•	•		•	•	•	•	•	•	•		•		•		•					•			•						•										•	F	105
38	Glimmerglass	South	83	•		•	•		•	•	•	•	•	•	•	•	•	•		•	•	•		•				•			•		•		•				•	•		•	•	B	107
39	Golden Beach	North	186	•	•		•		•	•	•	•	•	•		•		•		•	•	•					•			•		•		•		•	•	•	•	•		•		B	109
40	Golden Hill	West	50	•	•		•		•	•		•	•	•		•	•		•					•					•		•		•		•									M	111
41	Grass Point	North	77	•			•		•	•	•	•	•	•		•		•		•	•					•			•						•		•					•	•	F	113
42	Green Lakes	South	137	•		•	•		•	•	•	•	•	•	•		•		•	•	•				•			•		•	•		•	•	•						•	J	115
43	Hamlin Beach	West	264	•			•		•	•	•	•	•	•	•	•	•	•		•	•	•					•			•		•						•		•	B	117
44	Harriman - Beaver Pond	South	146	•			•		•	•	•	•	•	•	•		•		•		•							•		•				•		•					•	•	D	119
45	Harriman - Sebago Cabins	South	41		•	•	•	•	•		•				•		•		•		•					•		•		•				•							•	G	123
46	Hearthstone Point	North	241	•	•		•		•	•	•	•	•	•		•		•	•	•	•	•	•	•		•			•		•				•	•					•	G	125
47	Heckscher	L. I.	69	•			•		•	•	•	•	•	•		•		•		•					•			•		•											O	127
48	Higley Flow	North	135	•			•		•	•	•	•	•	•	•	•		•	•	•	•	•					•			•		•	•	•		•				•	•	E	129
49	Hither Hills	L. I.	167	•	•		•		•	•	•	•	•		•		•		•	•	•					•		•		•		•			•		•			•	•	J	131
50	Indian Lake Islands	North	51				•			•			•			•			•		•			•				•		•				•				•		•	E	133
51	Jacques Cartier	North	94	•			•		•	•	•	•	•	•		•		•		•					•			•		•		•	•									M	137
52	Keewaydin	North	39				•		•	•	•	•	•	•		•	•	•	•		•			•			•		•	•		•	•				•		•	J	139
53	Kenneth L. Wilson	South	62	•			•		•	•	•	•	•	•	•		•	•	•		•			•			•		•	•	•	•	•		•			•	J	141
54	Keuka Lake	West	150	•			•		•	•	•	•	•	•	•		•		•	•	•	•	•		•			•		•		•		•				K	143
55	Kring Point	North	86	•		•	•		•	•	•	•	•	•	•	•		•		•			•	•			•			•	•		•			•			•	•	C	145
56	Lake Durant	North	56	•	•		•		•	•		•	•	•	•			•		•			•	•			•	•		•	•	•	•							J	147
57	Lake Eaton	North	134	•	•		•		•	•		•	•	•	•			•		•	•	•	•					•			•		•						M	149
58	Lake Erie	West	102	•		•	•		•	•	•	•	•	•	•	•		•		•	•	•					•			•		•		•					P	151
59	Lake George Battleground	North	63	•	•		•		•	•	•	•	•	•	•	•		•		•	•	•	•					•			•		•	•		•			•	•	A	153
60	Lake George Islands	North	366			•				•	•		•		•		•				•														•			O	155
							•					•	•		•			•						•			•						•		•	•	•							O	157

State Map Location #	State Park or Public Campground	Map Region	Tent / Trailer Sites	Trailer Dump	Recycling	Cabins	Comfort Station-Flush Toilets	Pit / Vault / Solar Toilet	Showers	Potable/Drinking Water	Public Telephone	Pets Allowed	Handicapped Accessible	Picnic Area	Picnic Pavilion	Recreation Program	Hiking / Nature Trail	Exercise Course	Swimming / Beach	Swimming / Pool	Bath House	Fishing	Dock / Pier	Bicycling / Rollerblading	Ball Field / Soccer Field	Basketball Court	Horseshoe Pits	Playground	Tennis Courts	Volleyball Court	Golf Course	Hunting	Bridle Trails	Pond / Lake / Ocean	River / Stream / Creek	Boat Launch	Cartop Launch	Powerboats	Marina	Boat Rental	Cross Country Skiing	Ice Fishing	Ice Skating	Sledding Hills	Snowshoeing	Snowmobiling	Store / Concession	Regional Offices	Page Number
61	Lake Harris	North	88	●	●		●		●	●		●	●	●			●		●		●	●	●											●			●	●		●								P	161
62	Lake Taghkanic	South	61			●	●		●	●		●	●	●	●		●		●		●	●						●			●			●			●			●	●	●	●			●	●	I	163
63	Lakeside Beach	West	274	●		●		●	●	●		●	●	●	●		●				●			●	●	●	●	●	●			●		●						●						●	●	D	165
64	Letchworth	West	270	●		●	●		●	●	●	●	●	●	●	●		●			●		●		●			●		●		●			●	●	●					●		●		●	●	●	D	167
65	Lewey Lake	North	209	●	●		●		●	●	●	●	●		●			●		●		●	●	●											●		●		●		●								M	171
66	Limekiln Lake	North	254	●	●		●		●	●	●	●	●		●			●		●		●	●	●											●		●		●		●								M	173
67	Lincoln Pond	North	35	●			●		●	●	●		●		●			●		●		●	●												●		●	●			●								P	175
68	Little Pond	South	66	●	●			●	●	●	●		●		●			●		●			●												●		●				●								L	177
69	Little Sand Point	North	76	●			●			●	●	●		●			●		●			●	●												●		●		●		●								N	179
70	Long Point	North	86	●			●		●	●		●	●			●			●	●	●								●		●		●			●			●	●								J	181
71	Luzerne	North	166	●	●		●		●	●	●	●	●		●		●			●		●	●	●					●	●		●			●	●		●		●								O	183
72	Macomb Reservation	North	170	●			●		●	●	●	●	●	●	●		●	●	●	●	●	●	●	●				●						●	●		●			●		●		●	●			J	185
73	Mary Island	North	12			●			●			●			●							●	●												●		●			●									J	187
74	Max V. Shaul	South	29			●	●	●	●	●		●	●	●			●				●						●	●	●	●							●			●									H	189
75	Meacham Lake	North	224	●			●		●	●	●	●	●	●	●	●		●		●		●	●						●						●	●	●		●		●								P	191
76	Meadowbrook	North	62	●			●		●	●	●	●	●	●				●				●																											P	193
77	Mills - Norrie	South	51	●		●	●		●	●		●	●				●			●			●							●			●	●		●	●		●	●		●		●		●		I	195
78	Moffitt Beach	North	253	●	●		●		●	●		●	●	●		●		●		●		●	●						●						●		●		●		●								N	199
79	Mongaup Pond	South	142	●	●		●	●	●	●	●	●	●		●		●	●	●		●								●	●	●		●			●			●			●					●		K	201
80	Moreau Lake	North	148	●			●		●	●	●	●	●	●	●	●		●		●		●	●	●					●	●	●		●			●		●		●	●	●		●			●	●	H	203
81	Nick's Lake	North	104	●	●		●		●	●	●	●	●	●	●	●		●		●		●	●	●	●	●	●	●	●						●			●											Q	205
82	Northampton Beach	North	223	●	●		●		●	●	●	●	●	●	●	●		●		●		●	●						●						●		●		●		●								N	207
83	North-South Lake	South	202	●	●		●		●	●	●	●	●	●	●	●		●		●		●	●						●	●	●		●			●		●											L	209
84	Oquaga Creek	South	95	●			●		●	●	●	●	●	●	●	●		●		●		●	●	●				●					●			●		●		●		●	●		●	●		●	B	211
85	Paradox Lake	North	58	●	●		●		●	●	●	●	●		●			●		●		●	●												●		●		●		●	●	●	●					P	213
86	Pixley Falls	North	22			●		●	●	●		●	●	●			●					●				●		●					●	●		●						●				●			B	215
87	Point Comfort	North	65	●	●			●		●		●	●	●		●		●		●		●	●												●		●		●		●								N	217
88	Poke-O-Moonshine	North	25			●		●	●		●		●		●			●				●																											P	219
89	Poplar Point	North	21			●		●		●	●	●		●		●		●		●		●	●												●		●	●	●		●								N	221
90	Putnam Pond	North	63	●	●		●		●	●	●	●	●	●	●			●		●		●	●												●	●	●		●		●								P	223

State Map Location #	State Park or Public Campground	Map Region	Tent / Trailer Sites	Trailer Dump	Recycling	Cabins	Comfort Station-Flush Toilets	Pit / Vault / Solar Toilet	Showers	Potable/Drinking Water	Public Telephone	Pets Allowed	Handicapped Accessible	Picnic Area	Picnic Pavilion	Recreation Program	Hiking / Nature Trail	Exercise Course	Swimming / Beach	Swimming / Pool	Bath House	Fishing	Dock / Pier	Bicycling / Rollerblading	Ball Field / Soccer Field	Basketball Court	Horseshoe Pits	Playground	Tennis Courts	Volleyball Court	Golf Course	Hunting	Bridle Trails	Pond / Lake / Ocean	River / Stream / Creek	Boat Launch	Cartop Launch	Powerboats	Marina	Boat Rental	Cross Country Skiing	Ice Fishing	Ice Skating	Sledding Hills	Snowshoeing	Snowmobiling	Store / Concession	Regional Offices	Page Number
91	Robert Moses	North	168	●		●	●		●	●	●	●	●	●	●	●	●		●		●	●		●	●		●	●	●	●	●			●		●		●	●	●	●	●	●		●	●		J	225
92	Robert H. Treman	West	72	●		●	●		●	●		●	●	●	●	●		●		●		●	●					●		●					●						●							●	C	229
93	Rogers Rock	North	299	●	●		●		●	●	●	●	●			●		●		●		●	●		●			●							●		●		●		●								O	233
94	Rollins Pond	North	288	●	●		●		●	●	●	●	●			●		●		●		●						●							●		●	●	●		●								P	235
95	Sacandaga	North	137	●	●		●		●	●	●	●				●				●		●													●	●													N	237
96	Sampson	West	344	●	●		●		●	●	●	●	●	●	●	●	●	●		●		●	●		●	●	●	●	●		●				●		●		●	●		●			●	●	●	●	C	239
97	Saranac Lake Islands	North	79					●			●		●							●		●													●		●	●	●	●									P	241
98	Selkirk Shores	North	148	●	●		●		●	●	●	●	●	●		●		●		●		●	●					●							●	●		●			●						●	●	B	243
99	Sharp Bridge	North	40	●			●	●	●	●			●							●		●						●								●													P	247
100	Southwick	North	110	●			●		●	●		●	●			●	●	●	●	●		●	●		●			●							●		●			●					●			●	J	249
101	Stony Brook	West	125	●			●		●	●		●	●			●		●					●			●			●							●					●					●			●	C	251
102	Taconic - Copake Falls	South	112	●	●	●	●		●	●			●	●	●	●		●		●	●		●						●	●						●	●					●			●		●		I	255
103	Taconic - Rudd Pond	South	41		●			●	●	●	●		●					●		●	●		●						●							●		●			●	●		●					I	257
104	Taughannock Falls	West	74	●		●	●		●	●	●	●	●	●	●	●		●		●	●		●						●	●	●					●		●	●	●	●	●		●	●			●	C	259
105	Taylor Pond	North	30				●	●		●		●	●	●		●				●		●							●							●		●	●	●		●								P	261
106	Thompson's Lake	South	140	●			●		●	●	●	●	●			●	●		●		●							●								●		●			●	●	●							H	263
107	Tioga Point	North	25					●			●		●							●		●							●							●			●											M	265
108	Verona Beach	North	45	●			●		●	●	●	●	●	●	●	●			●		●	●		●		●	●		●		●	●	●									●	●			●	●	●	B	269
109	Watkins Glen	West	303	●			●		●	●			●	●	●	●			●		●	●							●		●	●	●			●					●			●	●			●	C	271
110	Wellesley Island	North	459	●		●	●		●	●	●	●	●	●	●	●		●		●		●	●	●	●			●							●		●	●	●	●	●	●	●	●			●	●	●	J	273
111	Wescott Beach	North	166	●			●		●	●	●	●	●	●		●		●		●	●		●	●			●								●		●		●	●		●			●		●	●	J	275
112	Whetstone Gulf	North	62	●			●		●	●	●	●	●	●			●	●	●		●	●		●							●						●		●	●		●			●	●			J	277
113	Wildwood	L. I.	320	●			●		●	●			●	●		●	●		●		●	●		●	●		●						●						●									●	E	279
114	Wilmington Notch	North	54	●	●		●		●	●		●				●				●																●													P	283
115	Woodland Valley	South	60	●	●		●		●	●	●	●	●	●		●				●																●													K	285

12

New York State Parks

Office of Parks and Recreation Regional Offices

Allegany Region

A   Office of Parks and Recreation – Allegany Region   (716) 354-9101
Salamanca, NY 14779

Central Region

B   Office of Parks and Recreation – Central Region   (315) 492-1756
Clark Reservation, Jamestown, NY 13078

Finger Lakes Region

C   Office of Parks and Recreation – Finger Lakes Region   (607) 387-7041
P. O. Box 1055, Trumansburg, NY 14886

Genesee Region

D   Office of Parks and Recreation –Genesee Region   (585) 493-3600
1 Letchworth State Park, Castile, NY 14427

Long Island Region

E   Office of Parks and Recreation – Long Island Region   (516) 669-1000
P. O. Box 247, Babylon, NY 11702

Niagara Frontier Region

F   Office of Parks and Recreation – Niagara Frontier Region   (716) 278-1770

Prospect Park, Niagara Falls, NY 14303

Palisades Region

G   Office of Parks and Recreation – Palisades Region   (914) 786-2701

Bear Mountain, NY 10911

Saratoga - Capital Region

H   Office of Parks and Recreation – Saratoga-Capital Region   (518) 584-2000

19 Roosevelt Drive, Saratoga Springs, NY 12866

Taconic Region

I   Office of Parks and Recreation – Taconic Region   (914) 889-4100

Staatsburg, NY 12580

Thousand Islands Region

J   Office of Parks and Recreation – Thousand Islands Region   (315) 482-2593

P. O. Box 247, Alexandria Bay, NY 13607

Adirondacks and Catskill Public Campgrounds

Department of Environmental Conservation Regional Offices

Region 1

K   Department of Environmental Conservation   (914) 256-3000

21 South Putts Corners Road, New Paltz, NY 12561

Region 2

L   Department of Environmental Conservation   (518) 327-2068

1150 North Wescott Road, Schenectady, NY 12306

Region 3

M   Department of Environmental Conservation   (518) 648-5616

Big Brook Road, Indian Lake, NY 12842

Region 4

N   Department of Environmental Conservation   (518) 863-8216

Main Street Extension, Northville, NY 12134

Region 5

O   Department of Environmental Conservation   (518) 623-3671
Hudson Street Extension, Warrensburg, NY 12885

Region 6

P   Department of Environmental Conservation   (518) 891-1370
Ray Brook, NY 12977

Region 7

Q   Department of Environmental Conservation   (315) 866-6330
255 North Main Street, Herkimer, NY 13350

Region 8

R   Department of Environmental Conservation   (315) 386-4546
30 Court Street, Canton, NY 13617

Special Services

ReserveAmerica Camping and Cabin Reservations

ReserveAmerica is the camping and cabin reservation system for all New York State Parks and Public Campgrounds. While reservations are not required, they are highly recommended, especially at popular campgrounds. To make a reservation by phone through **ReserveAmerica**, you may call between 2 days and 11 months prior to the 1st night of camping. Less than 2 days prior to your 1st nights stay, you need to contact the campground park office. There is a reservation service fee charged for each site reserved and there are restrictions for cancellations and refunds.

Reservations can be made by calling: **1-800-456-CAMP** or **1-800-456-2267**

Reservations can be made via the Internet: **http://www.reserveamerica.com**

Hours of operation:	March 15 – Labor Day	8 AM – 8 PM (EST) 7 days a week
		9 AM – 3 PM (EST) Saturday and Sunday
	Tuesday after Labor Day – March 14	9 AM – 5 PM (EST) Monday – Friday

Forms for camping and cabin reservations are also available by mail from or by calling:

State Parks
Albany, NY 12338

or

Department of Environmental Conservation
50 Wolf Road
Albany, NY 12233

Phone (518) 474-0456

Phone (518) 474-0456

Group Camping

Group Camping is available at Allegany, Beaverkill, Chenango Valley, Clarence Fahnestock, Darien Lake, Harriman, Higley Flow, Letchworth, Moreau Lake, Rogers Rock, Watkins Glen, and Wellesley Island state parks. Reservation procedures and details are available from the state parks or their regional offices.

Golden Park Program

Senior Citizens who are New York State residents and are at least 62 years of age have unlimited weekday and non-holiday access to all state parks. Discounts on certain fees are applicable by showing a driver's license or other identification.

Empire Passport

The **Empire Passport** provides unlimited vehicle entry to most New York State Parks and recreation areas during the calendar year from April 1 to March 31. This pass does not cover activity fees. Purchase of this passport can be made at most of the state parks or recreation areas or by mail from:

State Parks   Albany, NY 12238

Access Pass

The **Access Pass** is available to residents of New York with qualifying disabilities. This pass provides free entry and use of state parks and recreation areas and their facilities. It <u>does</u> <u>not</u> include those facilities and services that are concessionaire operated. Application forms are available from:

State Parks   Albany, NY 12238

General Information

Camping and Day Use

Almost all the state parks and public campgrounds offer facilities and activities for campers and day users. Campers are usually required to only pay fees for campsites, but are allowed throughout the park. Day users pay a daily fee and are required to leave by the park closing time. See the section on Special Services for information on discounts and passes.

Campsites

All sites, except where noted, have enough room for at least one tent, one vehicle, a rain or dining tarp, a picnic table and fireplace. Fireplaces are usually either a deep metal ring type or a three-sided stone or cement structure, and generally have a wide grate over them.

Some campgrounds have an additional fee for "prime sites", which are usually very popular or at the water's edge. Occasionally, the campgrounds add, eliminate, or rearrange campsites. The campsite information contained in this book is based on the configuration of the campground in the year 2000. Check with either **ReserveAmerica** or the campground for more specific information on these sites.

Drinking Water

Except where noted, drinking or potable water is available via spigots throughout the park. The designated spots are located on the campground maps. Most of the water systems are not insulated against freezing; and therefore, those parks open during the late fall and winter generally turn off the water systems when the temperature approaches freezing.

Comfort Stations and Showers

Comfort stations and shower are found at the majority of the campgrounds. The facilities vary in that sometimes the comfort stations and showers are combined into one building and in the other cases they are separate buildings. Comfort stations consist of a minimum of flush toilets and a sink. In some campgrounds, an electric outlet can be found in all comfort stations and in others, electric outlets can be found only where the shower facilities are located.

Recycling

An increasing number of parks realize the environmental benefit of recycling and they encourage campers to utilize the recycling centers where available. In addition to the campground effort to recycle, more and more of the day-use and picnic areas are designated as "Carry-In / Carry-Out".

Pet Policy

The following is a general guideline used by most of the state parks and public campground concerning pets:

1. Pets shall at all times be under the supervision of the owner or person having custody and shall be confined in a cage or on a leash not exceeding six feet in length.
2. Every dog shall be licensed under the laws of the state of residence of its owner and shall have a current rabies vaccination. The person having pet custody must be prepared to present a proof of compliance with this requirement.
3. No pet shall be allowed to be a nuisance or to interfere with the activities of any park patron.
4. Any person having custody of any pet shall be responsible for cleaning up and disposing of pet waste.

Picnic Areas

Picnic areas are usually found in scenic locations and / or near water. Fireplaces vary from a hibachi-style grill to a stone or cement fireplace. Rest rooms of some type are typically available near the picnic area.

Picnic Pavilions

Most of the state parks and public campgrounds have picnic pavilions (this is indicated on the summary page and campground map). Although some of the pavilions are enclosed, most are opened and covered. At specified campgrounds, picnic pavilions are reservable and calling the state park or public campground can reserve them.

Recreation Programs

Portions of the campgrounds have staffed recreations programs, which generally run from late June through Labor Day. Activities vary and are designed for all ages. See the Campground Profile Chart for those campgrounds, which participate in this activity.

Swimming

Almost all of the state parks and public campgrounds have a lifeguarded swimming area. The majority of the parks have sand beaches. Lifeguards are on duty starting from mid to late June through Labor Day.

Boating and Fishing

Boating and fishing are popular activities for campers as roughly 70% of the parks have boat launches of some type. Boat launches have a dock located with them unless they are a cartop launch. The term "cartop launch" means that there is no access for a trailer. Large boat owners may want to call ahead to check the launch facilities and conditions. Those parks only accessible by boat are designated in the campground summary. Some of the parks have a marina within or adjacent to the park for launching boats.

Fishing can either be from the shoreline, a dock or pier, or from a boat on the lake or river.

Boat Rental

Boat rental is available as noted on the campground summary page and it can include rowboats, canoes, paddleboats, and/or motorized boats. Rentals are either facilitated by the campground, a private vendor, or at a local marina. Please check with the specific campground concerning their boat rentals.

Winter Activities

Typical winter activities available at those parks open year-round include cross country skiing, snowshoeing, ice fishing, ice skating, sledding and snowmobiling. Many of the roads are plowed, and a few of the parks offer shelter and rest rooms.

Map Key

🏠	Bathhouse	Ⓟ	Parking Area
	Beach Area	🏕	Picnic Area
	Boat Launch with Dock		Picnic Pavilion
3	Cabin (number represents cabin #3)		Playground
C	Caretaker's Cabin	RC	Recycling Center
	Comfort Station (flush toilet & sink)	R	Registration
	Dock		Showers
25	Campsite - Non Electric		Swimming
(25)	Campsite - Electric		Telephone
	Fishing	T	Toilet - Pit, Vault, or Solar
	Handicapped Accessible		Trailer Dump
	Hiking / Nature Trail	•	Water - Potable / Drinking
	Lean - To		

Alger Island Public Campground

Petrie Road, Old Forge, NY 13420

(315) 369–3224

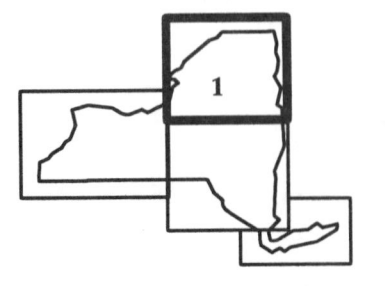

- Located 8 miles east of Old Forge off State Route 28 in the middle of Fourth Lake
- Open mid–May through Labor Day for camping
- **Boat Access Only** (island is approximately 1/2 mile from Fourth Lake Picnic Area which has a cartop launch only, for boats or trailers use the public launch at Inlet which is approximately 5 miles to the east)
- 15 Lean–To Sites (no electric, 6 persons per lean–to)
- 2 Tent Sites (not numbered)
- 45 Acres
- Pit Toilets
- Potable Water
- Pets Allowed
- Picnic Area
- Hiking Trail (around island)
- Swimming (no designated area)
- Fishing in Fourth Lake
- Boat Docks and Boat House
- Log Cabin

Note: Cribbing is rocks retained by wire mesh

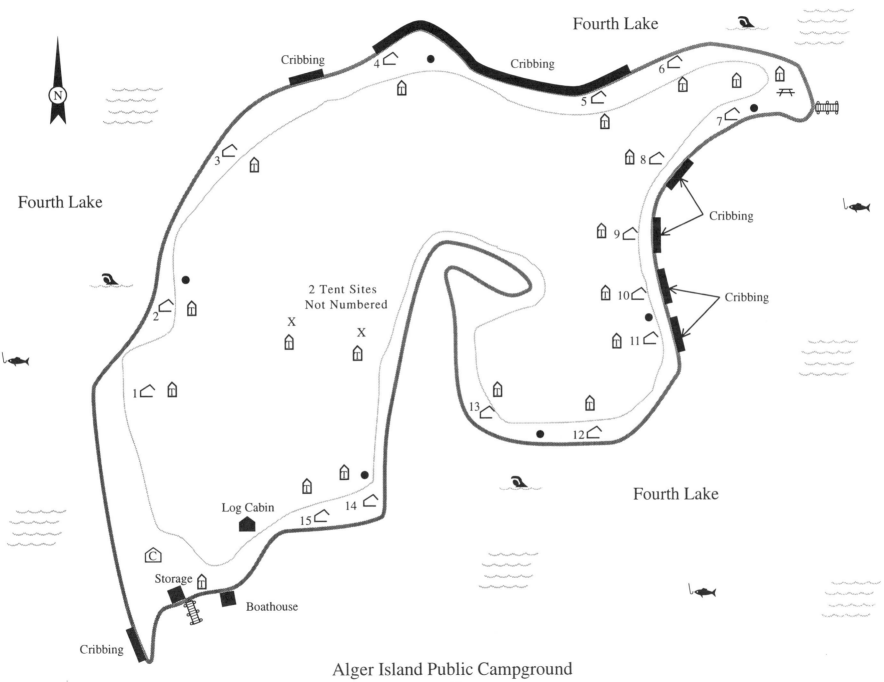

Fourth Lake

Cribbing

Fourth Lake

Cribbing

4

5

6

7

8

Cribbing

9

10

Cribbing

11

N

Fourth Lake

3

2

2 Tent Sites
Not Numbered

X

X

1

13

12

Fourth Lake

Log Cabin

14

15

C

Storage

Boathouse

Cribbing

Alger Island Public Campground

24

Allegany State Park

(see pages 27-30 for campground information and maps on Quaker and Red House Areas)

Quaker Cabin Area - Open All Year

Weller

Camp Turner

Barton

ASP Route 1

Camp 5

Ward

Amphitheater

ASP Route 3

Diehl Tent & Trailer Area

Ranger

Creekside

Pine Tree

Angle Buffalo

ASP Route 3

Washhouse

Hamlin

Horseshoe

Stony

Rental Office

Fancher

Parallel

Quaker Inn

Indian

Store

Reed

Kaiser

Tennis Courts

Brow

Circle

Maintenance Area

Ball Field

Coon

Gypsy

N

Red House Cabin Area - Open All Year

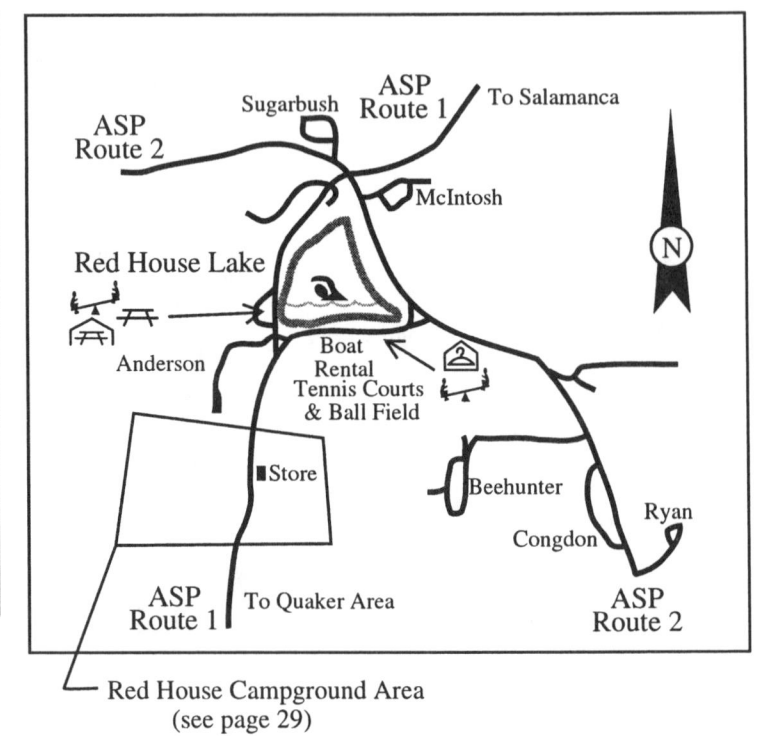

ASP Route 2

Sugarbush

ASP Route 1

To Salamanca

N

McIntosh

Red House Lake

Boat Rental

Anderson

Tennis Courts & Ball Field

Store

Beehunter

Ryan

Congdon

ASP Route 1

To Quaker Area

ASP Route 2

Red House Campground Area
(see page 29)

Notes: 1. ASP = Allegany State Parkway
2. Names represent cabin areas and most cabins have centrally located water and toilets

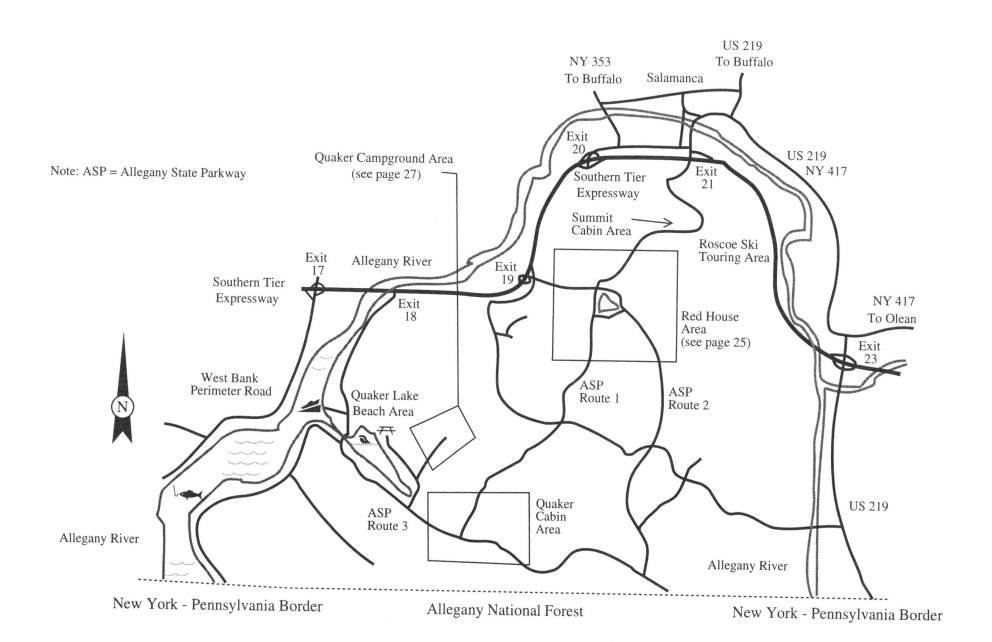

Note: ASP = Allegany State Parkway

Quaker Campground Area (see page 27)

NY 353 To Buffalo

US 219 To Buffalo

Salamanca

Exit 20

Southern Tier Expressway

US 219 NY 417

Summit Cabin Area

Exit 21

Roscoe Ski Touring Area

Exit 17

Allegany River

Southern Tier Expressway

Exit 19

Exit 18

Red House Area (see page 25)

NY 417 To Olean

Exit 23

West Bank Perimeter Road

Quaker Lake Beach Area

ASP Route 1

ASP Route 2

ASP Route 3

Quaker Cabin Area

Allegany River

US 219

Allegany River

New York - Pennsylvania Border

Allegany National Forest

New York - Pennsylvania Border

Allegany State Park

Allegany State Park – Quaker Area

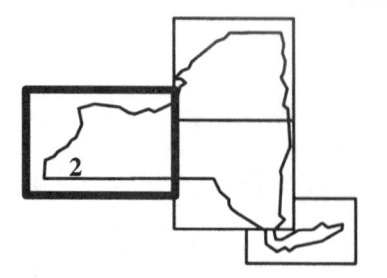

ASP Route 3, Salamanca, NY 14779

(716) 354–2182

- Located 15 miles southwest of Salamanca off State Park Route 280
- Open mid–May through mid–October for camping
- State Park is Open All Year
- 164 Tent & Trailer Sites (94 electric sites, trailer dump)
- 230 Cabins (see page 25 for locations)
- 32,500 Acres
- Comfort Station (flush toilets & sink) and Showers
- Potable Water
- Public Telephone
- Pets Allowed
- Handicapped Accessible
- Picnic Area (at Quaker Lake Beach Area)
- Picnic Pavilion (reservable at Quaker Cabin Area – Gypsy found on page 25)
- Recreation Program and Hunting
- Hiking and Nature Trails (within approximate 1/4 mile)
- Swimming with Sand Beach (at Quaker Lake – approximately 2 miles west)
- Fishing in Quaker Lake and Allegheny River
- Bicycling on Campground Roads, Playground and Tennis Courts (at Quaker Cabin Area)
- Bridle Trails (throughout the park at designated areas)
- Boat Launches (Quaker Lake and Allegheny Reservoir – approximately 3 miles northeast)
- Cross Country Skiing (Roscoe Ski Touring), Snowshoeing, Snowmobiling, and Sledding Hills
- Store and Quaker Inn

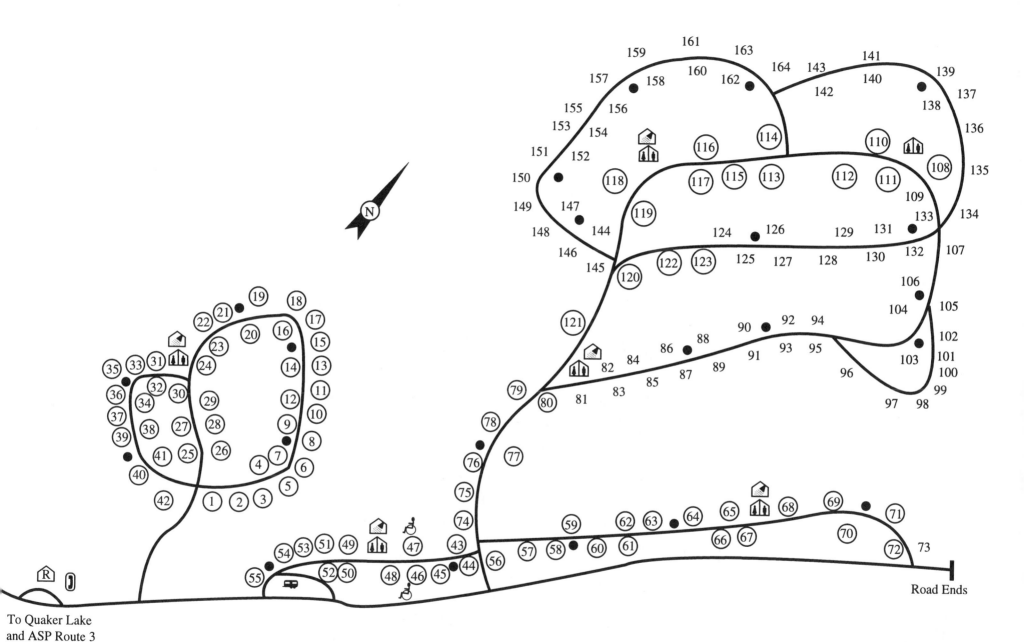

Allegany State Park - Quaker Area

28

Allegany State Park – Red House Area

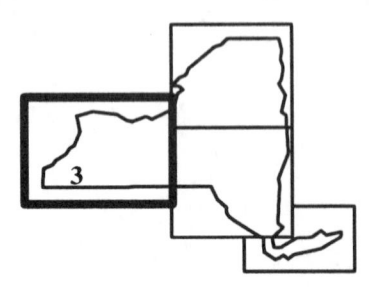

2373 ASP Route 1, STE 3, Salamanca, NY 14779

(716) 354–9121

- Located 6 miles southwest of Salamanca off State Park Route 17
- Open April through mid–December for camping
- State Park is Open All Year
- 139 Tent & Trailer Sites (66 electric sites, trailer dump)
- 144 Cabins (see page 26 for locations)
- 32,500 Acres
- Comfort Station (flush toilets & sink) and Showers
- Potable Water (throughout campground)
- Pets Allowed
- Handicapped Accessible
- Picnic Area (at Red House Lake) and Pavilions (2 reservable at Red House Lake)
- Recreation Program
- Hiking Trails (within approximately 1/4 mile)
- Swimming with Sand Beach (at Red House Lake – approximately 1 mile north)
- Bicycling on Campground Roads and Hunting
- Bridle Trails (throughout the park at designated areas)
- Fishing in Red House Lake, Stoddard Creek, and Allegany River
- Tennis, Basketball Courts, Horseshoe Pits, Baseball Fields, and Playground
- Boat Launch (no motor boats, cartop launch at Red House Lake)
- Rowboat, Paddleboat, and Bike Rental (at Red House Lake)
- Cross Country Skiing, Snowshoeing, Snowmobiling, and Sledding Hills
- Store

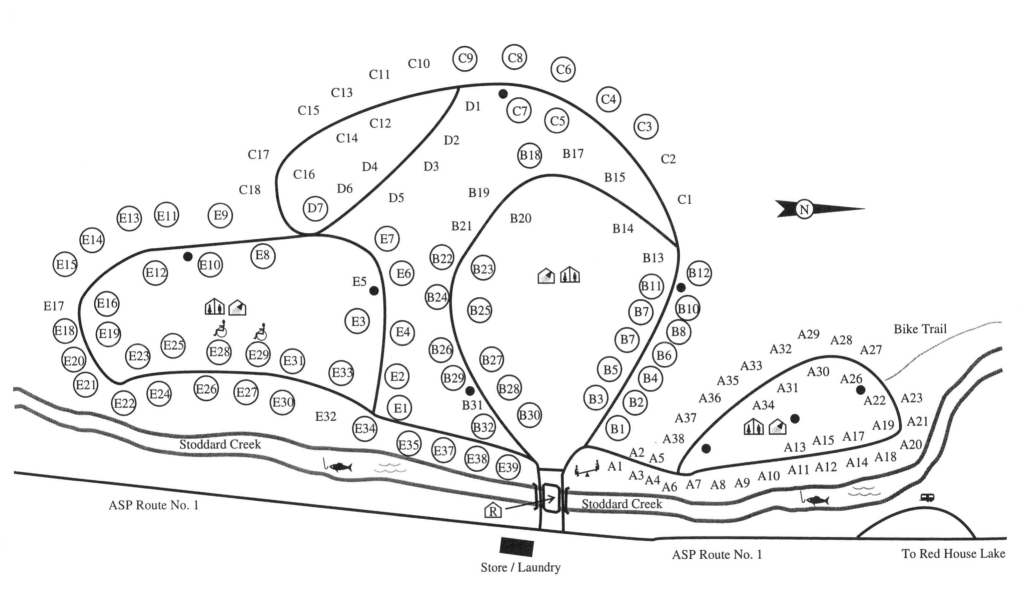

Allegany State Park - Red House Area

30

Ausable Point Public Campground

3346 Lake Shore Road, Peru, NY 12972

(518) 561–7080

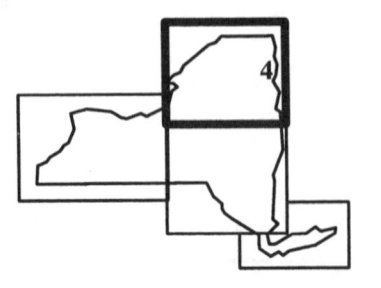

- Located 12 miles south of Plattsburgh or 3 miles north of Keeseville off US 9
- Open mid–May through mid–October for camping
- 120 Tent & Trailer Sites (43 electric sites, trailer dump, max RV 40 foot)
- 75 Acres
- Comfort Station (flush toilets & sink) and Showers
- Potable Water
- Pets Allowed
- Handicapped Accessible
- Picnic Area
- Picnic Pavilion (reservable)
- Swimming with Sand Beach and Bath House
- Fishing in Dead Creek, Ausable River, and Lake Champlain
- Bicycling and Rollerblading on Campground Roads
- Basketball, Volleyball and Playground
- Boat Launch (cartop only)
- Boat Rental (4 miles north off US 9)

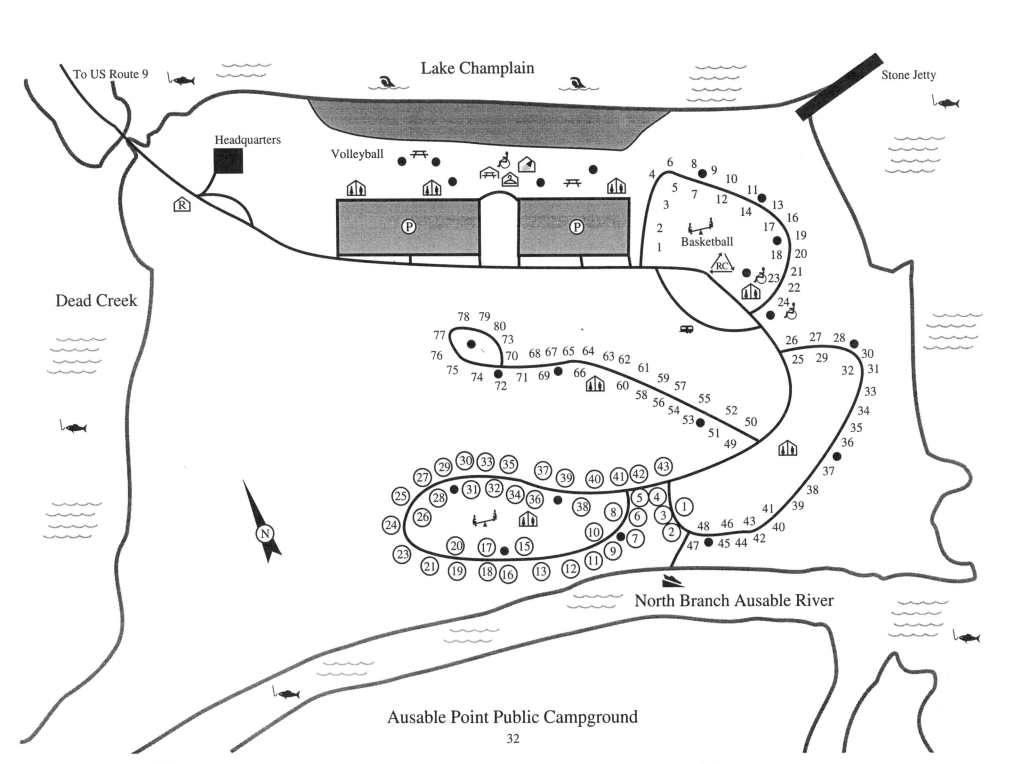

Lake Champlain

To US Route 9

Stone Jetty

Headquarters

Dead Creek

Volleyball

Basketball

RC

North Branch Ausable River

Ausable Point Public Campground

N

32

Bear Spring Mountain Public Campground

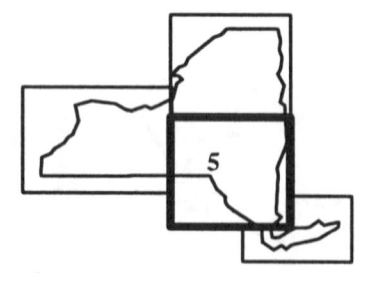

HC 63, Box 30, Downsville, NY 13755

(607) 865–6989

- Located 5 miles southeast of Walton off Route 206
- Open mid–May through mid–October for camping
- 41 Tent & Trailer Sites (no electric sites, trailer dump)
- 31 Acres
- Vault and Solar Toilets
- Potable Water (throughout campground)
- Public Telephone
- Pets Allowed
- Handicapped Accessible
- Picnic Areas
- Picnic Pavilion (reservable)
- Hiking Trails
- Swimming with Sand Beach and Bath House
- Fishing in Launt Pond and East Trout Brook
- Dock
- Hunting
- Bridle Trails (24 miles on adjacent wildlife area)
- Boat Launch (no motors boats)
- Rowboat and Canoe Rental (at park office)
- Horse Stalls, Corral, and Stud Pen
- Cross Country Skiing

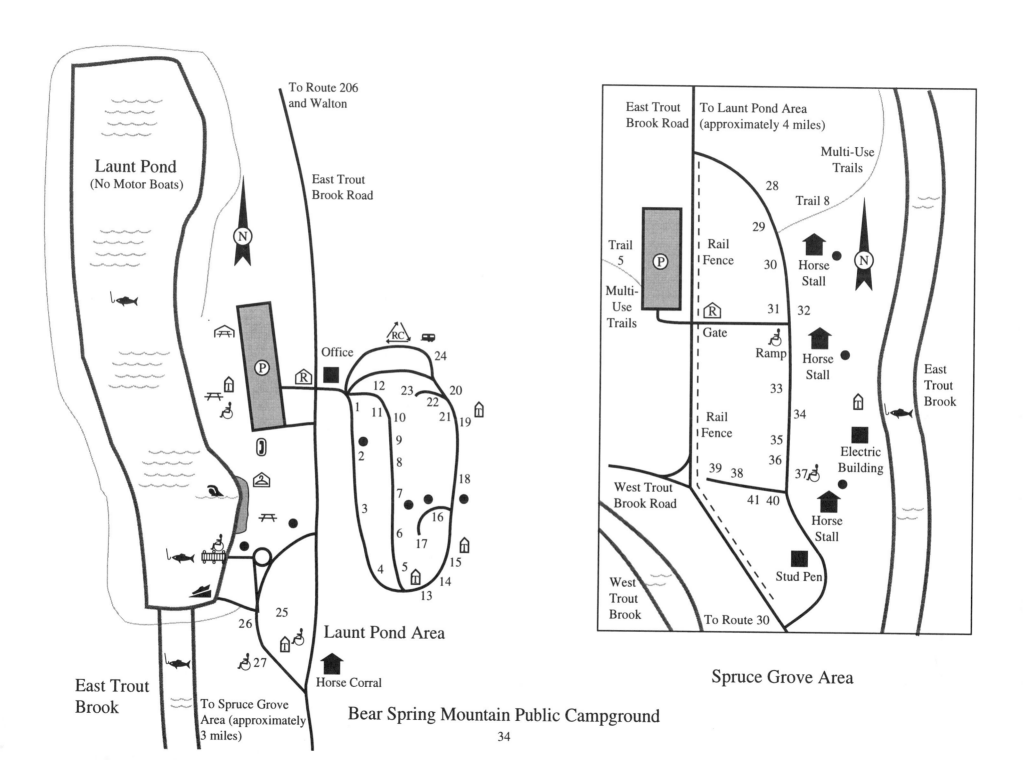

Launt Pond
(No Motor Boats)

To Route 206
and Walton

East Trout
Brook Road

N

Office

RC

Office

24

12
23
20
1
11
10
22
21
19
9
2
8
18
7
16
3
17
6
4
5
14
13
15

25
26
27

East Trout
Brook

To Spruce Grove
Area (approximately
3 miles)

Horse Corral

Launt Pond Area

East Trout
Brook Road

To Launt Pond Area
(approximately 4 miles)

Multi-Use
Trails

28

Trail 8

29

Trail
5

Rail
Fence

P

30

Horse
Stall

N

31
32

Multi-
Use
Trails

R

Gate

Ramp

33

Horse
Stall

East
Trout
Brook

Rail
Fence

34

35

36

Electric
Building

39
38

37

West Trout
Brook Road

41
40

Horse
Stall

West
Trout
Brook

Stud Pen

To Route 30

Spruce Grove Area

Bear Spring Mountain Public Campground

Beaverkill Public Campground

RR 3, Box 243, Roscoe, NY 12776

(914) 439–4281

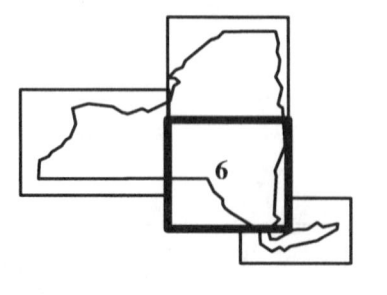

- Located 7 miles northwest of Livingston Manor off State Route 151 or 6 miles northeast of Roscoe off State Route 206
- Open mid–May through Labor Day for camping
- 107 Tent & Trailer Sites (no electric sites, trailer dump)
- 62 Acres
- Comfort Station (flush toilets & sink) and Showers
- Potable Water
- Pets Allowed
- Picnic Area
- Hiking Trails (within approximately 6 miles)
- Swimming and Bath House
- Fishing in Beaverkill River
- Day Use Area

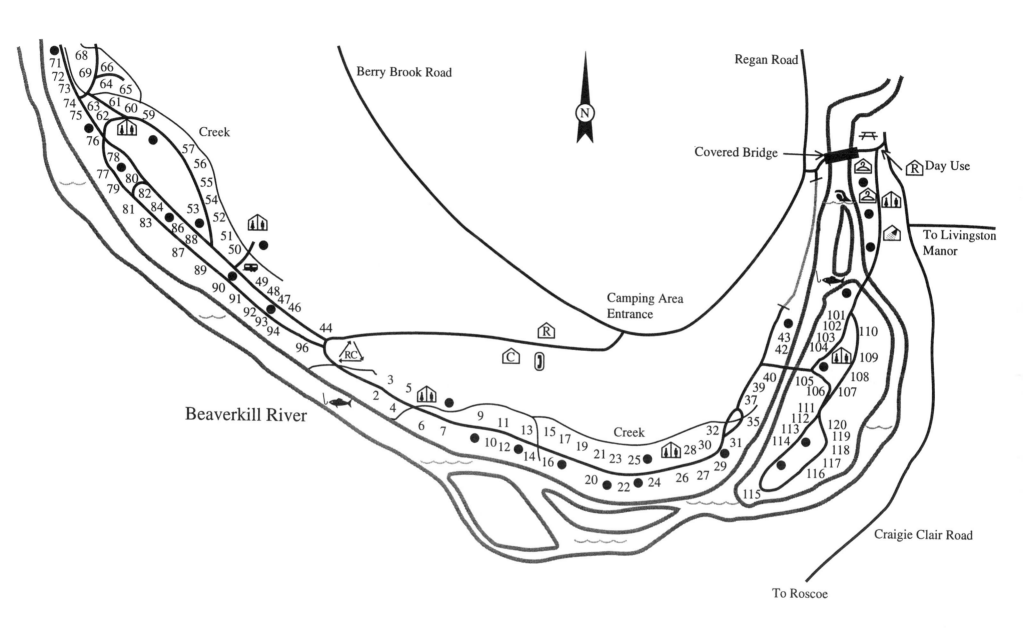

Beaverkill Public Campground

Bowman Lake State Park

745 Bliven Sherman Road, Oxford, NY 13830

(607) 334–2718

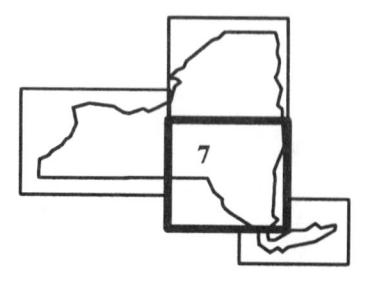

- Located 8 miles northwest of Oxford off State Route 220
- State Park is Open All Year for camping
- 210 Tent & Trailer Sites (no electric sites, 158 trailer sites, trailer dump)
- 653 Acres
- Comfort Station (flush toilets & sink) and Showers
- Potable Water
- Public Telephone
- Handicapped Accessible
- Picnic Areas
- Picnic Pavilion (reservable)
- Recreation Program
- Hiking Trails, Nature Trails and Nature Center
- Swimming with Sand Beach and Bath House
- Fishing in Bowman Lake
- Hunting
- Bicycling on Campground Roads
- Basketball Court and Playgrounds
- Boat Launch (no motors boats and permit required)
- Rowboat and Paddleboat Rental (at boat house)
- Cross Country Skiing, Warming Center, and Snowmobiling
- Snack Bar

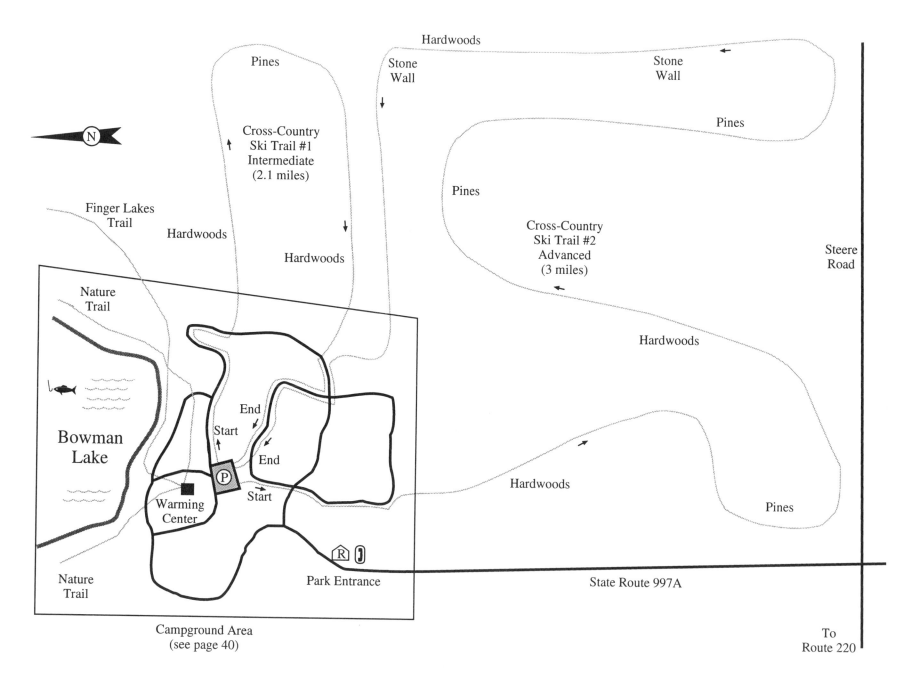

N

Hardwoods

Pines

Stone
Wall

Stone
Wall

Pines

Cross-Country
Ski Trail #1
Intermediate
(2.1 miles)

Pines

Finger Lakes
Trail

Hardwoods

Cross-Country
Ski Trail #2
Advanced
(3 miles)

Steere
Road

Hardwoods

Nature
Trail

Hardwoods

Bowman
Lake

End

Start

End

Hardwoods

Warming
Center

P

Start

Pines

R

Nature
Trail

Park Entrance

State Route 997A

Campground Area
(see page 40)

To
Route 220

Bowman Lake State Park

Bowman Lake State Park

(see page 37 for campground information and main park map)

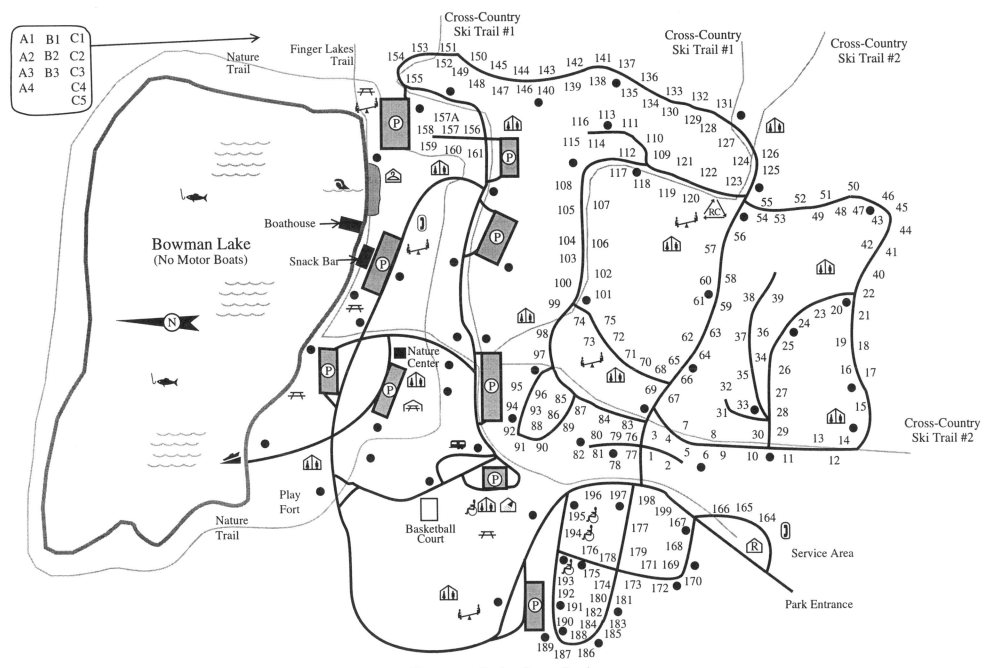

Bowman Lake State Park

Brown Tract Pond Public Campground

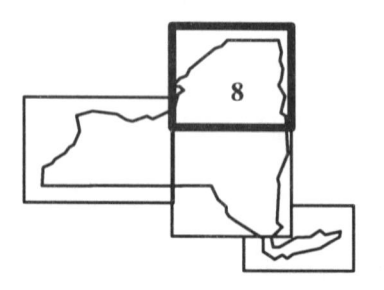

State Route 28, Raquette Lake, NY 13436

(315) 354–4412

- Located 2 miles west of Raquette Lake Village or 7 miles east of Eagle Bay off State Route 28
- Open mid–May through Labor Day for camping
- 90 Tent & Trailer Sites (no electric sites, trailer dump)
- 20 Acres
- Pit Toilets
- Potable Water
- Pets Allowed
- Picnic Area
- Hiking Trails (within approximately 1 mile)
- Swimming with Sand Beach and Bath House
- Fishing in Lower Brown Tract Pond
- Bicycling on Campground Roads
- Boat Launch (no motor boats)
- Rowboat and Canoe Rental (at park office)

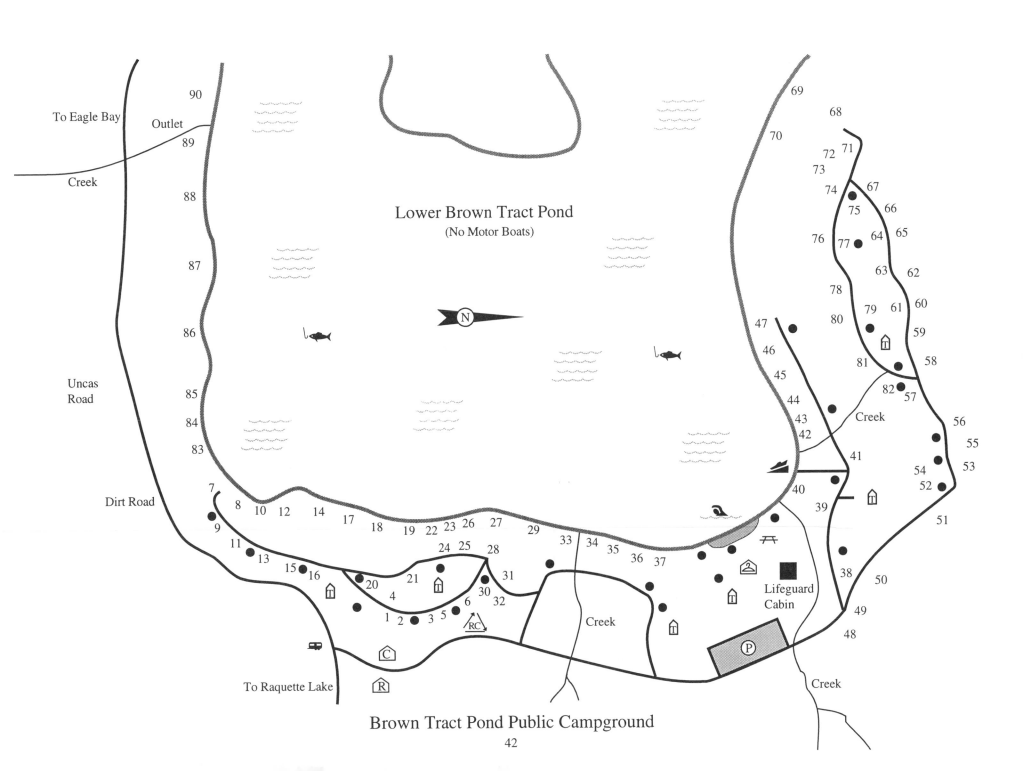

Lower Brown Tract Pond
(No Motor Boats)

To Eagle Bay

Outlet

Creek

Uncas Road

Dirt Road

Lifeguard Cabin

Creek

Creek

Creek

To Raquette Lake

Brown Tract Pond Public Campground

42

Buck Pond Public Campground

HCR 1, Box 9A, Onchiota, NY 12968

(518) 891–3449

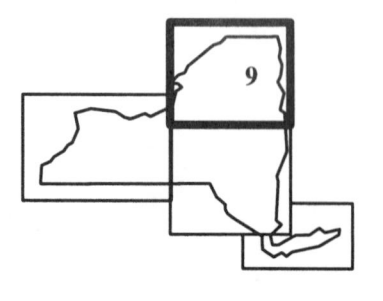

- Located 8 miles east of Paul Smiths off Franklin County Road 30
- Open mid–May through Labor Day for camping
- 114 Tent & Trailer Sites (no electric sites, trailer dump)
- Island sites I1 and I2 require boat for access
- 150 Acres
- Comfort Station (flush toilets & sink) and Showers
- Potable Water
- Public Telephone
- Pets Allowed
- Handicapped Accessible
- Picnic Area
- Hiking Trails (within approximately 3 miles)
- Swimming with Sand Beach and Bath House
- Fishing in Lake Kushaqua and Buck Pond
- Bicycling on Campground Roads
- Boat Launch (trailer launch on Lake Kushaqua and cartop launch on Buck Pond)
- Rowboat and Canoe Rental (at park office)

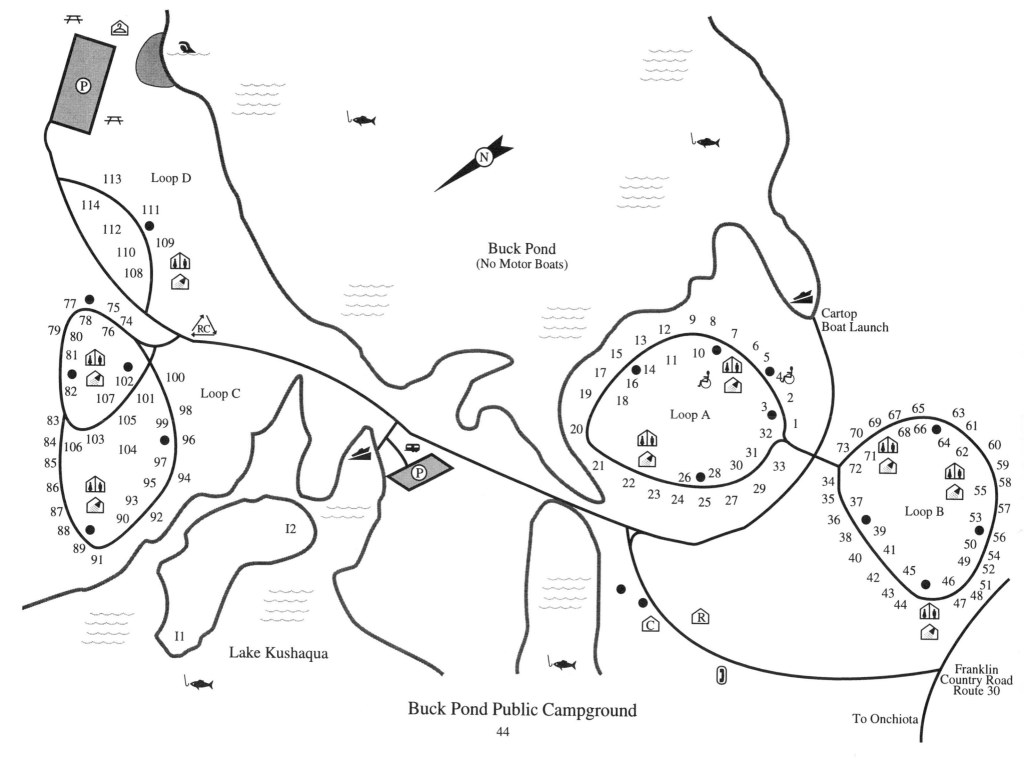

Loop D

Loop C

Loop A

Loop B

Buck Pond
(No Motor Boats)

Lake Kushaqua

Cartop
Boat Launch

Franklin
Country Road
Route 30

To Onchiota

Buck Pond Public Campground

44

Burnham Point State Park

c/o 36661 Cedar Point State Park Drive, Clayton, NY 13624

(315) 654–2324

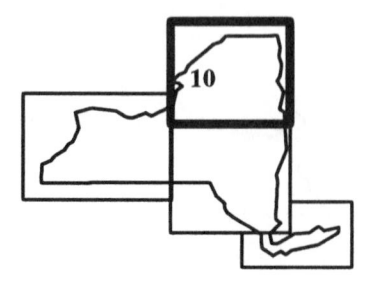

- Located 4 miles northeast of Cape Vincent or 9 miles southwest of Clayton off State Route 12E
- Open mid–May through mid–September for camping
- 49 Tent & Trailer Sites (18 electric sites, trailer dump)
- 12 Acres
- Comfort Station (flush toilets & sink)
- Potable Water
- Public Telephone
- Pets Allowed
- Handicapped Accessible
- Picnic Areas
- Picnic Pavilion (reservable)
- Fishing in St. Lawrence River
- Playground
- Hunting (by DEC permit only)
- Docks
- Boat Launch (at Cedar Point State Park)
- Ice Available

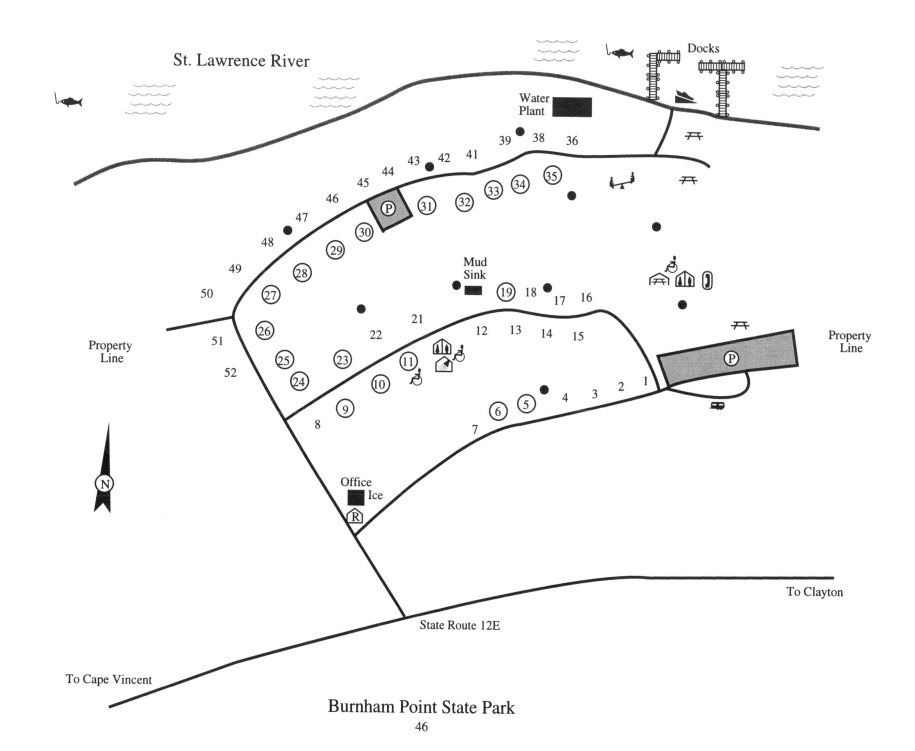

St. Lawrence River

Docks

Water
Plant

39 38 36

43 42 41

44

45

46 33 34 35

47 P 31 32

30

48 29

49 28

27 Mud
Sink

26 19 18 17 16

51 22 21

52 25 23 12 13 14 15

24 11

10

9 6 5 4 3 2 1

8

7

N

Property
Line

Property
Line

Office
Ice

R

To Clayton

State Route 12E

To Cape Vincent

Burnham Point State Park

Buttermilk Falls State Park

c/o Robert Treman State Park, RD #10, Ithaca, NY 14850

(607) 273–5761

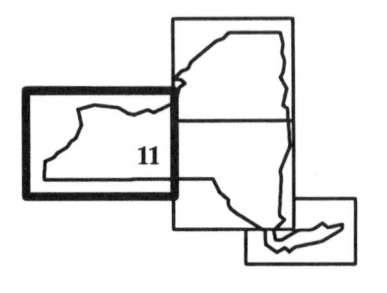

- Located 6 miles south of Ithaca or 25 miles northeast of Elmira off State Route 13
- Open mid–May through October for camping
- State Park is Open All Year
- 45 Tent & Trailer Sites (no electric sites, trailer dump)
- 7 Cabins
- 751 Acres
- Comfort Station (flush toilets & sink) and Showers
- Potable Water (throughout campground)
- Pets Allowed
- Handicapped Accessible
- Picnic Areas
- Picnic Pavilion and Lean To Shelters
- Recreation Program
- Hiking and Nature Trail
- Swimming in Lower Gorge Pool and Bath House
- Fishing in Buttermilk Creek and Treman Lake
- Hunting (fall archery)
- Ball Field and Playground
- Limited Cross Country Skiing at the Upper Park
- Concession, Ice Available, and Vending

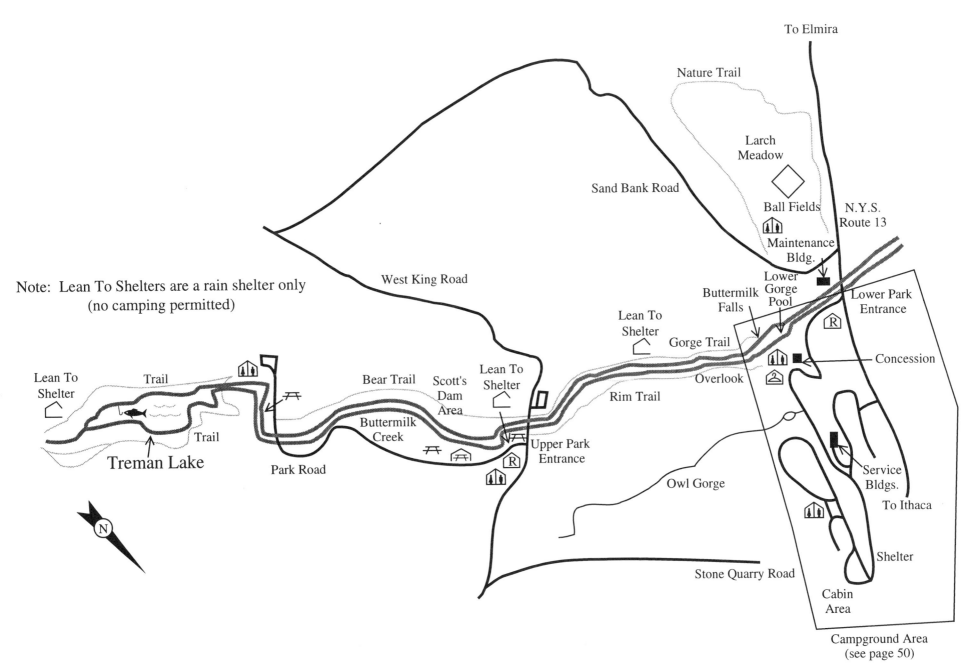

Note: Lean To Shelters are a rain shelter only (no camping permitted)

To Elmira

Nature Trail

Larch Meadow

Sand Bank Road

Ball Fields

N.Y.S. Route 13

Maintenance Bldg.

Lower Gorge Pool

Buttermilk Falls

Lower Park Entrance

West King Road

Lean To Shelter

Gorge Trail

Concession

Overlook

Lean To Shelter

Trail

Bear Trail

Scott's Dam Area

Lean To Shelter

Rim Trail

Service Bldgs.

Lean To Shelter

Buttermilk Creek

Upper Park Entrance

To Ithaca

Trail

Treman Lake

Park Road

Owl Gorge

Shelter

N

Cabin Area

Stone Quarry Road

Campground Area (see page 50)

Buttermilk Falls State Park

48

Buttermilk Falls State Park

(see page 47 for campground information and main park map)

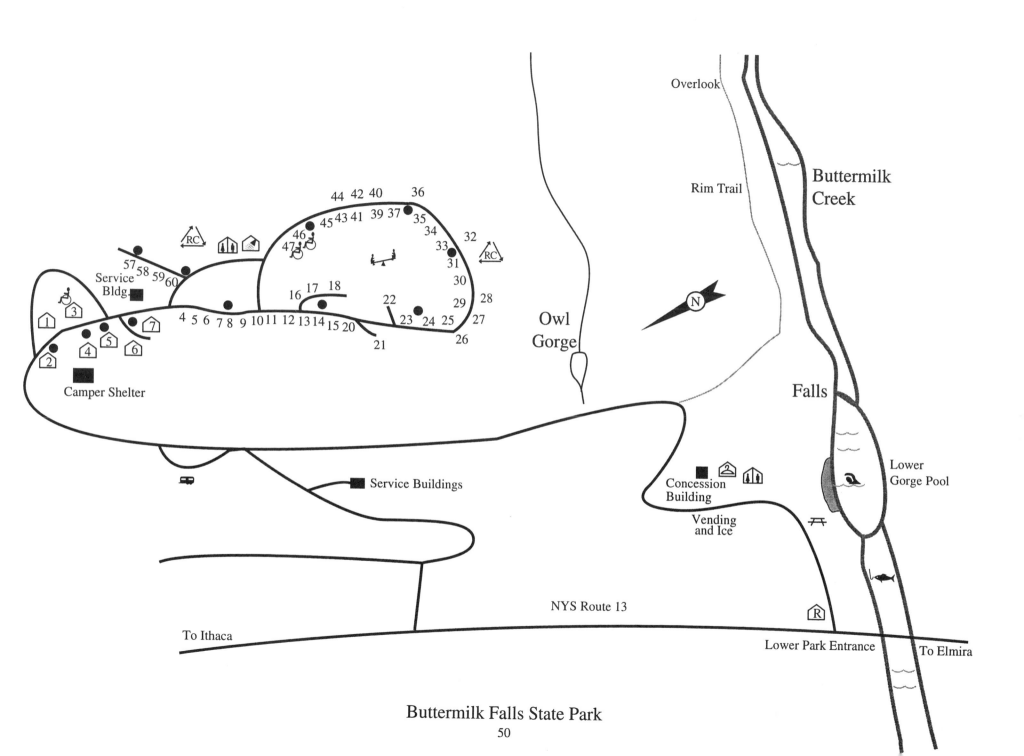

Buttermilk Falls State Park

50

Canoe Point State Park

c/o Cedar Point State Park, 36661 Cedar Point State Park Dr., Clayton, NY 13624

(315) 654–2522

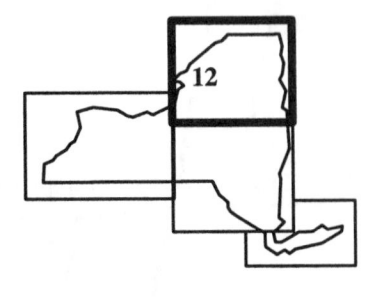

- Located 3.5 miles southwest from Wellesley Island on Grindstone Island
- Open mid–May through Labor Day for camping
- **Boat Access Only**
- 25 Tent Sites (no electric sites)
- 6 Cabins (1 is Handicapped Accessible)
- 70 Acres
- Comfort Station (flush toilets & sink)
- Potable Water
- Pets Allowed
- Handicapped Accessible
- Picnic Area
- Picnic Pavilion
- Fishing in St. Lawrence River
- Hunting
- Docks and Floating Docks
- Horseshoe Pits

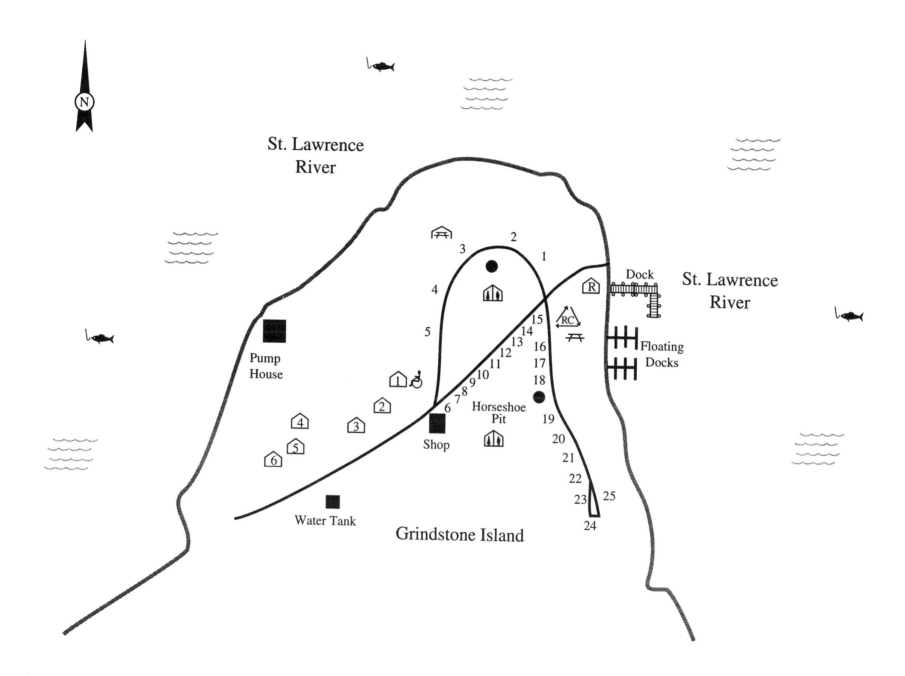

N

St. Lawrence
River

St. Lawrence
River

Dock

Floating
Docks

RC

Pump
House

Horseshoe
Pit

Shop

Water Tank

Grindstone Island

Canoe Point State Park

52

Caroga Lake Public Campground

3043 State Highway 29A, Gloversville, NY 12078

(518) 835–4241

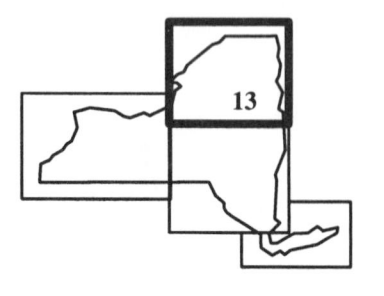

- Located in the town of Caroga Lake or 9 miles northwest of Gloversville off State Route 29A
- Open mid–May through Labor Day for camping
- 162 Tent & Trailer Sites (no electric sites, trailer dump)
- 40 Acres
- Comfort Station (flush toilets & sink), Pit Toilet, and Showers
- Potable Water
- Public Telephone
- Pets Allowed
- Handicapped Accessible
- Picnic Area
- Hiking Trails (within approximately 6 miles)
- Swimming with Sand Beach and Bath House
- Fishing in East Caroga Lake
- Bicycling on Campground Roads
- Exercise Course with 18 Stations
- Boat Launch

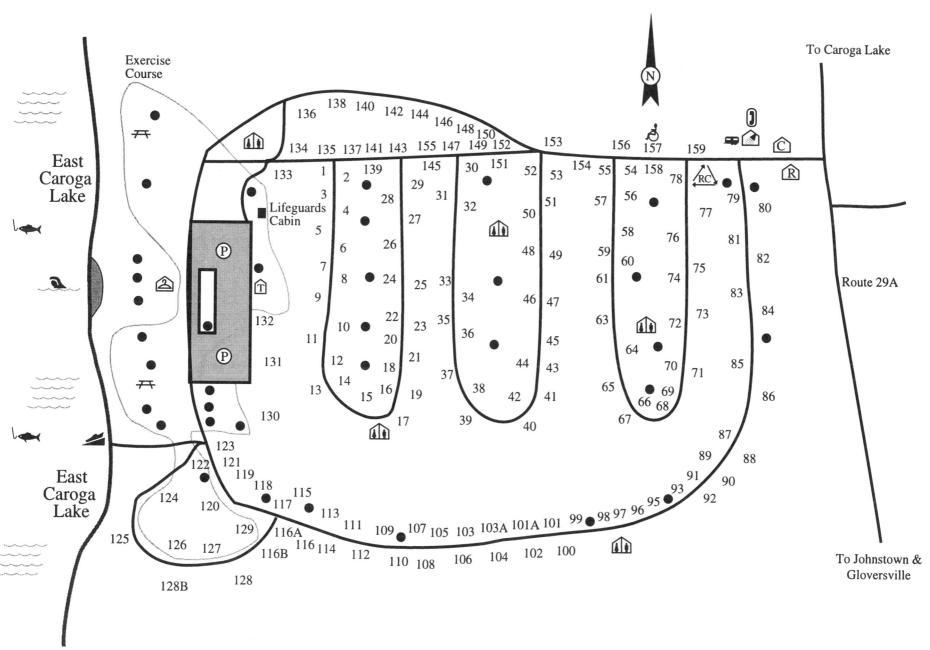

Caroga Lake Public Campground

Cayuga Lake State Park

2678 Lower Lake Road, Seneca Falls, NY 13148

(315) 568–5163

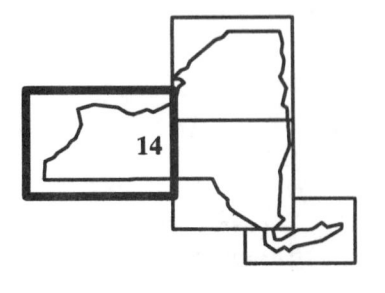

- Located 4 miles southeast of Seneca Falls or 34 miles north of Ithaca off State Route 89
- Open May through October for camping
- State Park is Open All Year
- 286 Tent & Trailer Sites (36 electric sites, trailer dump)
- 14 Cabins
- 142 Acres
- Comfort Station (flush toilets & sink) and Showers
- Potable Water (throughout campground)
- Public Telephone
- Pets Allowed
- Handicapped Accessible
- Picnic Area
- Picnic Pavilions (1 open, 2 enclosed – one located on 2nd floor of bath house)
- Hiking Trail (within state park)
- Recreation Program
- Swimming with Sand Beach and Bath House
- Fishing in Cayuga Lake
- Baseball Field, Playground and Volleyball
- Boat Launch
- Cross Country Skiing, Ice Fishing, Snowmobiling, and Sledding Hills

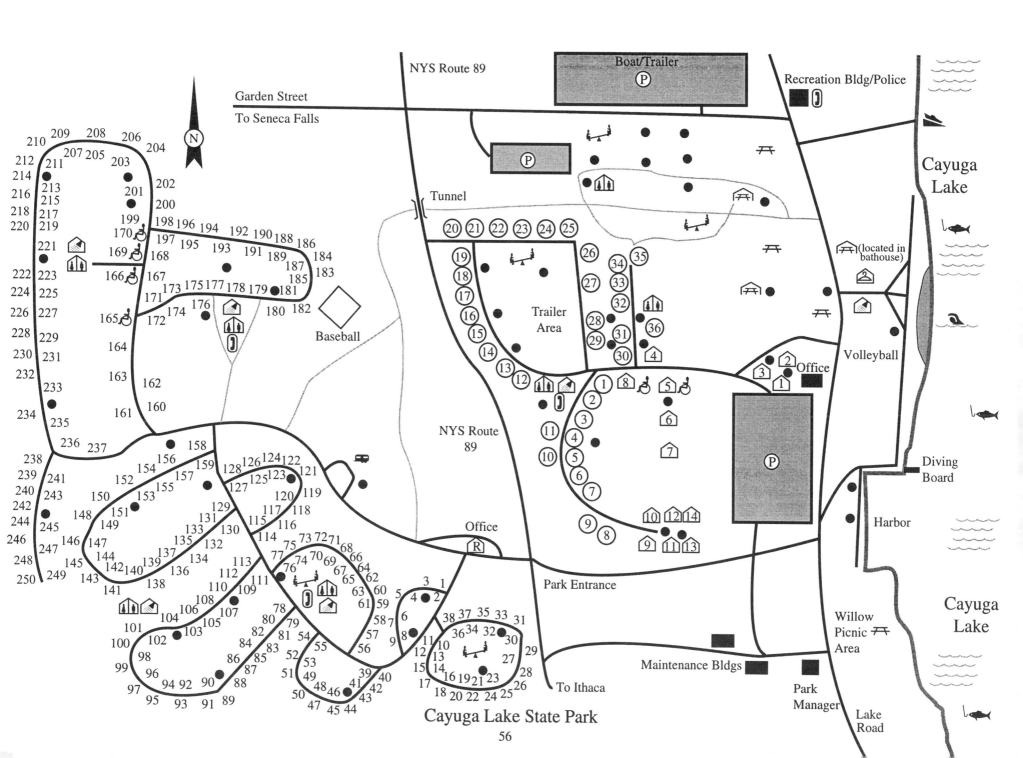

Cayuga Lake State Park

56

Cedar Island State Park

c/o Cedar Point State Park, 36661 Cedar Point State Park Dr., Clayton, NY 13624

(315) 654–2522

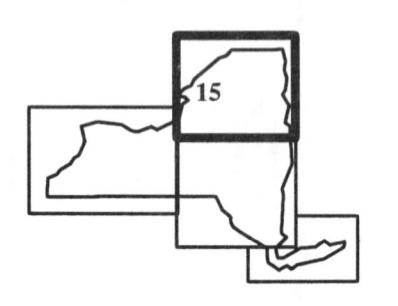

- Located in the Chippewa Bay on the St. Lawrence River
- Open mid–May through Labor Day for camping
- **Boat Access Only** (located 10 miles northeast of Alexandria Bay)
- 18 Tent Sites (no electric sites)
- 10 Acres
- Comfort Station (flush toilets & sink)
- Potable Water
- Pets Allowed
- Picnic Area
- Picnic Pavilion
- Fishing in St. Lawrence River
- Hunting
- Docks and Floating Docks

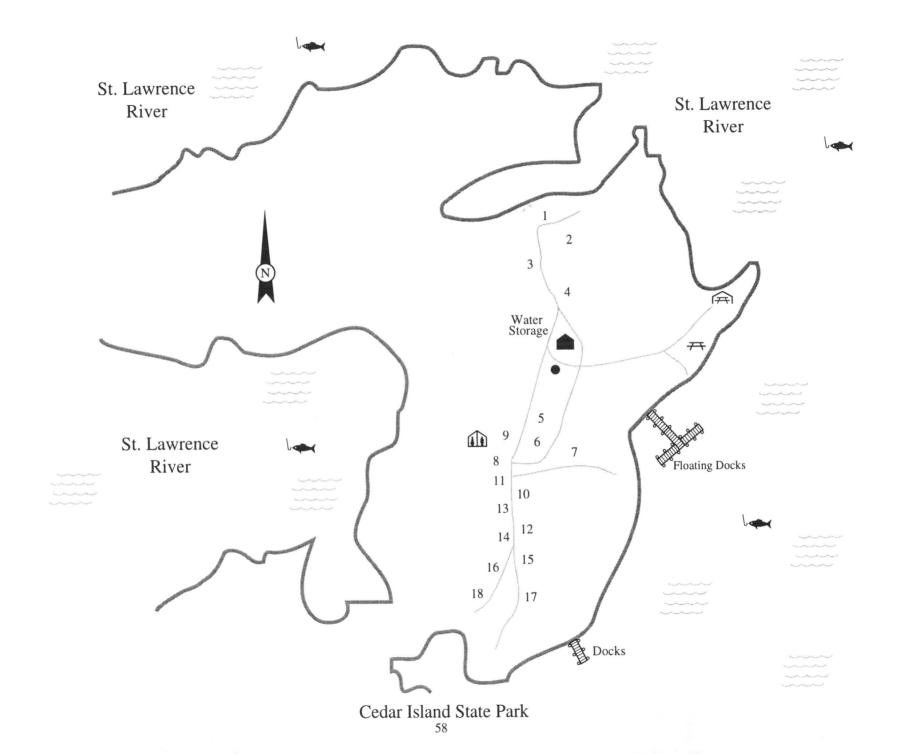

St. Lawrence
River

St. Lawrence
River

St. Lawrence
River

N

Water
Storage

1
2
3
4
5
9
6
8
7
11
10
13
14
12
16
15
18
17

Floating Docks

Docks

Cedar Island State Park
58

Cedar Point State Park

36661 Cedar Point State Park Dr., Clayton, NY 13624

(315) 654–2522

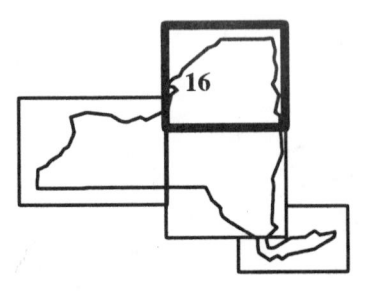

- Located 7 miles southwest of Clayton off State Route 12E
- Open May through mid–October for camping
- 174 Tent & Trailer Sites (58 electric sites, 33 full trailer hookup sites, trailer dump)
- 46 Acres
- Comfort Station (flush toilets & sink) and Showers
- Potable Water
- Pets Allowed
- Handicapped Accessible
- Picnic Area
- Picnic Pavilion (located in the recreation building – reservable)
- Recreation Program
- Swimming with Sand Beach and Bath House
- Fishing in St. Lawrence River
- Docks
- Bicycling on Campground Roads
- Duck Hunting (in season with permit only)
- Horseshoe Pits and Playground
- Boat Launch and Marina (pump out and fuel)
- Boat Rental (at marina)
- Raft

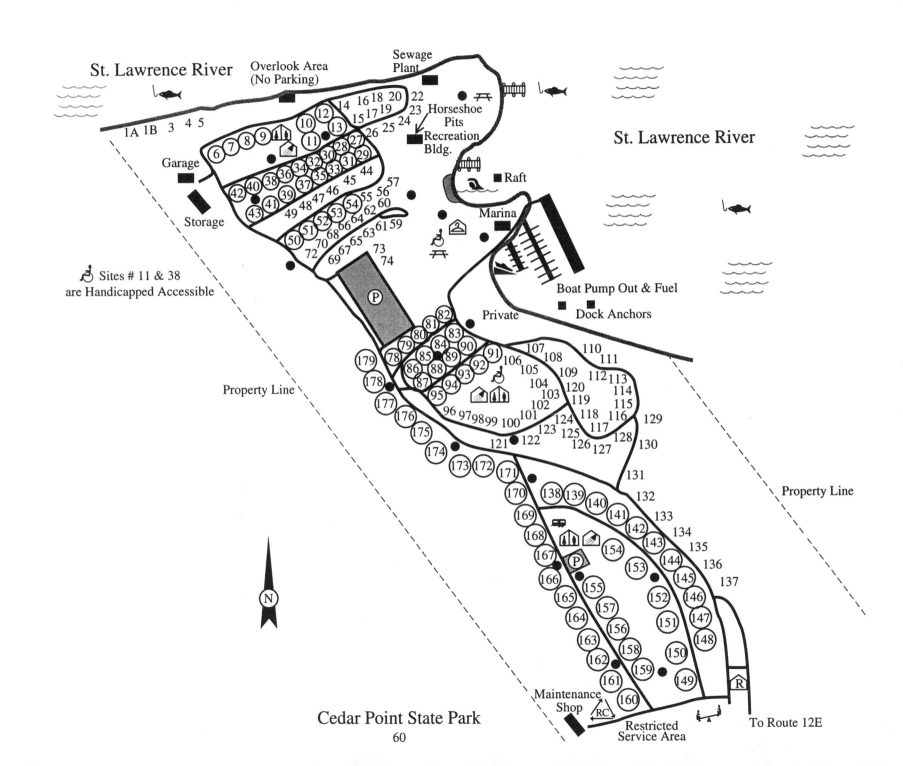

St. Lawrence River

Overlook Area (No Parking)

Sewage Plant

St. Lawrence River

Horseshoe Pits

Recreation Bldg.

Garage

Raft

Storage

Marina

Sites # 11 & 38 are Handicapped Accessible

Boat Pump Out & Fuel

Dock Anchors

Private

Property Line

Property Line

N

Maintenance Shop

Restricted Service Area

To Route 12E

Cedar Point State Park

60

Chenango Valley State Park

153 State Park Road, Chenango Forks, NY 13746

(607) 648–5251

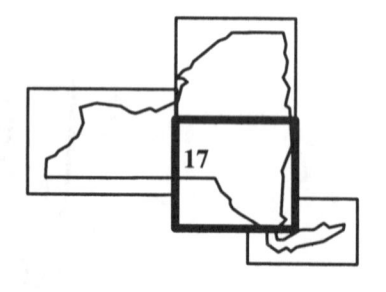

- Located 12 miles northeast of Binghamton off State Route 369 or 2 miles south of Chenango Forks off Pigeon Hill Road
- Open mid–April through October for camping
- State Park is Open All Year
- 216 Tent & Trailer Sites (51 electric sites, trailer dump)
- 24 Cabins
- 1,075 Acres
- Comfort Station (flush toilets & sink) and Showers
- Potable Water
- Public Telephone
- Pets Allowed
- Handicapped Accessible
- Picnic Areas
- Picnic Pavilions (3 reservable)
- Recreation Program
- Nature Trails
- Swimming with Sand Beach
- Fishing in Chenango River, Chenango Lake, and Lily Lake
- Bicycling on Campground Roads and Playground
- 18 Hole Golf Course, Clubhouse, and Food
- Rowboat Rental (at boat house on Chenango Lake)
- Cross Country Skiing, Ice Skating, and Sledding Hills

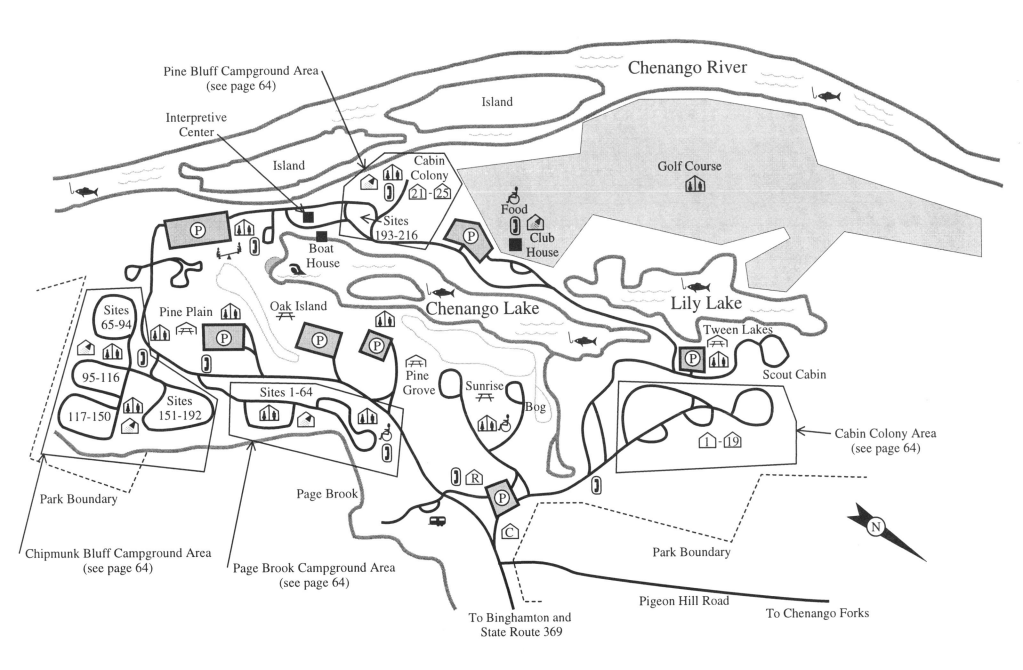

Chenango River

Pine Bluff Campground Area (see page 64)

Interpretive Center

Island

Island

Cabin Colony
21 - 25

Golf Course

Food
Club House

Sites 193-216

P

P

Boat House

Chenango Lake

Lily Lake

Pine Plain

Oak Island

Sites 65-94

P

P

P

Tween Lakes

Scout Cabin

95-116

Sites 1-64

Sites 151-192

Pine Grove

Sunrise

Bog

117-150

Park Boundary

Page Brook

R

P

Cabin Colony Area (see page 64)

1 - 19

N

Chipmunk Bluff Campground Area (see page 64)

Page Brook Campground Area (see page 64)

C

Park Boundary

Pigeon Hill Road

To Binghamton and State Route 369

To Chenango Forks

Chenango Valley State Park

Chenango Valley State Park

(see page 61 for campground information and main park map)

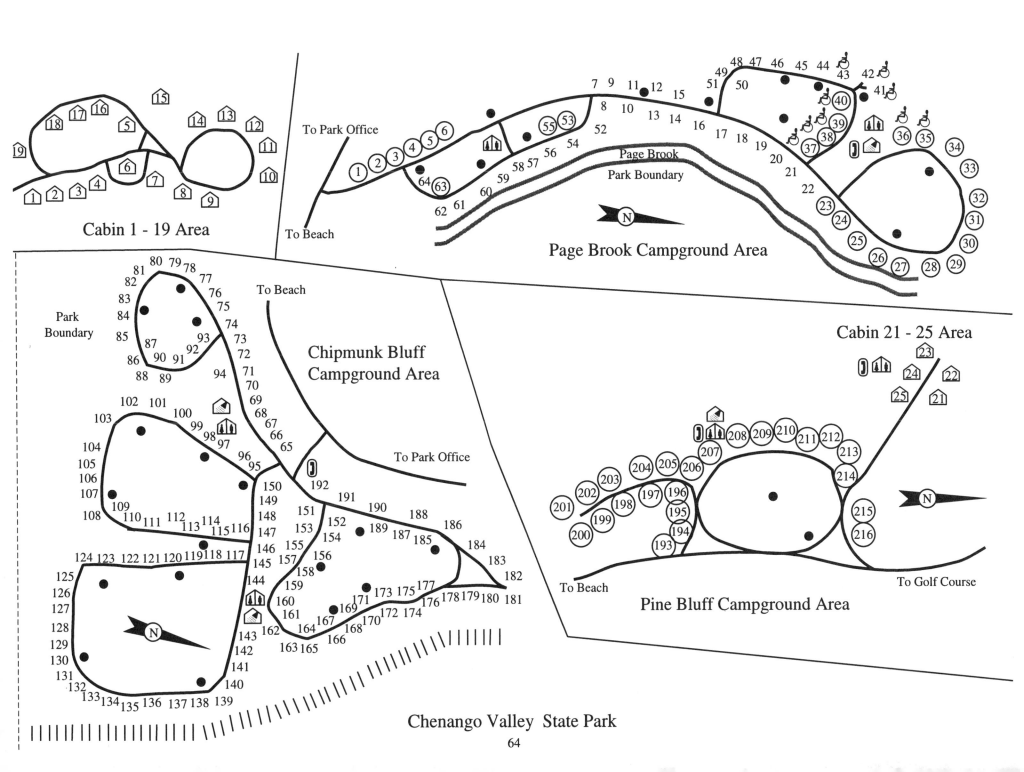

Cabin 1 - 19 Area

Page Brook Campground Area

Chipmunk Bluff
Campground Area

Cabin 21 - 25 Area

Pine Bluff Campground Area

Chenango Valley State Park

64

Chittenango Falls State Park

2300 Rathbun Road, Cazenovia, NY 13035

(315) 655–9620

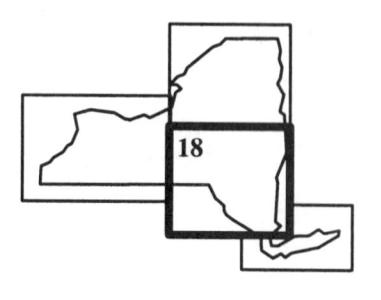

- Located 4 miles north of Cazenovia or 6 miles south of Chittenango off State Route 13
- Open mid–May through mid–October for camping
- 22 Tent & Trailer Sites (no electric sites, max RV 22 foot)
- 192 Acres
- Comfort Station (flush toilets & sink) and Showers
- Potable Water
- Public Telephone
- Pets Allowed
- Handicapped Accessible
- Picnic Areas
- Picnic Pavilion (reservable)
- Hiking Trails
- Fishing in Chittenango Creek
- Baseball Field, Sand Volleyball Court, and Horseshoe Pits

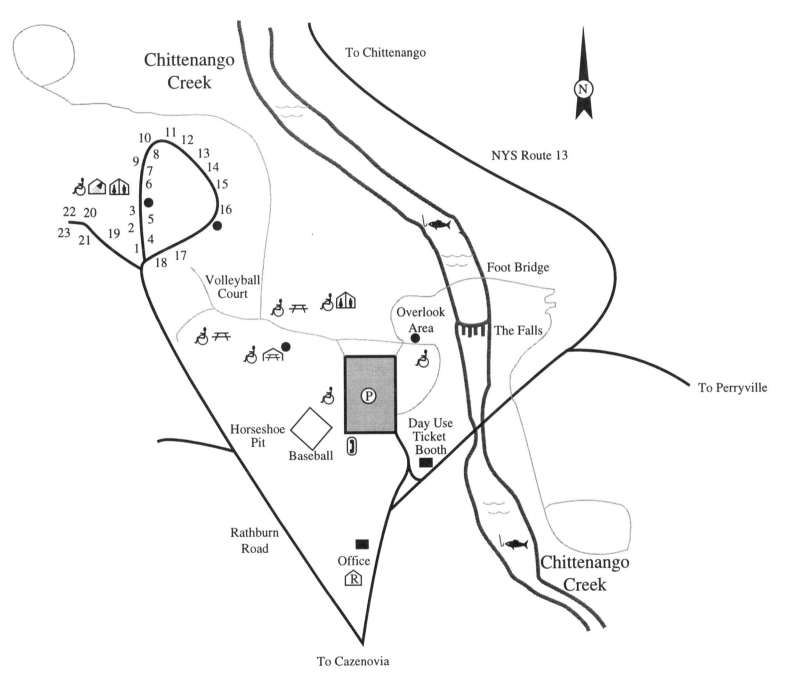

Chittenango Creek

To Chittenango

N

NYS Route 13

10 11 12
     8   13
9   14
   7   15
   6
22 20   3   16
          5
23 21 19 2   4
          1
        18 17

Volleyball
Court

Foot Bridge

Overlook
Area

The Falls

To Perryville

Horseshoe
Pit

P

Baseball

Day Use
Ticket
Booth

Rathburn
Road

Office
R

To Cazenovia

Chittenango
Creek

Chittenango Falls State Park

66

Clarence Fahnestock Memorial State Park

Route 301, Carmel, NY 10512

(845) 225–7207

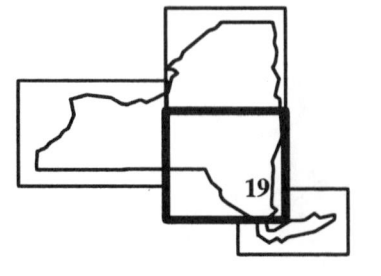

- Located 8 miles east of Cold Spring off State Route 301 or 10 miles north of Shrub Oak off the Taconic State Parkway
- Open mid–April through mid–December for camping
- State Park is Open All Year
- 80 Tent & Trailer Sites (no electric sites)
- 6,532 Acres
- Comfort Station (flush toilets & sink) and Showers
- Potable Water
- Handicapped Accessible
- Picnic Area
- Picnic Pavilion (at Canopus Beach)
- Recreation Program
- Hiking and Nature Trails
- Nature Center
- Swimming with Sand Beach (at Canopus Lake)
- Fishing in Canopus Lake, Pelton Pond, Duck Pond, and John Allen Pond
- Hunting
- Mountain Bike Trail, Bridle Trails, and Playground
- Boat Launch on Canopus Lake (cartop launch, park permit required, no gas motors)
- Rowboat Rental (at Canopus Lake)
- Cross Country Skiing, Ice Skating, Snowshoeing, and Snowmobiling
- Winter Camping and Food

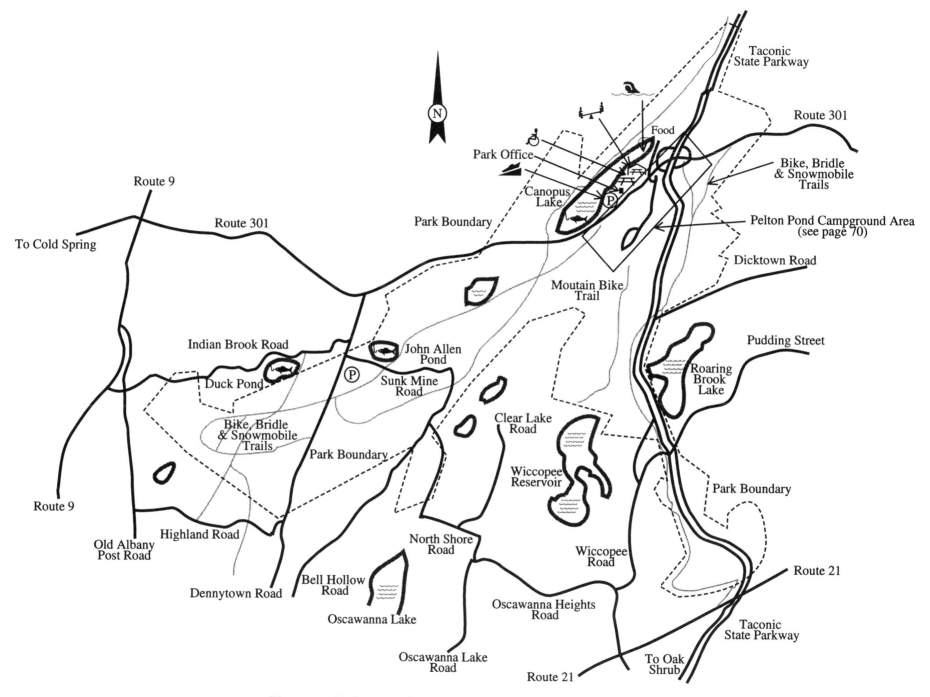

Clarence Fahnestock Memorial State Park

Clarence Fahnestock Memorial State Park

(see page 67 for campground information and main park map)

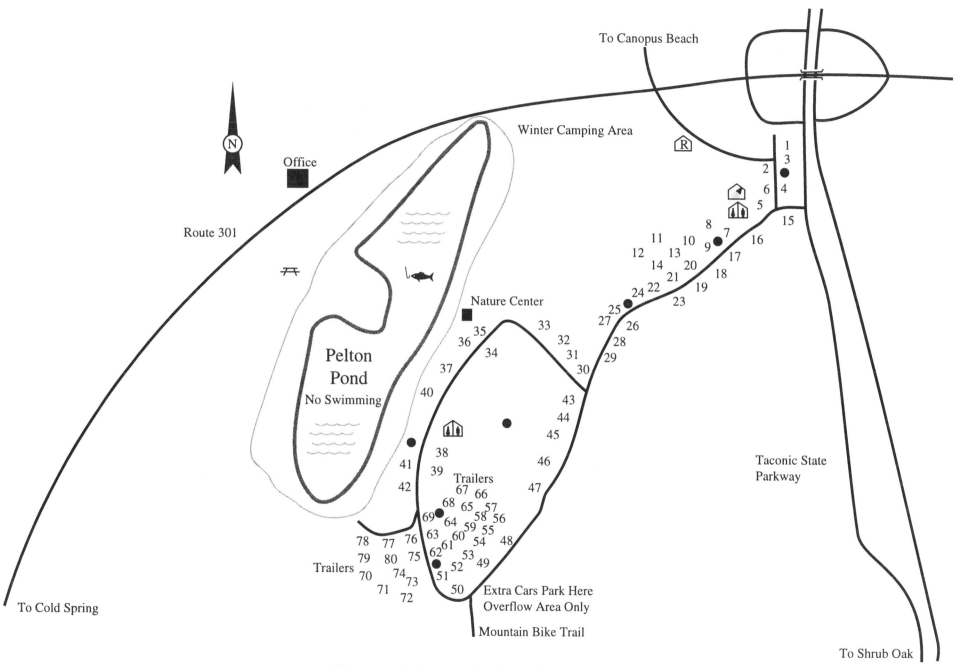

Clarence Fahnestock Memorial State Park

Coles Creek State Park

P. O. Box 442, Waddington, NY 13694

(315) 388–5636

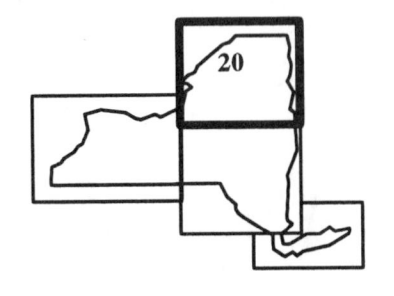

- Located 4 miles northeast of Waddington off State Route 37
- Open mid–May through mid–October for camping
- 229 Tent & Trailer Sites (153 electric sites, trailer dump)
- 1,800 Acres
- Comfort Station (flush toilets & sink) and Showers
- Potable Water
- Public Telephone
- Pets Allowed
- Handicapped Accessible
- Picnic Areas
- Picnic Pavilion (2 sections in the concession building)
- Recreation Program
- Swimming with Sand Beach
- Fishing in St. Lawrence River
- Hunting
- Bicycling on Campground Roads
- Baseball Field and Playground
- Boat Launch and Marina (located at Coles Creek Marina – just north of the park entrance on Route 37)
- Boat Rental (locally)
- Concession

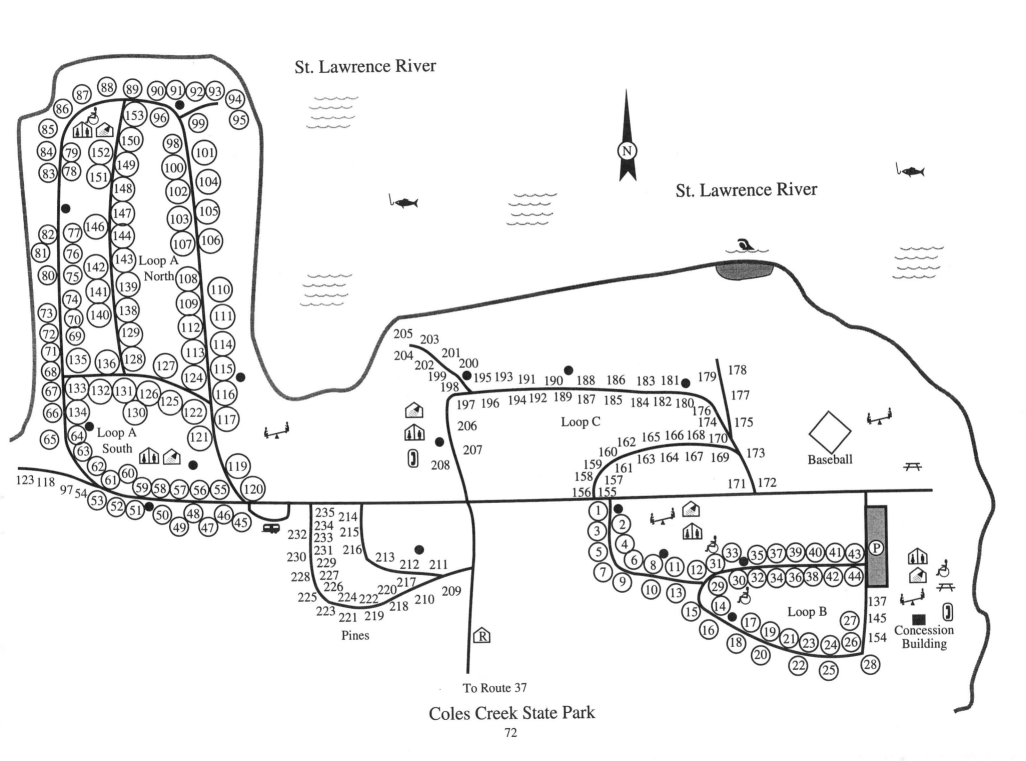

St. Lawrence River

St. Lawrence River

N

Loop A North

Loop A South

Loop C

Baseball

Loop B

Concession Building

Pines

To Route 37

Coles Creek State Park

72

Cranberry Lake Public Campground

243 Lone Pine Road, Cranberry Lake, NY 12927

(315) 848–2315

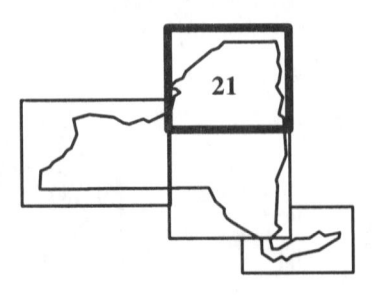

- Located 1 mile south of Cranberry Lake off State Route 3
- Open mid–May through October for camping
- 165 Tent & Trailer Sites (no electric sites, trailer dump)
- Comfort Station (flush toilets & sink) and Showers
- Potable Water
- Public Telephone
- Pets Allowed
- Handicapped Accessible
- Picnic Area
- Recreation Program
- Hiking Trails
- Swimming with Sand Beach and Bath House
- Fishing in Cranberry Lake
- Dock
- Bicycling and Rollerblading on Campground Roads
- Boat Launch (near Cranberry Lake dam – 1.5 miles north)
- Amphitheater

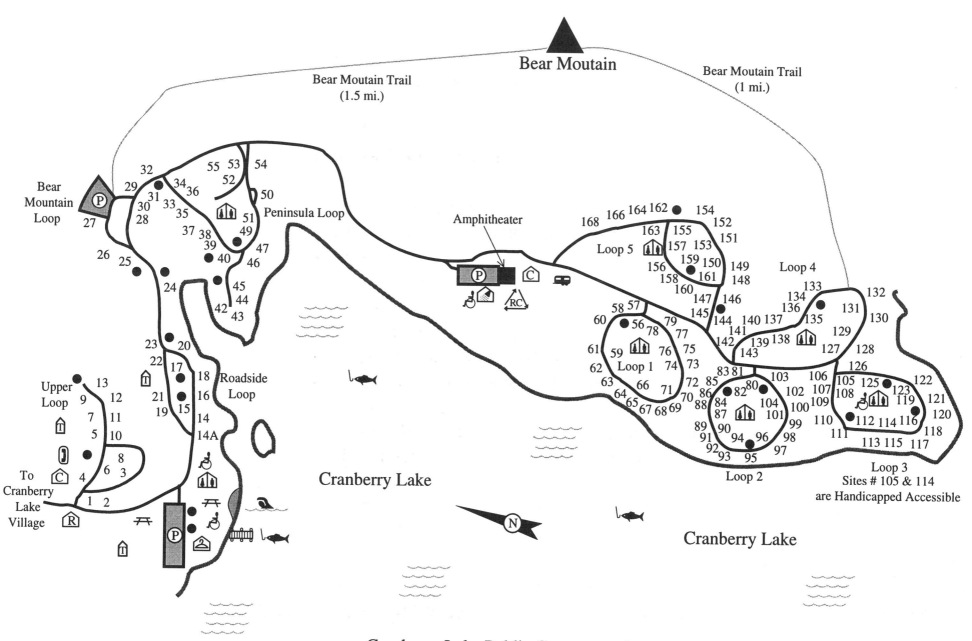

Cranberry Lake Public Campground

74

Crown Point Reservation Public Campground

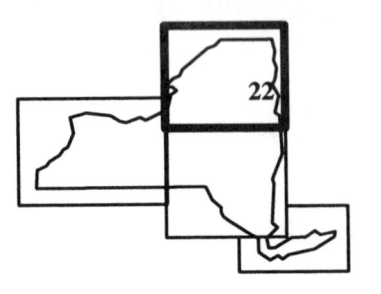

Route 9N, P. O. Box 218, Crown Point, NY 12928

(518) 597–3603

- Located 8 miles north of Crown Point off State Route 9N (adjacent to Lake Champlain toll bridge to Vermont)
- Open late–April through mid–October for camping
- 66 Tent & Trailer Sites (no electric sites, trailer dump, max RV 40 foot)
- 39 Acres
- Comfort Station (flush toilets & sink) and Showers
- Potable Water (throughout campground)
- Public Telephone
- Pets Allowed
- Handicapped Accessible
- Picnic Area
- Swimming (nearby at Port Henry Public Beach – 8 miles northwest)
- Fishing in Lake Champlain
- Pier
- Bicycling on Campground Roads
- Playground
- Boat Launch
- Champlain Monument Lighthouse
- Grenadier's Redoubt (Old Fort Ruins)

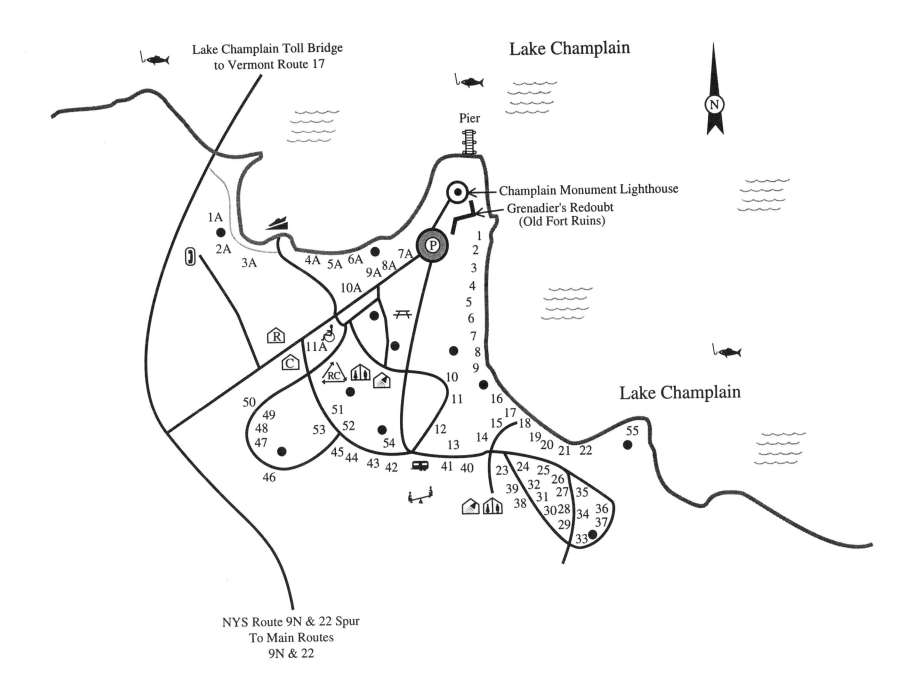

Lake Champlain Toll Bridge
to Vermont Route 17

Lake Champlain

Pier

Champlain Monument Lighthouse

Grenadier's Redoubt
(Old Fort Ruins)

N

1A
2A
3A
4A 5A 6A
7A
8A
9A
10A
11A

R
C
RC

1
2
3
4
5
6
7
8
9
10
11
16
17
15 18
19
20 21 22
55

Lake Champlain

50
49
48
47
46
51
52
53
54
45 44 43 42 41 40
12
13
14
23 24 25
26
27
39 32 31
38 3028
29
35
34 36
33 37

NYS Route 9N & 22 Spur
To Main Routes
9N & 22

Crown Point Reservation Public Campground

Cumberland Bay State Park

152 Cumberland Head Road, Plattsburgh, NY 12901

(518) 563–5240

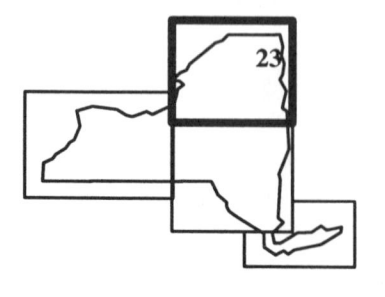

- Located 2 miles north of Plattsburgh off State Route 314
- Open May through mid–October for camping
- 207 Tent & Trailer Sites (18 electric sites, trailer dump)
- 319 Acres
- Comfort Station (flush toilets & sink) and Showers
- Potable Water (throughout campground)
- Public Telephone
- Pets Allowed
- Handicapped Accessible
- Picnic Area
- Recreation Program
- Swimming with Sand Beach
- Fishing in Lake Champlain (fishing not allowed on beach area)
- Bicycling on Campground Roads
- Basketball, Volleyball Court, Horseshoe Pits, and Playground
- Cross Country Skiing (at Point Au Roche State Park – 6 miles north)
- Recreation Room and Camp Store

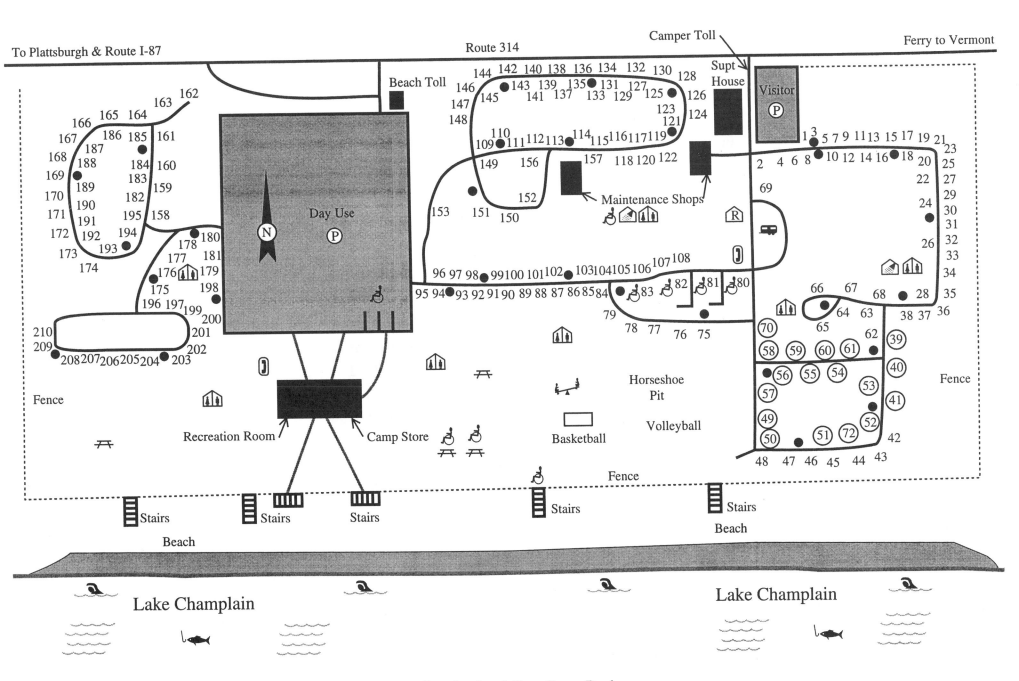

To Plattsburgh & Route I-87

Route 314

Camper Toll

Ferry to Vermont

Beach Toll

Supt House

Visitor P

Day Use P

N

Maintenance Shops

R

Recreation Room

Camp Store

Horseshoe Pit

Volleyball

Basketball

Fence

Fence

Stairs   Stairs   Stairs   Stairs   Stairs

Beach

Beach

Lake Champlain

Lake Champlain

Cumberland Bay State Park

Darien Lakes State Park

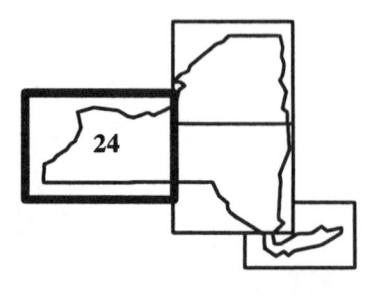

10289 Harlow Road, Darien Center, NY 14040

(845) 547–9242

(845) 547–9481 (winter)

- Located 2 miles west of Darien Center or 3 miles east of Alden off US 20
- Open All Year for camping
- 155 Tent & Trailer Sites (45 electric sites, trailer dump)
- 1,846 Acres
- Comfort Station (flush toilets & sink) and Showers
- Potable Water
- Public Telephone
- Pets Allowed (Loop A only)
- Handicapped Accessible
- Picnic Areas
- Picnic Pavilions (2 reservable)
- Hiking Trails
- Swimming with Sand Beach
- Fishing in Harlow Lake
- Bicycling on Campground Roads
- Basketball and Volleyball Courts, Ball Fields, and Playground
- Bridle Trails (the entire park east of Elevenmile Creek)
- Hunting for Small & Large Game (permit required, no firearms April 1st through Labor Day)
- Darien Lakes Amusement Park located 3 miles east of State Park
- Cross Country Skiing, Warming Hut, Ice Skating, and Snowmobiling

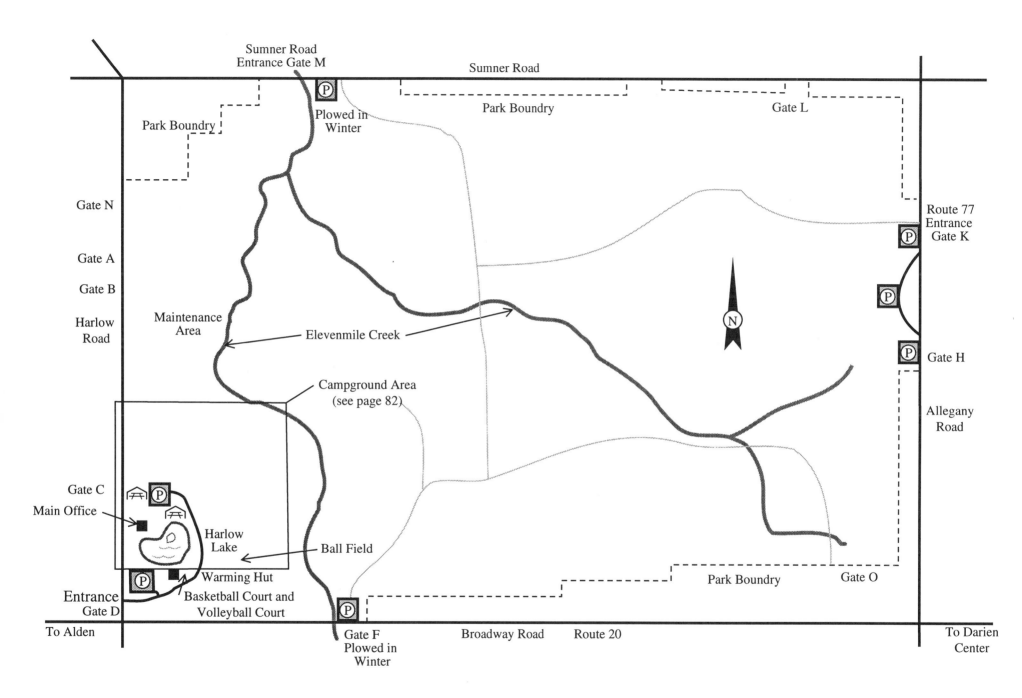

Sumner Road
Entrance Gate M

Sumner Road

Park Boundry

Gate L

Park Boundry

Plowed in
Winter

Gate N

Route 77
Entrance
Gate K

Gate A

Gate B

Harlow
Road

Maintenance
Area

Elevenmile Creek

N

Gate H

Allegany
Road

Campground Area
(see page 82)

Gate C

Main Office

Harlow
Lake

Ball Field

Park Boundry

Gate O

Warming Hut

Entrance
Gate D

Basketball Court and
Volleyball Court

Gate F
Plowed in
Winter

To Alden

Broadway Road   Route 20

To Darien
Center

Darien Lakes State Park

Darien Lakes State Park

(see page 79 for campground information and main park map)

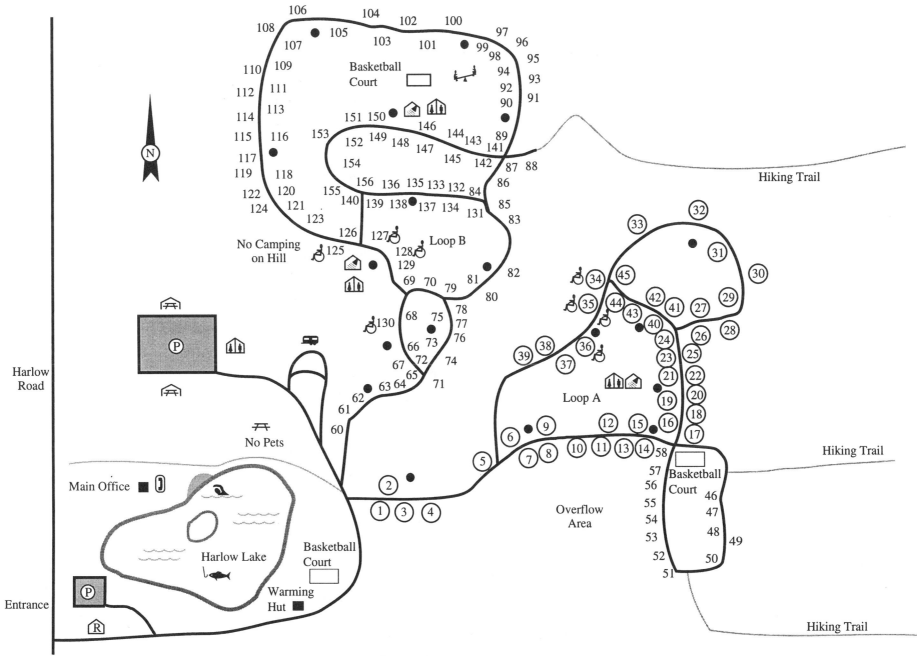

Darien Lakes State Park

Delta Lake State Park

8797 State Route 46, Rome, NY 13440

(315) 337–4670

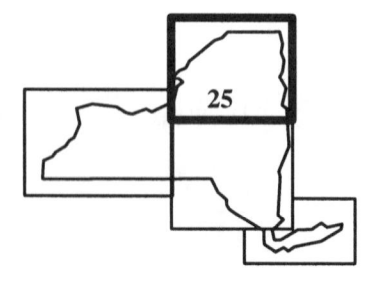

- Located 6 miles north of Rome or 15 miles south of Boonville off State Route 46
- Open May through mid–October for camping
- State Park is Open All Year
- 101 Tent & Trailer Sites (no electric sites, trailer dump)
- 400 Acres
- Comfort Station (flush toilets & sink) and Showers
- Potable Water (throughout campground)
- Public Telephone
- Pets Allowed
- Handicapped Accessible
- Picnic Area
- Picnic Pavilions (3 reservable)
- Recreation Program
- Hiking and Nature Trails
- Swimming with Sand Beach and Bath House
- Fishing in Delta Lake
- Bicycling on Campground Roads
- Baseball Field, Basketball Court (dirt court), Horseshoe Pits, and Playground
- Boat Launch
- Rowboat and Canoe Rental (across the lake at local marina)
- Cross Country Skiing, Ice Fishing, Snowshoeing, and Snowmobiling
- Concessions

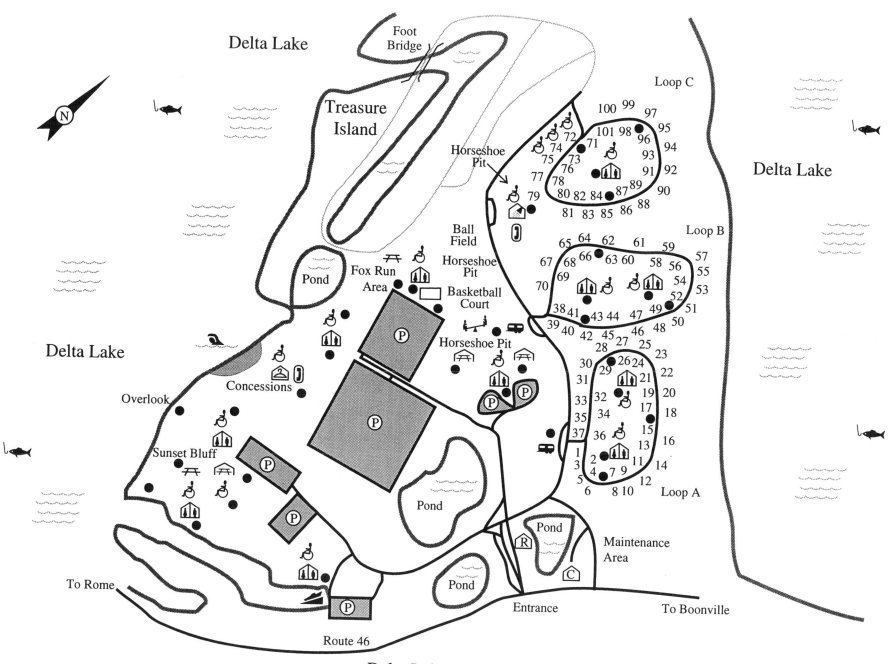

Delta Lake

Foot Bridge

Delta Lake

Treasure Island

N

Horseshoe Pit

Loop C

100 99 97
101 98 95
72 71   96 94
74   93
73   91 92
75 76   89
77 78 80 82 84 87 90
79 81 83 85 86 88

Delta Lake

Ball Field

Horseshoe Pit

Loop B

65 64 62 61 59
67 68 66 63 60   57
69   58 56
70   54 55
38 41 43 44 47 49 52 53
39 40 42 45 46 48 50 51
28 27 25 51

Fox Run Area

Basketball Court

Pond

Delta Lake

P

Horseshoe Pit

P P P

30 29 26 24 23
31   21 22
33 32 19 20
35 34 17 18
37 36 15 16
1 2 13
3   11 14
5 4 7 9
6 8 10 12   Loop A

Overlook

Concessions

P

Sunset Bluff

P

P

Pond

P

Pond

R

Pond

C

Maintenance Area

To Rome

P

Pond

Entrance

To Boonville

Route 46

Delta Lake State Park

Devil's Tombstone Public Campground

P. O. Box 6, Hunter, NY 12122

(845) 688–7160

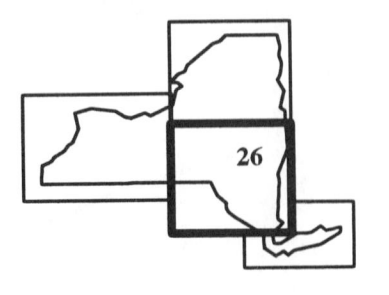

- Located 4 miles south of Hunter or 8 miles northeast of Phoenicia off State Route 214
- Open mid–May through Labor Day for camping
- 24 Tent & Trailer Sites (no electric sites)
- 24 Acres
- Pit Toilets
- Potable Water
- Public Telephone
- Pets Allowed
- Handicapped Accessible
- Picnic Area at Notch Lake
- Recreation Program
- Hiking Trails
- Playground

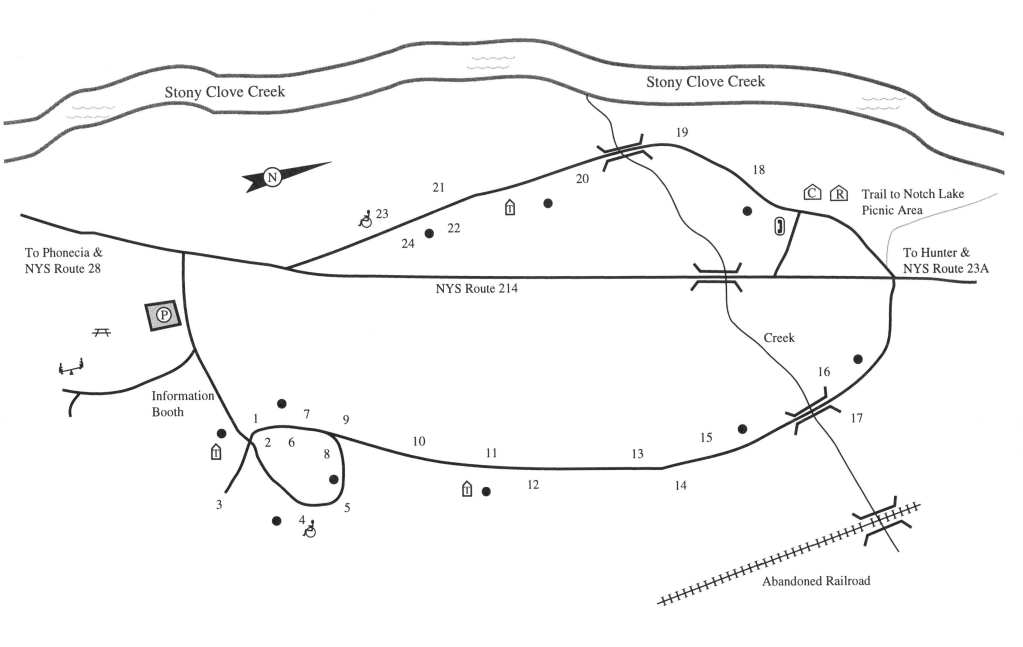

Stony Clove Creek

Stony Clove Creek

N

19

18

21

20

C R Trail to Notch Lake
Picnic Area

23

22

24

To Phonecia &
NYS Route 28

NYS Route 214

To Hunter &
NYS Route 23A

P

Creek

16

Information
Booth

1 7 9

2 6 10

8

11 13 15 17

3 12 14

4 5

Abandoned Railroad

Devil's Tombstone Public Campground

De Wolf Point State Park

45920 County Route 191, Fineview, NY 13640

(315) 482–2012

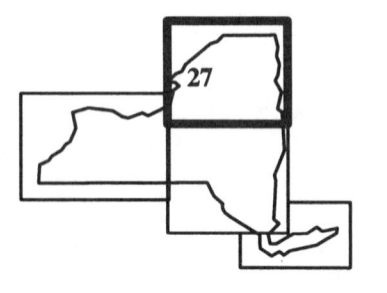

- Located 2 miles north of Thousand Islands Bridge on Wellesley Island (Exit 51)
- Open May through mid–September for camping
- State Park is Open All Year
- 14 Tent & Trailer Sites (no electric sites, max RV 20 foot)
- 14 Cabins
- 13 Acres
- Comfort Station (flush toilets & sink) and Showers
- Potable Water (throughout campground)
- Pets Allowed
- Handicapped Accessible
- Picnic Area
- Swimming and Recreation Programs at Wellesley Island State Park
  (approximately 7 miles west – free access)
- Fishing in the Lake of the Isles and St. Lawrence River
- Boat Launch (gravel) and Dock

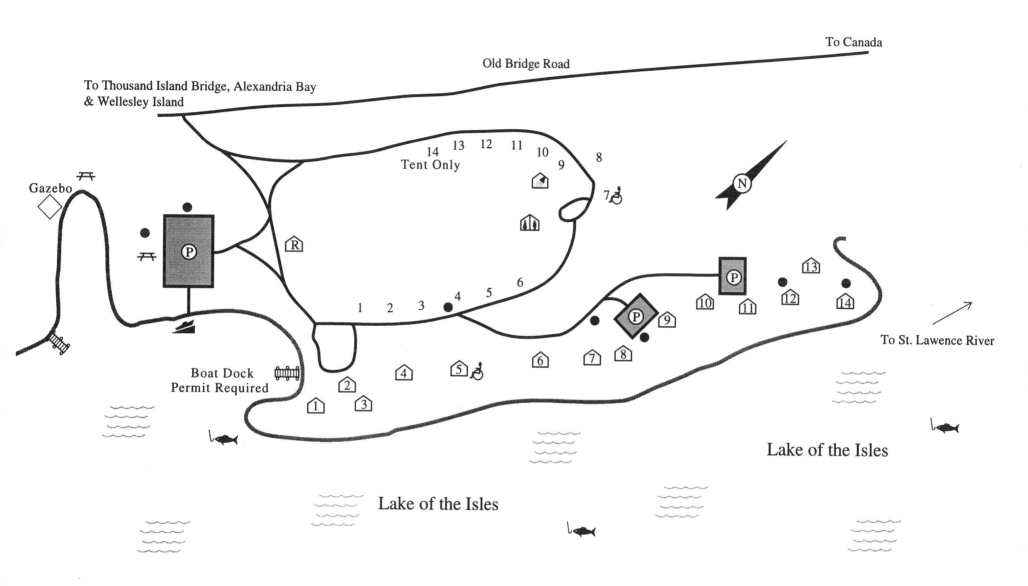

To Canada

Old Bridge Road

To Thousand Island Bridge, Alexandria Bay
& Wellesley Island

Gazebo

N

Tent Only

14   13   12   11   10   8
9
7

P

R

6

1   2   3   4   5

P

P

13

10   11   12   14

To St. Lawence River

6   7   8   9

Boat Dock
Permit Required

4   5

2

1   3

Lake of the Isles

Lake of the Isles

De Wolf Point State Park

88

Eagle Point Public Campground

Route 9, Pottersville, NY 12860

(518) 494–2220

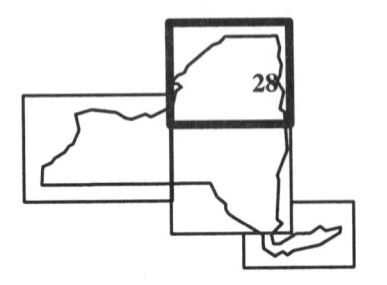

- Located 2 miles north of Pottersville or 6 miles south of Schroon Lake off State Route 9
- Open mid–May through Labor Day for camping
- 71 Tent & Trailer Sites (no electric sites, 55 trailer sites, trailer dump, max RV 40 foot)
- 25 Acres
- Comfort Station (flush toilets & sink) and Showers
- Potable Water
- Public Telephone
- Pets Allowed
- Handicapped Accessible
- Picnic Area
- Swimming with Sand Beach and Bath House
- Fishing in Schroon Lake
- Boat Launch (cartop launch)

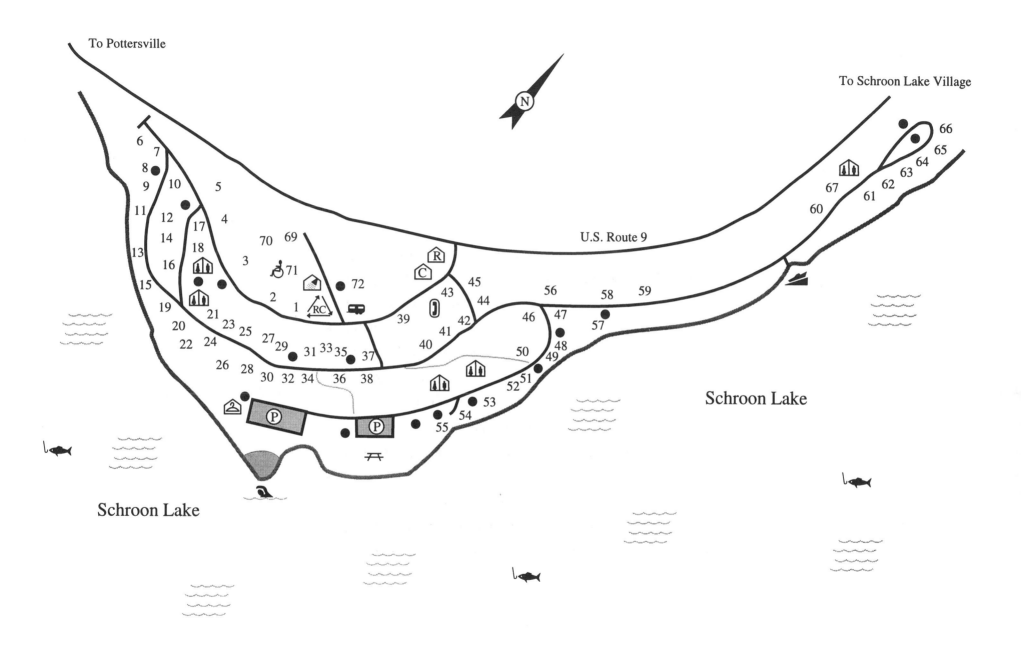

Eagle Point Public Campground

Eel Weir State Park

P. O. Box 380, Morristown, NY 13664

(315) 393–1138

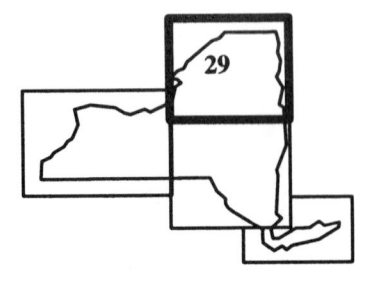

- Located 5 miles south of Ogdensburg or 10 miles east of Morristown off State Route 79
- Open Memorial Day through Labor Day for camping
- 34 Tent & Trailer Sites (no electric sites)
- 16 Acres
- Comfort Station (flush toilets & sink) and Showers
- Potable Water (throughout campground)
- Public Telephone
- Pets Allowed
- Handicapped Accessible
- Picnic Area
- Picnic Pavilion (reservable)
- Fishing in Oswegatchie River and Black Lake (approximately 2 miles south)
- Boat Launch (cartop launch)

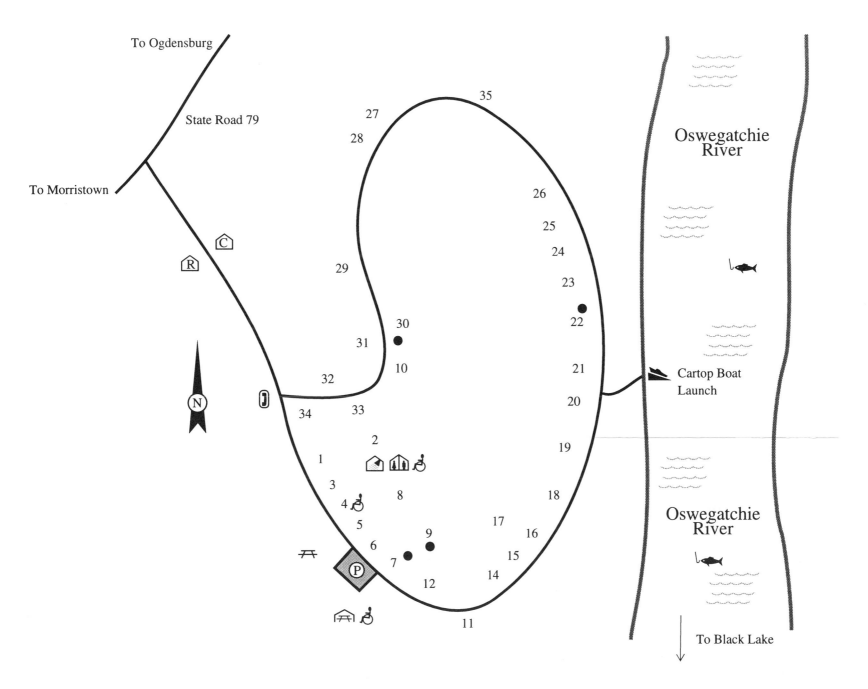

To Ogdensburg

State Road 79

To Morristown

Ⓒ

Ⓡ

Ⓝ

Ⓓ

27

28

35

26

25

24

23

29

22

30

31

10

21

32

20

34

33

19

2

1

3

8

18

4

5

17

16

9

6

15

7

14

12

11

Oswegatchie River

Cartop Boat Launch

Oswegatchie River

To Black Lake

Eel Weir State Park

92

Eighth Lake Public Campground

Route 28, Inlet, NY 13360

(315) 354–4120

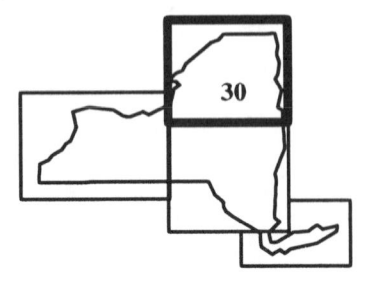

- Located 6 miles east of Inlet or 5 miles west of Raquette Lake off State Route 28
- Open mid–April through mid–October for camping
- 111 Tent & Trailer Sites (no electric sites, trailer dump, max RV 30 foot)
- 75 Acres
- Comfort Station (flush toilets & sink) and Showers
- Potable Water
- Public Telephone
- Pets Allowed
- Handicapped Accessible
- Picnic Areas
- Hiking Trails (within approximately 2 miles)
- Swimming with Sand Beach and Bath House (Eighth Lake only)
- Fishing in Seventh and Eighth Lakes
- Dock (on Seventh Lake)
- Bicycling and Rollerblading on Campground Roads
- Boat Launch (launch for Seventh Lake is 2 miles south on Route 28)
- Boat and Canoe Rental (at park office)

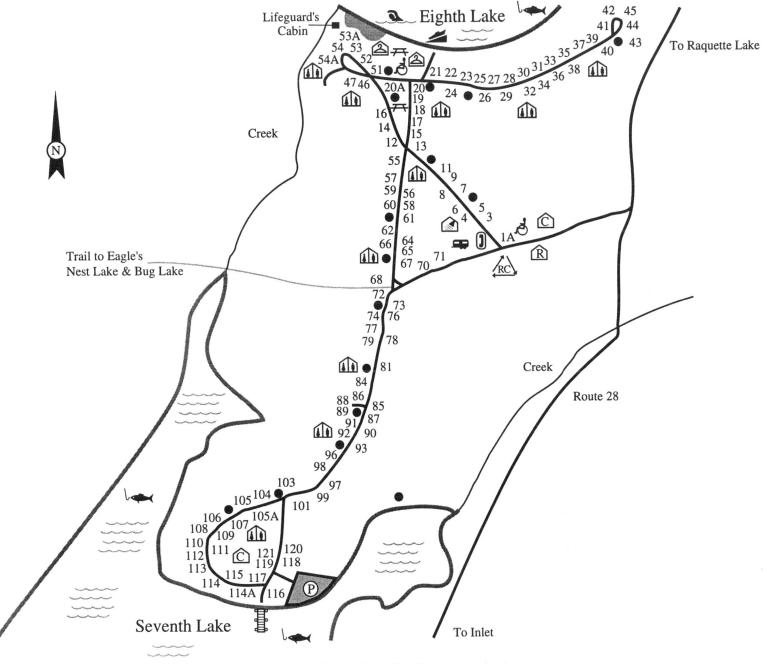

Lifeguard's Cabin

Eighth Lake

To Raquette Lake

Creek

Trail to Eagle's
Nest Lake & Bug Lake

Creek

Route 28

Seventh Lake

To Inlet

Eighth Lake Public Campground

94

Evangola State Park

Shaw Road, Irving, NY 14081

(716) 549-1760

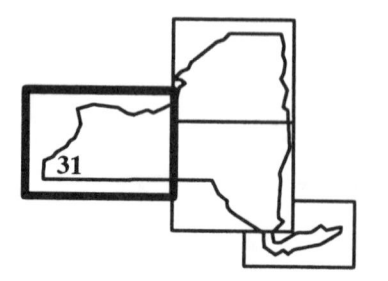

- Located 4 miles southwest of Angola or 4 miles north of Irving off State Route 5
- Open mid–April through mid–October for camping
- State Park is Open All Year
- 122 Tent & Trailer Sites (37 electric sites, trailer dump)
- 733 Acres
- Comfort Station (flush toilets & sink)
- Potable Water
- Public Telephone
- Pets Allowed
- Handicapped Accessible
- Picnic Areas
- Picnic Pavilions (5 reservable)
- Recreation Program and Hall
- Hiking Trails
- Swimming with Sand Beach and Bath House
- Fishing in Lake Erie
- Bicycling and Rollerblading on Campground Roads
- Hunting
- Tennis Courts, Soccer & Baseball Fields, Basketball Court, Horseshoe Pits, and Playground
- Cross Country Skiing and Snowmobiling
- Snack Bar

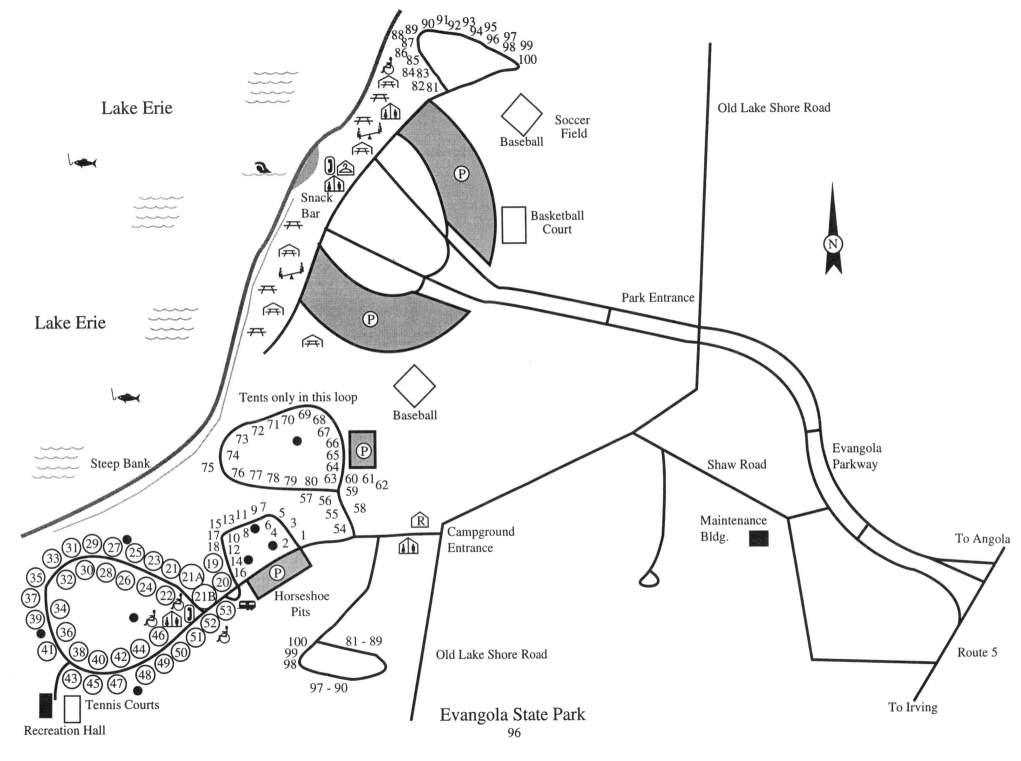

Lake Erie

Lake Erie

90 91 92 93 94 95
88 89 96 97
87 98 99
86 85 100
84 83
82 81

Old Lake Shore Road

Soccer Field

Baseball

P

Basketball Court

N

Snack Bar

P

P

Park Entrance

Baseball

Tents only in this loop

73 72 71 70 69 68
67
66
65
64
60 61 62
59
74
75
76 77 78 79 80 63
57 56
55 58
54

P

Shaw Road

Evangola Parkway

Maintenance Bldg.

Steep Bank

15 13 11 9 7
17 10 8 5
18 12 6 4 3
14 2 1
19
16 20

R

Campground Entrance

To Angola

31 29 27
33 25
23
35 30 28 26 24 21 21A
32 22 21B
37
34
39 36
41 38 40 42 44 46 51 50
43 45 47 48 49 52 53

P

Horseshoe Pits

Old Lake Shore Road

Route 5

100
99
98
97 - 90
81 - 89

Tennis Courts

Recreation Hall

Evangola State Park

To Irving

96

Fair Haven Beach State Park

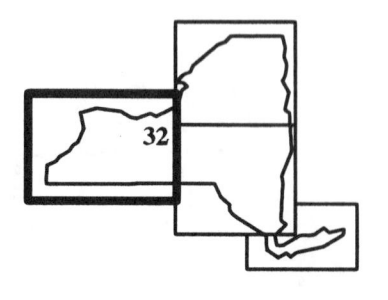

Route 104A, P. O. Box 16, Fair Haven, NY 13064

(315) 947–5205

- Located 1 mile north of Fair Haven off State Route 104A
- Open April through October for camping
- State Park is Open All Year
- 185 Tent & Trailer Sites (46 electric sites, trailer dump)
- 32 Cabins (6 cabins with wood heat for winter camping)
- 865 Acres
- Comfort Station (flush toilets & sink) and Showers
- Potable Water
- Public Telephone
- Pets Allowed
- Handicapped Accessible
- Picnic Areas and Picnic Pavilions (3 reservable)
- Recreation Program and Building, and Store
- Hiking and Nature Trails
- Swimming with Sand Beach and Bath House
- Fishing in Little Sodus Bay, Sterling Pond, and Lake Ontario
- Hunting
- Dock (on Little Sodus Bay) and Marina (approximately 1 mile south on Little Sodus Bay)
- Bicycling on Campground Roads, Baseball, and Playground
- Boat Launch (Little Sodus Bay and small boat launch on Sterling Pond)
- Boat Rental (at park office for Sterling Pond only)
- Cross Country Skiing, Ice Fishing, Ice Skating, Snowshoeing, and Snowmobiling

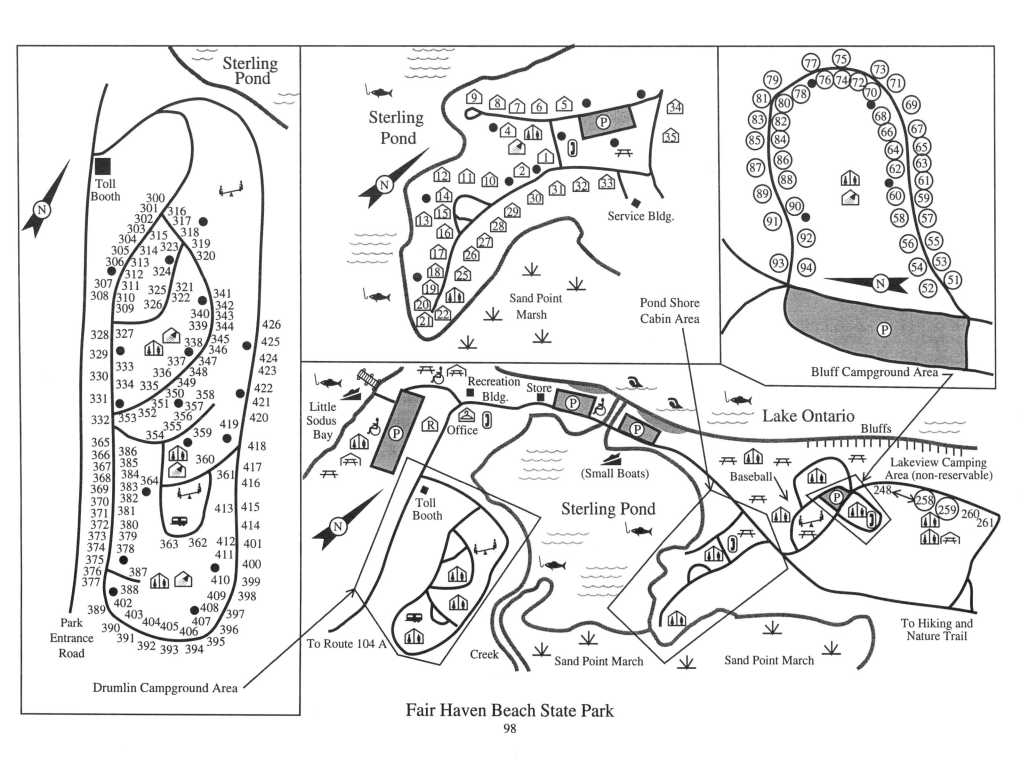

Sterling Pond

Sterling Pond

Toll Booth

300
301
302
303
304
305
306
307
308
309
310
311
312
313
314
315
316
317
318
319
320
321
322
323
324
325
326
327
328
329
330
331
332
333
334
335
336
337
338
339
340
341
342
343
344
345
346
347
348
349
350
351
352
353
354
355
356
357
358
359
360
361
362
363
364
365
366
367
368
369
370
371
372
373
374
375
376
377
378
379
380
381
382
383
384
385
386
387
388
389
390
391
392
393
394
395
396
397
398
399
400
401
402
403
404
405
406
407
408
409
410
411
412
413
414
415
416
417
418
419
420
421
422
423
424
425
426

Park Entrance Road

Drumlin Campground Area

9 8 7 6 5
4
1 2
12 11 10
14
13 15
16
17
18
19
20
21 22
30
31 32 33
29
28
27
26
25
34
35

Service Bldg.

Sand Point Marsh

77 75
79 76 74 72 73
81 80 78 71
83 82 70 69
85 84 68
86 66 67
88 64 65
87 62 63
89 60 61
91 90 59
92 58 57
93 94 56 55
54 53
52 51

Pond Shore Cabin Area

Bluff Campground Area

Little Sodus Bay

Recreation Bldg.
Store
Office

Toll Booth

(Small Boats)

Sterling Pond

Lake Ontario
Bluffs

Baseball

Lakeview Camping Area (non-reservable)

248
258 259 260
261

To Route 104 A

Creek

Sand Point March

Sand Point March

To Hiking and Nature Trail

Fair Haven Beach State Park

Fillmore Glen State Park

1686 State Route 38, Moravia, NY 13118

(315) 497–0130

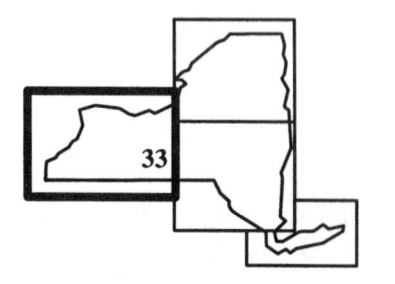

- Located 1 mile south of Moravia or 8 miles north of Groton off State Route 38
- Open mid–May through mid–October for camping
- State Park is Open All Year
- 70 Tent & Trailer Sites (no electric sites, trailer dump)
- 3 Cabins
- 938 Acres
- Comfort Station (flush toilets & sink) and Showers
- Potable Water (throughout campground)
- Pets Allowed
- Handicapped Accessible
- Picnic Areas
- Picnic Pavilions (3 reservable and 1 first come basis)
- Recreation Program
- Hiking Trails and Gorge Hikes
- Swimming in Gorge Pool
- Fishing (in Owasco Lake – boat launch approximately 5 miles north on Route 38)
- Hunting
- Rollerblading in General Park Area Only
- Baseball and Soccer Field, Horseshoe Pits, and Playground
- 18 Hole Golf Course (1 mile south of the park)
- Cross Country Skiing and Snowmobiling

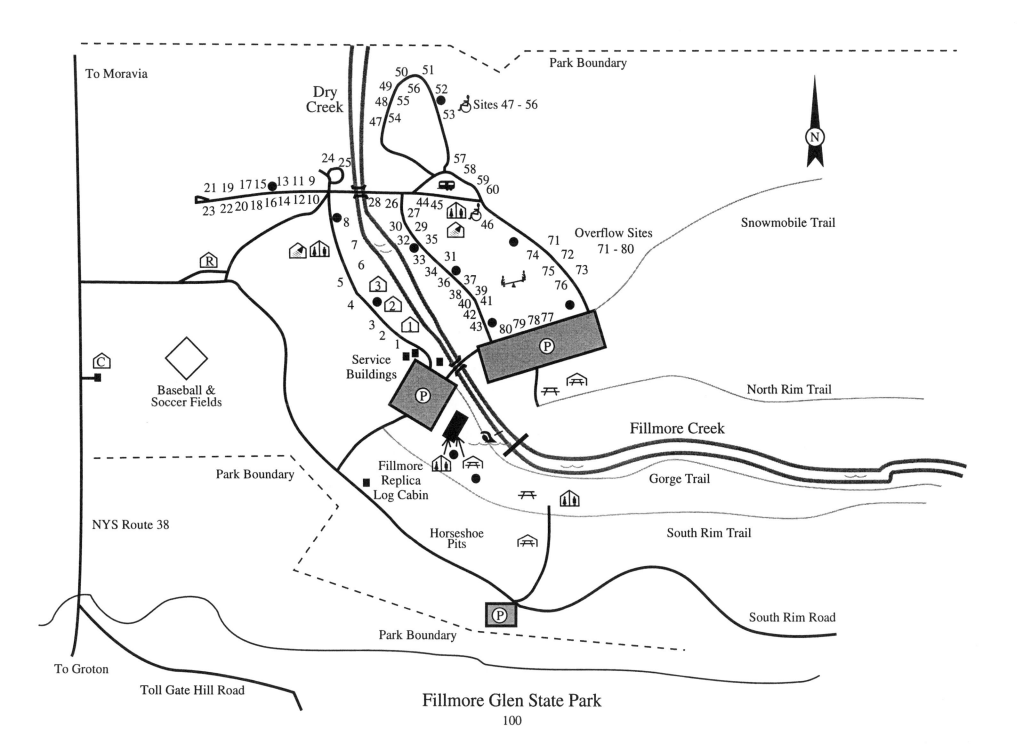

To Moravia

Dry Creek

50 51
49 56 52
48 55
47 54 53

Sites 47 - 56

N

Park Boundary

57
58
59 60

Snowmobile Trail

24 25

21 19 17 15 13 11 9
23 22 20 18 16 14 12 10

28 26
27 44 45
30 29 46
32 35
33 31
34
36 37
38 39
40 41
42
43

71
74 72
75 73
76

80 79 78 77

Overflow Sites
71 - 80

8

7
6
5
4
3 2
3 2
1

R

C

Baseball &
Soccer Fields

Service
Buildings

P

P

Fillmore Creek

North Rim Trail

Gorge Trail

South Rim Trail

Fillmore
Replica
Log Cabin

Horseshoe
Pits

NYS Route 38

Park Boundary

P

South Rim Road

Park Boundary

To Groton

Toll Gate Hill Road

Fillmore Glen State Park

Fish Creek Pond Public Campground

Star Route, Box 75, Saranac Lake, NY 12983

(518) 891–4560

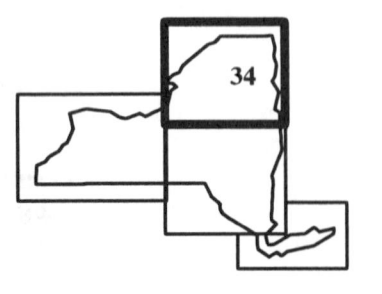

- Located 12 miles northeast of Tupper Lake or 17 miles west of Saranac Lake off State Route 30
- Open mid–April through mid–November for camping
- 355 Tent & Trailer Sites (no electric sites, trailer dump, max RV 40 foot)
- 121 Acres
- Comfort Station (flush toilets & sink) and Showers
- Potable Water
- Public Telephone
- Pets Allowed
- Handicapped Accessible
- Picnic Areas
- Picnic Pavilions (2 reservable)
- Recreation Program
- Hiking Trails
- Swimming with Sand Beach and Bath House
- Fishing in Fish Creek and Square Ponds
- Bicycling on Campground Roads
- Basketball, Playground and Volleyball
- Boat Launch
- Boat Rental (at adjacent Rollins Pond Public Campground)
- Amphitheater
- Recreation Office

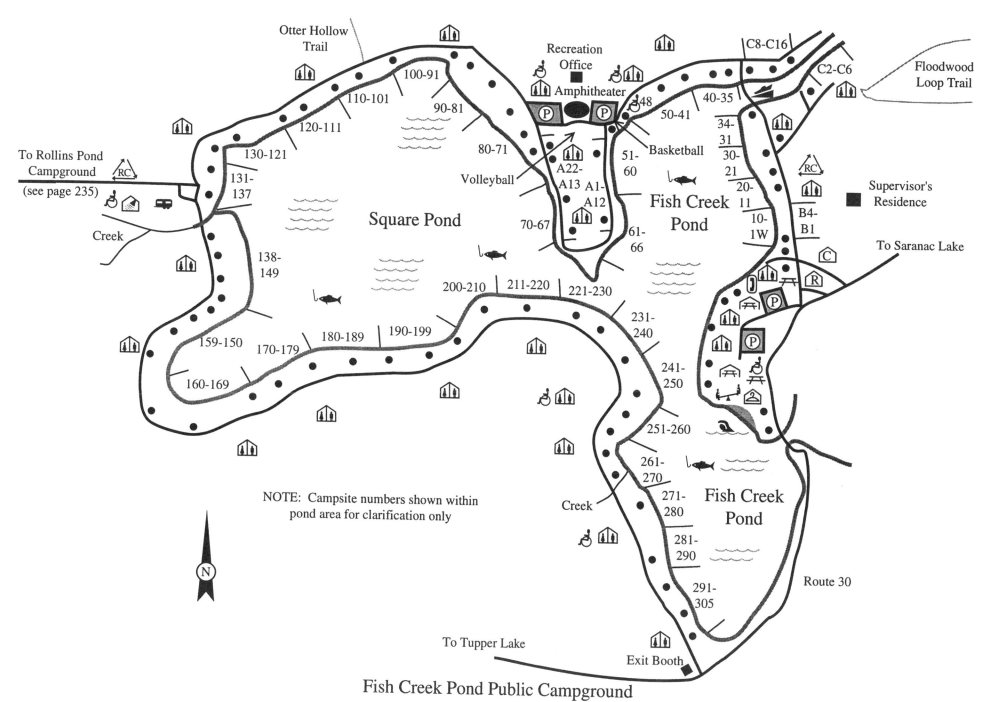

Otter Hollow Trail

Recreation Office

C8-C16

C2-C6

Floodwood Loop Trail

Amphitheater

100-91

110-101

120-111

130-121

To Rollins Pond Campground (see page 235)

RC

131-137

Creek

90-81

80-71

Volleyball

A22-A13

A1-A12

70-67

48

50-41

51-60

Basketball

40-35

34-31

30-21

20-11

10-1W

B4-B1

Fish Creek Pond

RC

Supervisor's Residence

To Saranac Lake

C

R

Square Pond

138-149

200-210

211-220

221-230

231-240

P

159-150

170-179

180-189

190-199

241-250

251-260

160-169

261-270

271-280

Creek

281-290

Fish Creek Pond

291-305

Route 30

NOTE: Campsite numbers shown within pond area for clarification only

N

To Tupper Lake

Exit Booth

Fish Creek Pond Public Campground

Forked Lake Primitive Public Campground

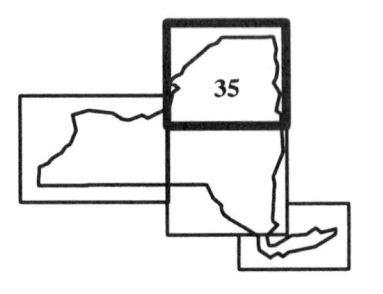

County Road 20, Long Lake, NY 12847

(518) 624–6646

- Located 5 miles southwest of Deerland Village or 5 miles southwest of Long Lake off State Route 30
- Open mid–May through Labor Day for camping
- **Primitive Campground** (minimal facilities, access to sites 3 – 35, 63 – 78, and 69A is by hiking trail or boat only, access to sites 36 – 62 is by boat only)
- 77 Tent Sites (no electric sites)
- 27 Acres
- Pit Toilet (at all sites)
- Potable Water
- Picnic Area
- Hiking Trails (within approximately 5 miles)
- Swimming (no designated area)
- Fishing in Forked Lake
- Boat Launch (gravel launch)
- Boat and Canoe Rental (at park office)

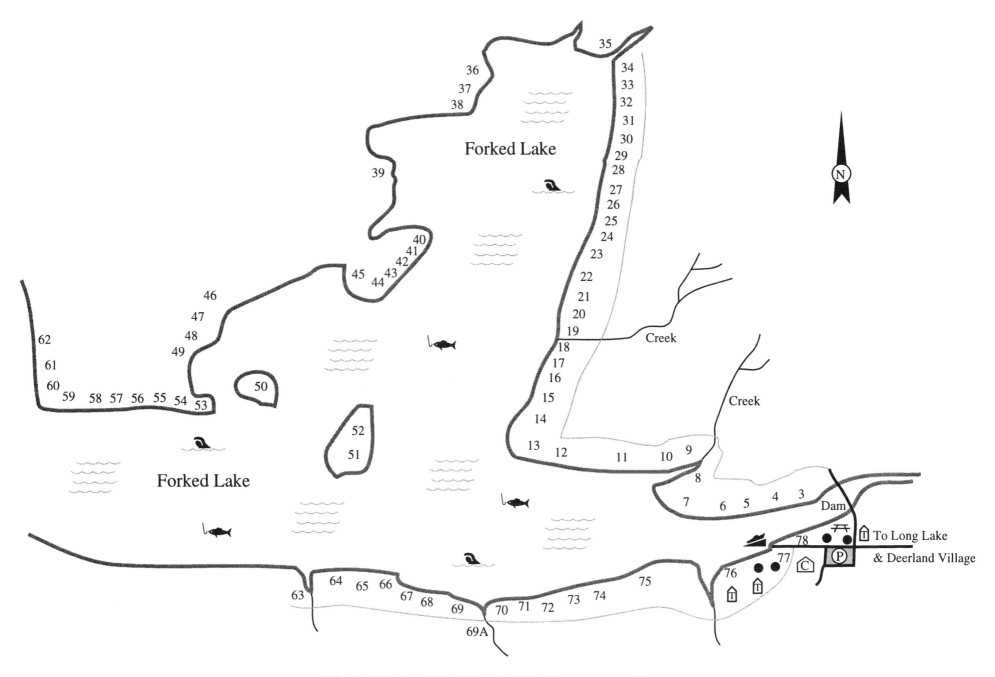

Forked Lake

Forked Lake

Creek

Creek

Dam

To Long Lake
& Deerland Village

N

Forked Lake Primitive Public Campground

Four Mile Creek State Park

One Four Mile Drive, Youngstown, NY 14174

(716) 745–3802

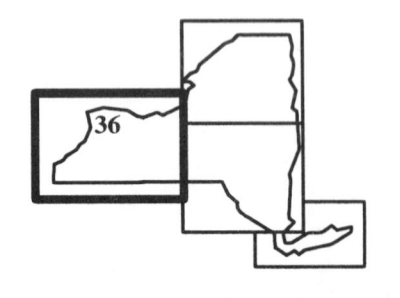

- Located 3 miles east of Youngstown off State Route 18
- Open mid–April through mid–October for camping
- 278 Tent & Trailer Sites (119 electric sites, trailer dump)
- 248 Acres
- Comfort Station (flush toilets & sink)
- Potable Water
- Pets Allowed
- Handicapped Accessible
- Picnic Pavilion
- Recreation Program
- Fishing in Lake Ontario and Four Mile Creek
- Playground
- Store

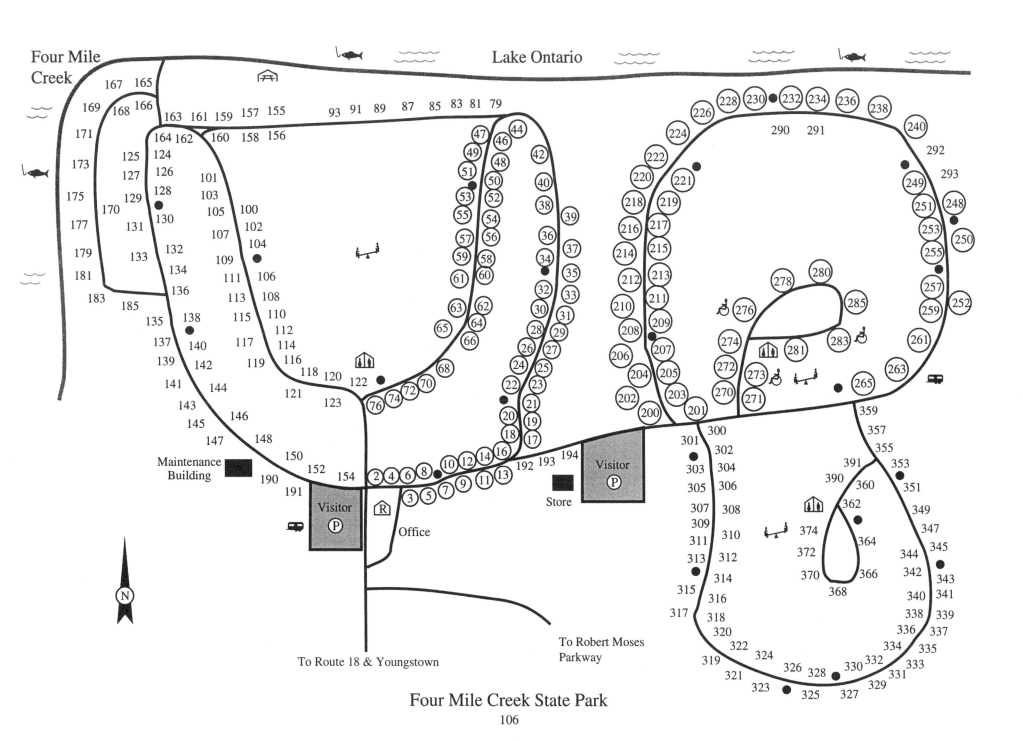

Four Mile Creek State Park

106

Gilbert Lake State Park

18 CCC Road, Laurens, NY 13796

(607) 432–2114

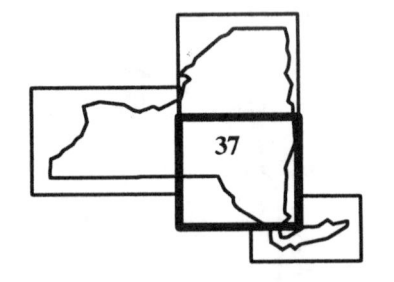

- Located 10 miles north of Oneonta or 4 miles north of Laurens off State Route 12
- Open mid–May through mid–October for camping
- State Park is Open All Year
- 221 Tent & Trailer Sites (17 electric sites, trailer dump)
- 1,590 Acres
- 33 Cabins
- Comfort Station (flush toilets & sink) and Showers
- Potable Water
- Public Telephone
- Pets Allowed
- Handicapped Accessible
- Picnic Area and Pavilions (3 reservable)
- Recreation Program
- Hiking and Nature Trails, Nature Center, and Concessions
- Swimming with Sand Beach and Bath House
- Fishing in Gilbert Lake
- Hunting (archery only)
- Bicycling on Campground Roads
- Softball Field, Basketball, Horseshoe Pits, Playground, Volleyball, and Frisbee Golf Course
- Boat Launch (cartop launch, permit required)
- Rowboat Rental (at concession building)
- Cross Country Skiing and Snowmobiling

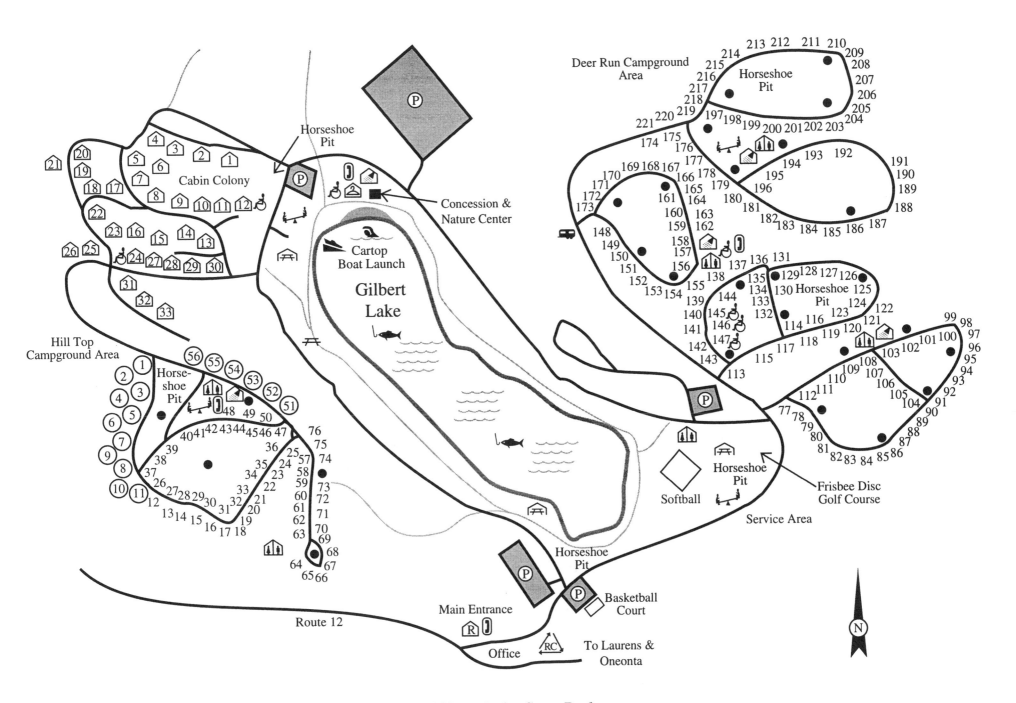

Gilbert Lake State Park

108

Glimmerglass State Park

1527 County Highway 31, Cooperstown, NY 13326

(607) 547–8662

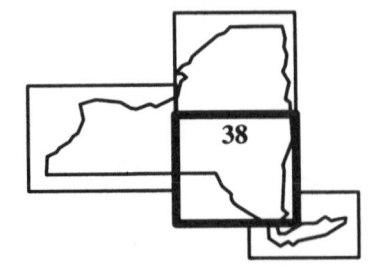

- Located 8 miles north of Cooperstown off County Route 31
- Open May through mid–October for camping
- State Park is Open All Year
- 83 Tent & Trailer Sites (no electric sites, 10 primitive sites, trailer dump)
- 593 Acres
- Comfort Station (flush toilets & sink) and Showers
- Potable Water
- Public Telephone
- Pets Allowed
- Handicapped Accessible
- Picnic Area
- Picnic Pavilion (2 reservable pavilions and 3 reservable tents)
- Recreation Program
- Hiking Trails
- Swimming with Sand Beach and Bath House
- Fishing in Otsego Lake
- Bicycling on Campground Roads
- Baseball Field, Basketball Court, Volleyball, Horseshoe Pits, and Playground
- Boat Launch (cartop launch, public launch in Cooperstown – 7 miles south)
- Primitive Winter Camping (self–contained units only) and Hyde Hall Mansion
- Cross Country Skiing, Ice Fishing, Ice Skating, Snowtubing Hill, and Snowmobiling

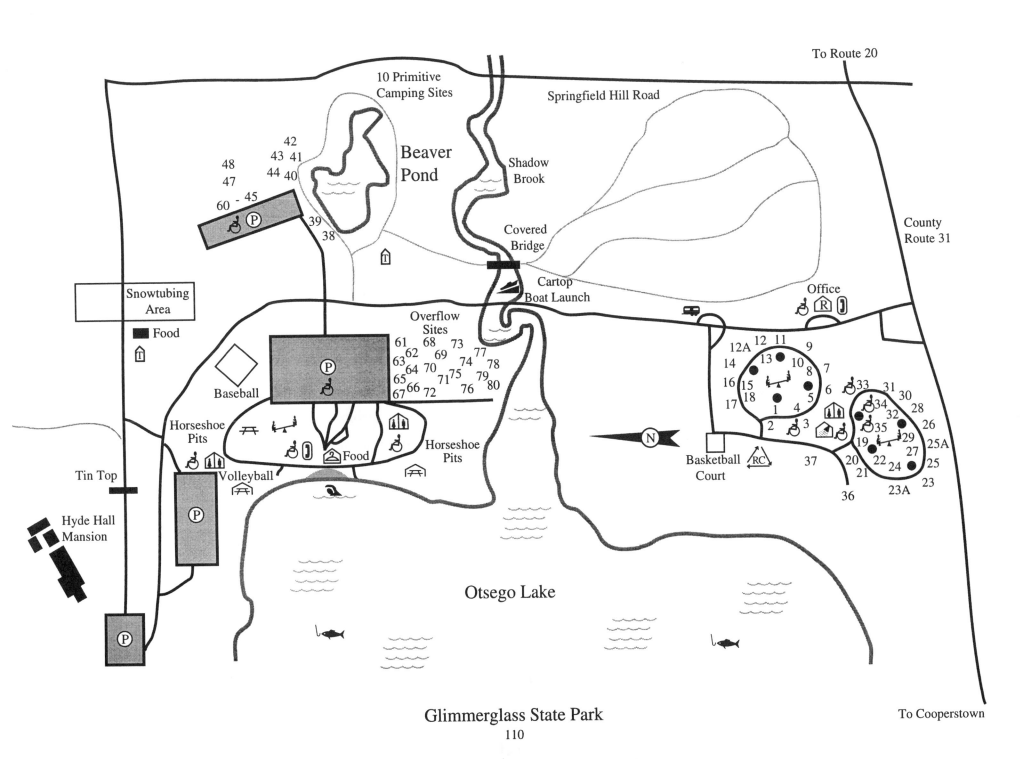

Glimmerglass State Park

110

Golden Beach Public Campground

State Route 28, Raquette Lake Village, NY 13436

(315) 354–4230

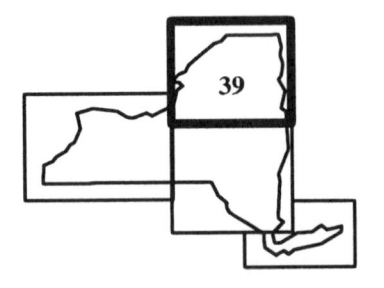

- Located 4 miles east of Raquette Lake Village or 9 miles west of Blue Mountain Lake off State Route 28
- Open mid–May through Labor Day for camping
- 186 Tent & Trailer Sites (no electric sites, trailer dump)
- 40 Acres
- Comfort Station (flush toilets & sink) and Showers
- Potable Water
- Public Telephone
- Pets Allowed
- Handicapped Accessible
- Picnic Area
- Hiking Trails (within approximately 4 miles)
- Swimming with Sand Beach and Bath House
- Fishing in Raquette Lake
- Bicycling on Campground Roads
- Boat Launch
- Boat and Canoe Rental (at Raquette Lake Village)
- Cabin

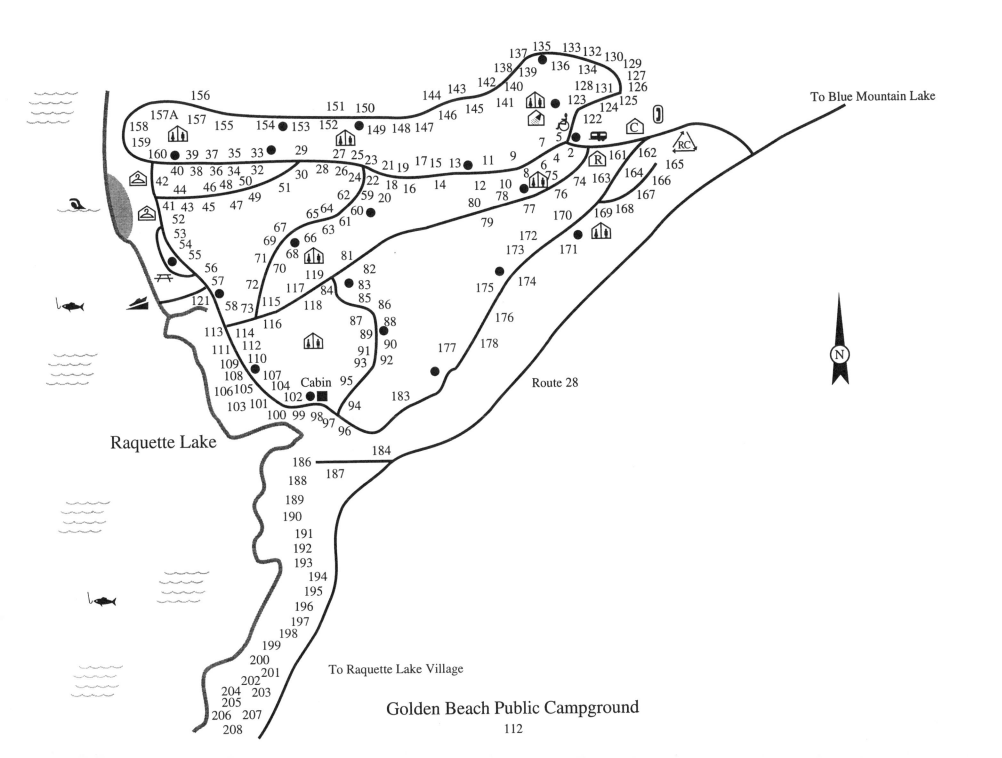

To Blue Mountain Lake

Raquette Lake

Route 28

To Raquette Lake Village

Golden Beach Public Campground

112

Golden Hill State Park

9691 Lower Lake Road, Barker, NY 14012

(716) 795–3855

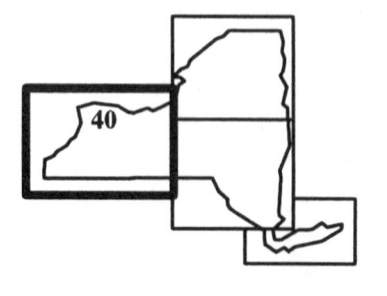

- Located 2 miles north of County Line off Lower Lake Road
- Open late–April through mid–October for camping
- 55 Tent & Trailer Sites (21 electric sites, trailer dump)
- 510 Acres
- Comfort Station (flush toilets & sink) and Showers
- Potable Water (throughout campground)
- Handicapped Accessible
- Picnic Area (at boat launch area)
- Picnic Pavilions (3 reservable)
- Recreation Program and Hall
- Hiking Trails (throughout park)
- Fishing in Lake Ontario
- Hunting (after campground is closed, small game only)
- Bicycling on Campground Roads
- Horseshoe Pits
- Playground
- Boat Launch (approximately 1/2 mile east of the park off Lower Lake Road)
- Cross Country Skiing, Snowshoeing and Snowmobiling
- Lighthouse

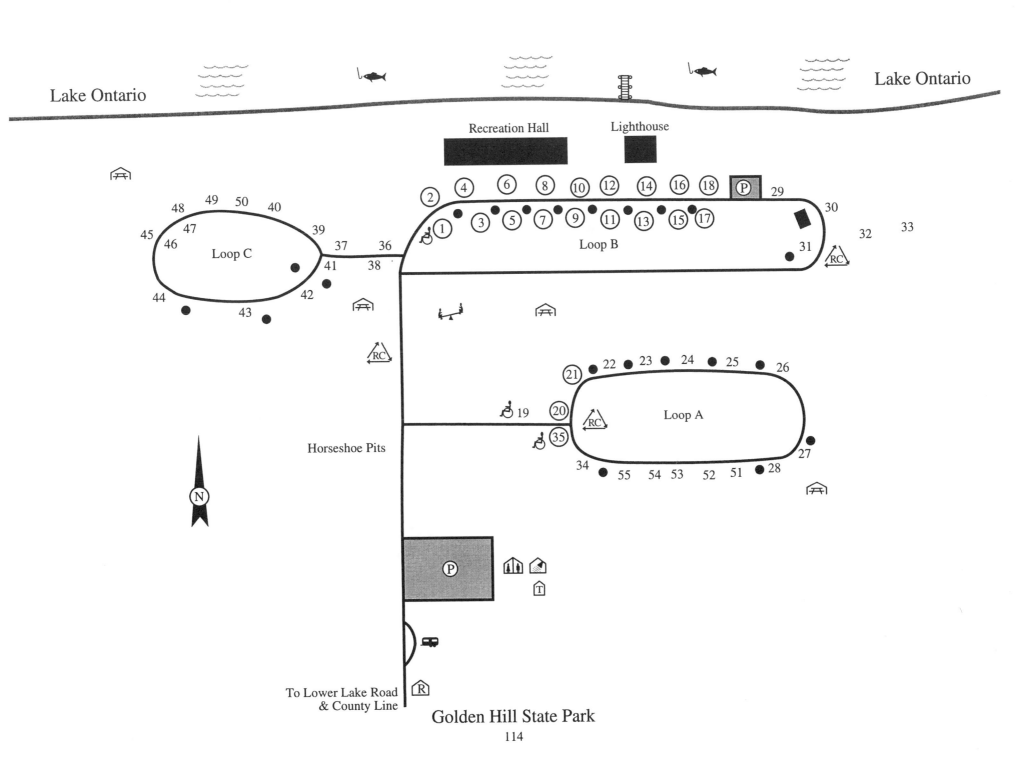

Lake Ontario

Lake Ontario

Recreation Hall

Lighthouse

Loop C

Loop B

Loop A

Horseshoe Pits

N

To Lower Lake Road
& County Line

Golden Hill State Park

114

Grass Point State Park

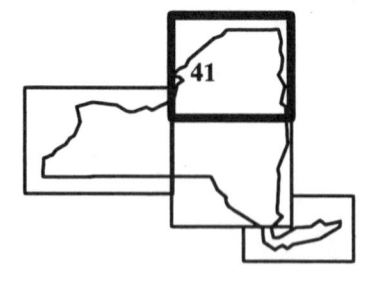

c/o Cedar Point State Park, 36661 Cedar Point State Park Dr., Clayton, NY 13624

(315) 686–4472

- Located 6 miles southwest of Alexandria Bay or 5 miles northeast of Clayton
  off State Route 12
- Open mid–May through mid–September for camping
- 77 Tent & Trailer Sites (22 electric sites, trailer dump)
- 65 Acres
- Comfort Station (flush toilets & sink) and Showers
- Potable Water
- Public Telephone
- Pets Allowed
- Handicapped Accessible
- Picnic Area
- Picnic Pavilion (reservable)
- Swimming with Sand Beach
- Fishing in St. Lawrence River
- Hunting (waterfowl in season with permit only)
- Playground
- Docks and Pier
- Boat Launch and Marina (32 slips)
- Boat Trailer Parking
- Cross Country Skiing
- Store

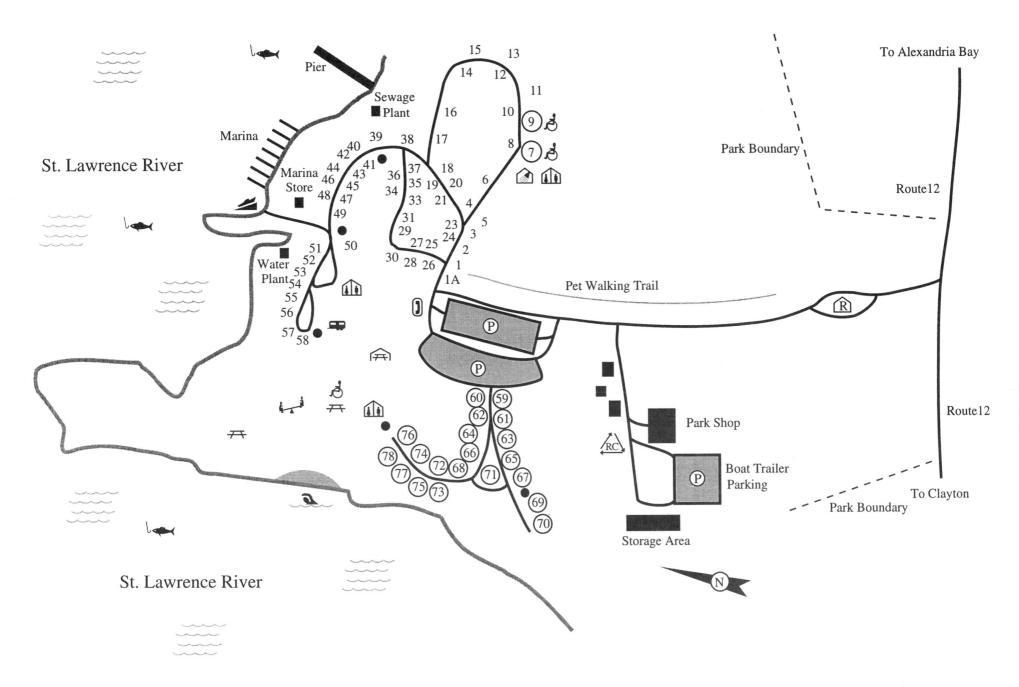

Grass Point State Park

116

Green Lakes State Park

7900 Green Lakes Road, Fayetteville, NY 13066

(315) 637–6111

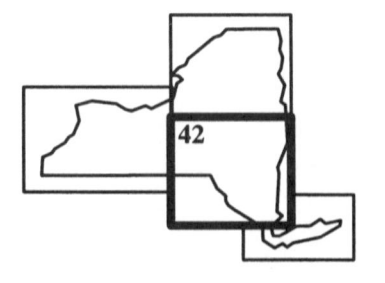

- Located 4 miles northeast of Fayetteville off State Route 290
- Open mid–May through mid–October for camping
- State Park is Open All Year
- 137 Tent & Trailer Sites (42 electric sites, trailer dump)
- 7 Cabins
- 1,835 Acres
- Comfort Station (flush toilets & sink) and Showers
- Potable Water
- Public Telephone
- Pets Allowed
- Handicapped Accessible
- Picnic Areas (1 reservable) and Pavilions (2 reservable)
- Recreation Program
- Hiking and Nature Trails
- Swimming with Sand Beach and Bath House (concessions)
- Fishing in Green Lake
- Bicycling on Campground Roads (mountain biking on designated off road trails)
- Softball Field, Basketball Court, Frisbee Golf Course, and Playground
- 18 Hole Golf Course and Clubhouse (with restaurant)
- Rowboat and Paddleboat Rental (Memorial Day to Labor Day – no private boats)
- Cross Country Skiing and Snowshoeing

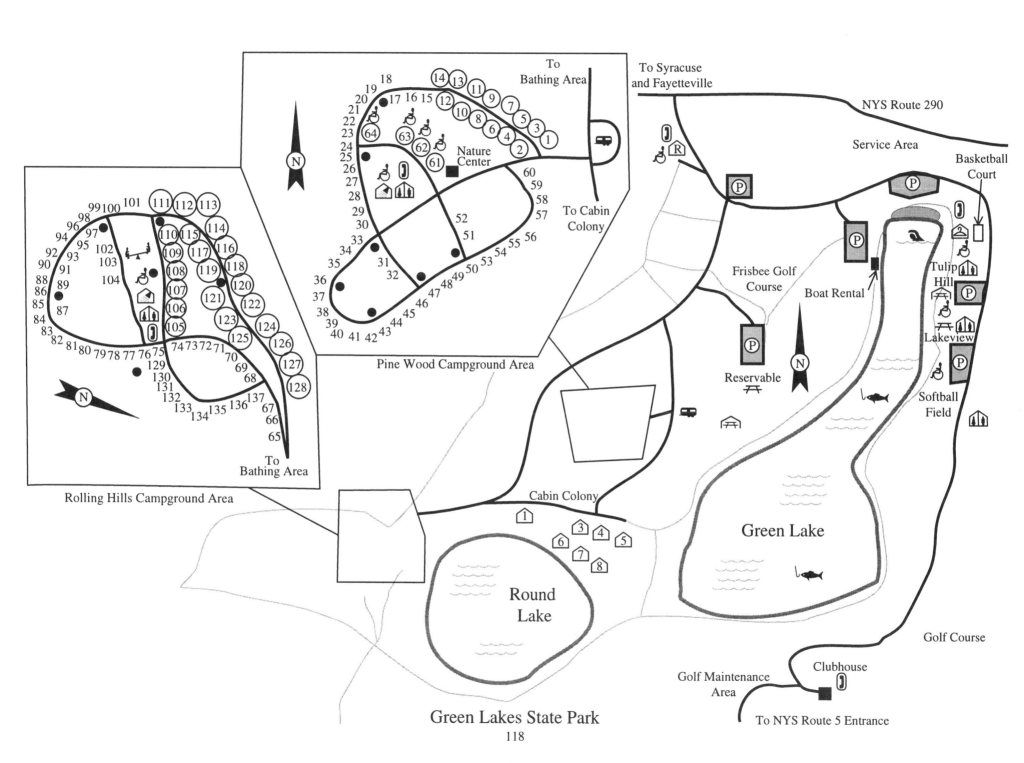

Pine Wood Campground Area

Rolling Hills Campground Area

To Bathing Area

To Syracuse and Fayetteville

NYS Route 290

Service Area

Basketball Court

To Cabin Colony

Nature Center

Frisbee Golf Course

Boat Rental

Tulip Hill

Lakeview

Reservable

Softball Field

Cabin Colony

Green Lake

Round Lake

Golf Course

Golf Maintenance Area

Clubhouse

To NYS Route 5 Entrance

Green Lakes State Park

118

Hamlin Beach State Park

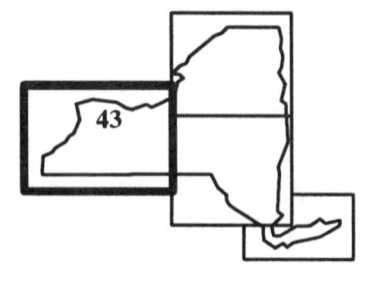

1 Camp Road, Hamlin, NY 14464

(845) 964–2121

- Located 5 miles north of Hamlin or 21 miles northwest of Rochester off Lake Ontario State Parkway
- Open All Year for camping
- 264 Tent & Trailer Sites (264 electric sites, trailer dump, max RV 35 foot)
- 1,200 Acres
- Comfort Station (flush toilets & sink) and Showers
- Potable Water
- Public Telephone
- Pets Allowed (sites 1–73 only)
- Handicapped Accessible
- Picnic Areas
- Picnic Pavilions (4 reservable)
- Recreation Program and Hall
- Hiking and Nature Trails
- Swimming with Sand Beach and Bath House
- Fishing in Lake Ontario
- Bicycling on Campground Roads
- Baseball Field, Basketball Court, Horseshoe Pits, and Playground
- Boat Launch (cartop launch)
- Cross Country Skiing and Snowmobiling
- Group Camping Area
- Camp Store

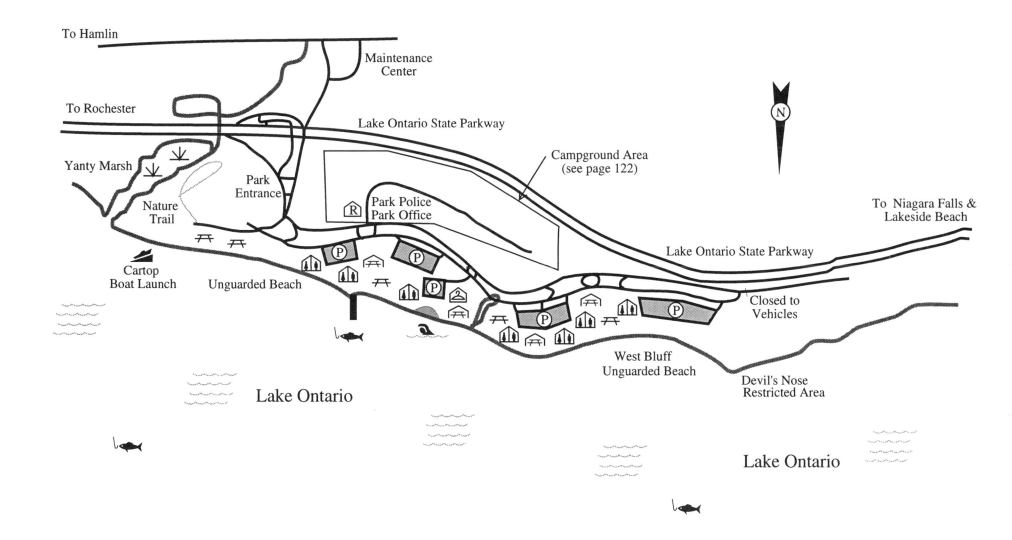

To Hamlin

Maintenance Center

To Rochester

Lake Ontario State Parkway

N

Yanty Marsh

Campground Area (see page 122)

Park Entrance

Nature Trail

Park Police Park Office

R

To Niagara Falls & Lakeside Beach

Cartop Boat Launch

Unguarded Beach

P

P

P

Lake Ontario State Parkway

P

P

Closed to Vehicles

West Bluff Unguarded Beach

Lake Ontario

Devil's Nose Restricted Area

Lake Ontario

Hamlin Beach State Park

Hamlin Beach State Park

(see page 119 for campground information and main park map)

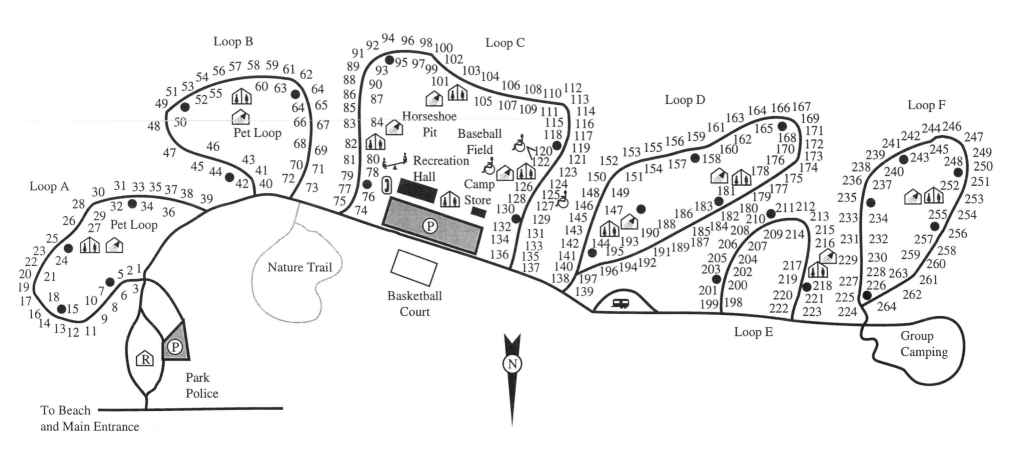

Loop B

Loop C

Loop D

Loop F

Loop A

Horseshoe Pit

Baseball Field

Recreation Hall

Camp Store

Pet Loop

Pet Loop

Nature Trail

Basketball Court

Loop E

Group Camping

Park Police

To Beach
and Main Entrance

N

NOTE: ALL CAMPSITES
ARE ELECTRIC

Hamlin Beach State Park

Harriman State Park – Beaver Pond

800 County Road, Route 106, Stony Point, NY 10980

(914) 947–2792

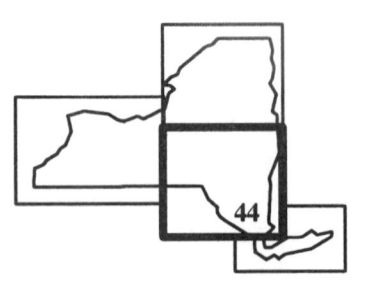

- Located 5 miles west of Stony Point off County Road 106
- Open mid–April through mid–October for camping
- State Park is Open All Year
- 146 Tent & Trailer Sites (no electric sites, 7 trailer sites, trailer dump, 55 tent platform sites, max RV 40 foot)
- 25 Acres
- Comfort Station (flush toilets & sink) and Showers
- Potable Water (throughout campground)
- Public Telephone
- Handicapped Accessible (ground sites only)
- Picnic Area
- Recreation Program
- Hiking Trails (within approximately 4 miles)
- Swimming with Sand Beach and Bath House
- Fishing in Lake Welch
- Boat Launch (cartop launch, electric motors only, permit required)
- Paddleboat Rental (at beach area)
- Snowmobiling (snowmobile must be registered at Lake Welch)
- Recreation Building
- Laundry

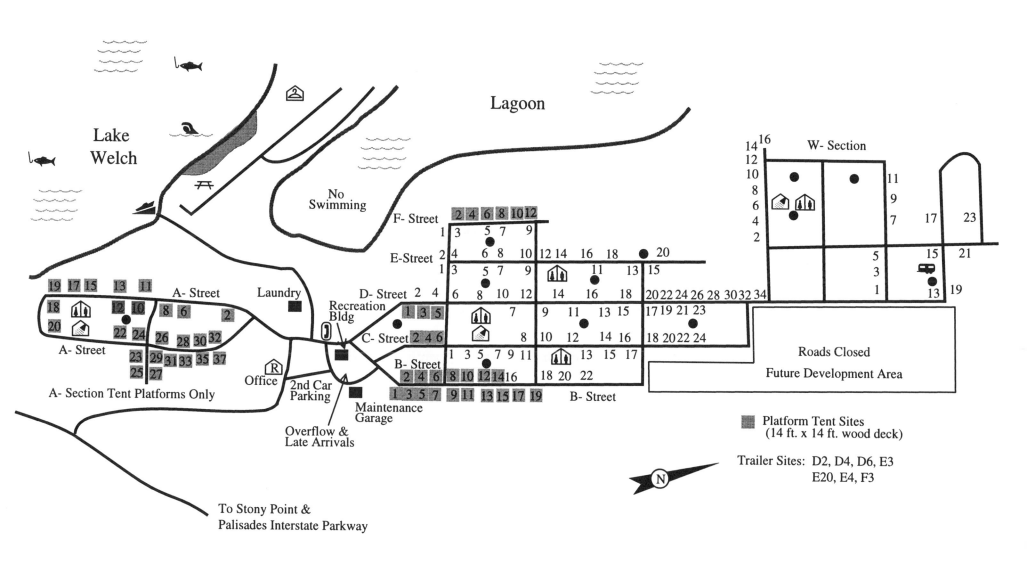

Lake Welch

Lagoon

No Swimming

W- Section

F- Street

E-Street

D- Street

Laundry

Recreation Bldg

C- Street

A- Street

A- Street

A- Section Tent Platforms Only

Office

2nd Car Parking

Overflow & Late Arrivals

Maintenance Garage

B- Street

B- Street

Roads Closed

Future Development Area

To Stony Point & Palisades Interstate Parkway

Platform Tent Sites
(14 ft. x 14 ft. wood deck)

Trailer Sites: D2, D4, D6, E3
E20, E4, F3

N

Harriman State Park – Beaver Pond

Harriman State Park – Sebago Cabin Complex

7 Lake Drive, Bear Mountain, NY 10911

(845) 351–9808

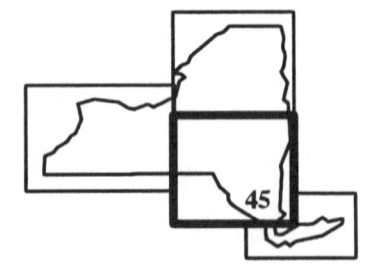

- Located 6 miles west of Sloatsburg or 10 miles south of Bear Mountain off Seven Lakes Parkway
- Open mid–April through mid–October for camping
- 41 Cabins
- 50 Acres
- Comfort Station (flush toilets & sink), Pit Toilets, and Showers
- Potable Water (throughout campground)
- Handicapped Accessible
- Picnic Area (located at each cabin and restricted to those staying in cabins)
- Recreation Program
- Hiking Trails (within approximately 1 mile)
- Swimming with Sand Beach
- Fishing in Lake Sebago
- Dock
- Bicycling on Campground Roads
- Baseball Field, Basketball Court, Horseshoe Pit, Playground, and Tennis Courts
- Boat Launch (electric motors only, permit required)
- Rowboat Rental
- Cross Country Skiing
- Recreation Hall
- Laundry
- Store and Bonfire Pit

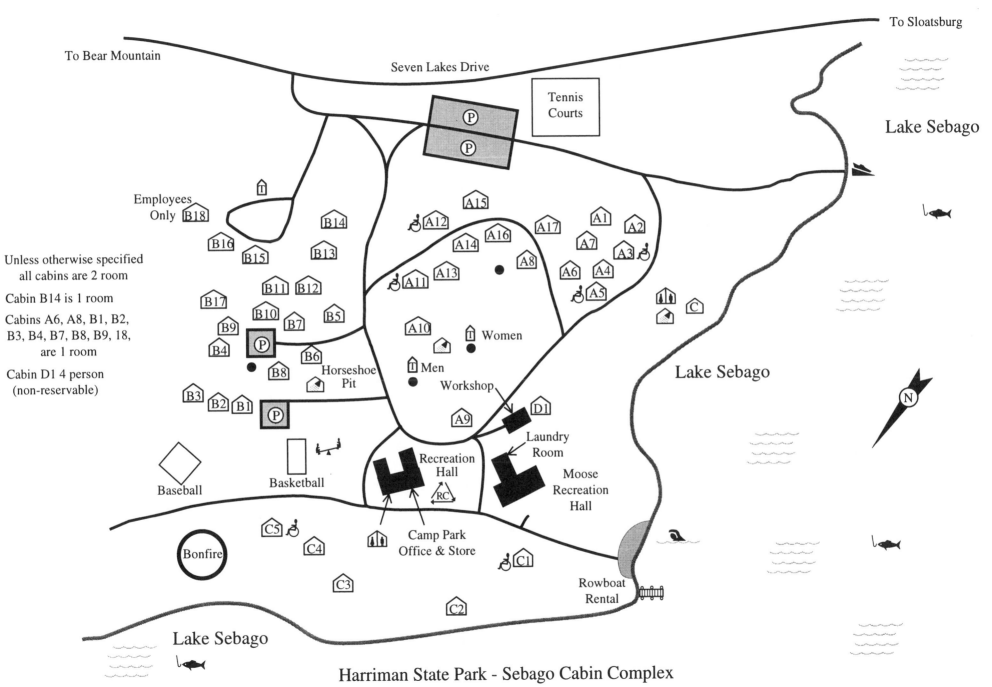

To Sloatsburg

To Bear Mountain

Seven Lakes Drive

Tennis Courts

Lake Sebago

P

P

Employees Only

B18

T

B14

A15

A12

A17

A1

A2

B16

B13

A16

A7

A3

B15

A14

A8

Unless otherwise specified all cabins are 2 room

B11

B12

A11

A13

A6

A4

Cabin B14 is 1 room

B17

B10

B5

A5

Cabins A6, A8, B1, B2, B3, B4, B7, B8, B9, 18, are 1 room

B9

B7

C

Cabin D1 4 person (non-reservable)

B4

P

A10

T Women

B6

Horseshoe Pit

T Men

Lake Sebago

B8

B3

B2

B1

P

Workshop

D1

A9

Laundry Room

Baseball

Basketball

Recreation Hall

RC

Moose Recreation Hall

C5

Camp Park Office & Store

C4

C1

Bonfire

C3

Rowboat Rental

C2

Lake Sebago

Harriman State Park - Sebago Cabin Complex

126

Hearthstone Point Public Campground

Route 9N, Lake George, NY 12885

(518) 668–5193

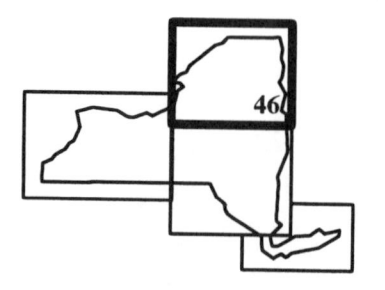

- Located 2 miles north of Lake George Village or 2 miles south of Diamond Point off State Route 9N
- Open mid–May through Labor Day for camping
- 241 Tent & Trailer Sites (no electric sites, 175 trailer sites, trailer dump,max 40 foot RV)
- 89 Acres
- Comfort Station (flush toilets & sink) and Showers
- Potable Water
- Public Telephone
- Pets Allowed
- Handicapped Accessible
- Picnic Area
- Swimming with Sand Beach
- Fishing in Lake George
- Bicycling on Campground Roads
- Boat Launch (nearby marina)

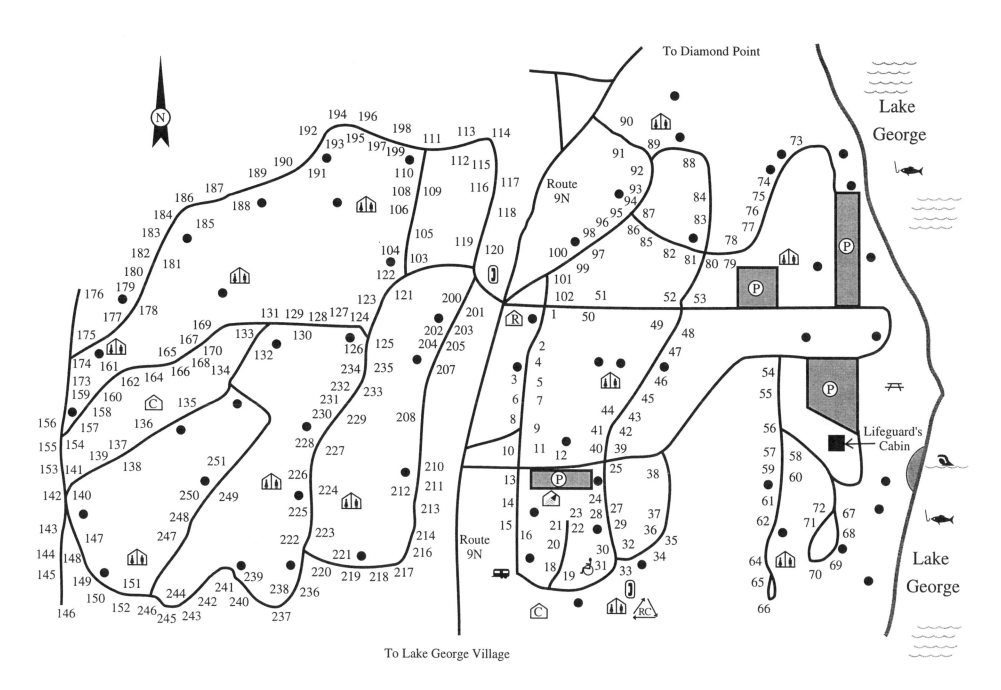

Lake George

To Diamond Point

Route 9N

Route 9N

To Lake George Village

Lifeguard's Cabin

Lake George

Hearthstone Point Public Campground

128

Heckscher State Park

P. O. Box 160, East Islip, NY 11730

(631) 581–2100

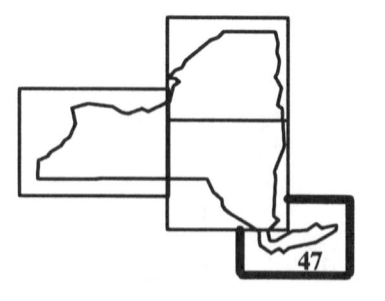

- Located 2 miles south of East Islip or 50 miles east of New York City off
  Southern State Parkway
- Open Memorial Day through Labor Day for camping
- State Park is Open All Year
- 69 Tent & Trailer Sites (no electric sites, trailer dump)
- 1,657 Acres
- Comfort Station (flush toilets & sink) and Showers
- Potable Water
- Handicapped Accessible
- Picnic Areas
- Picnic Pavilion (reservable by permit only)
- Recreation Program
- Hiking Trails
- Swimming with Sand Beach and Pool (pool open mid – June until Labor Day)
- Fishing in Great South Bay and Nicoll Bay
- Bicycling on Campground Roads
- Ball Fields, Basketball Court, and Playground
- Boat Launch (powerboats and hand launch boats)
- Cross Country Skiing and Snowshoeing
- Refreshment Stand

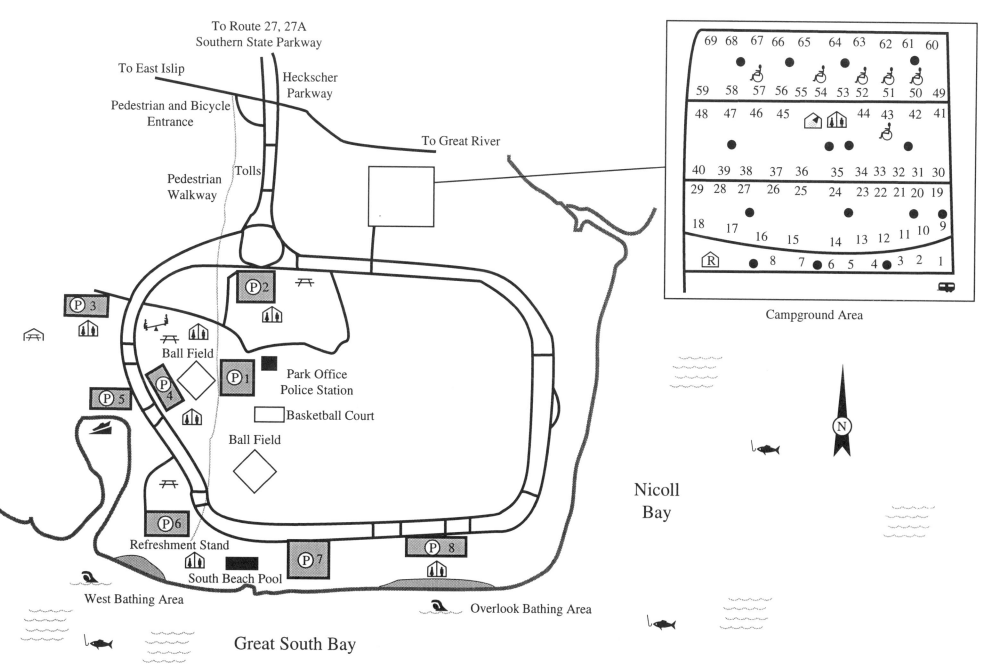

Campground Area

Nicoll
Bay

Ball Field

Park Office
Police Station

Basketball Court

Ball Field

Refreshment Stand

South Beach Pool

West Bathing Area

Overlook Bathing Area

Great South Bay

To Route 27, 27A
Southern State Parkway

To East Islip

Heckscher
Parkway

Pedestrian and Bicycle
Entrance

To Great River

Pedestrian
Walkway

Tolls

Heckscher State Park

Higley Flow State Park

442 Cold Brook Drive, Colton, NY 13625

(315) 262–2880

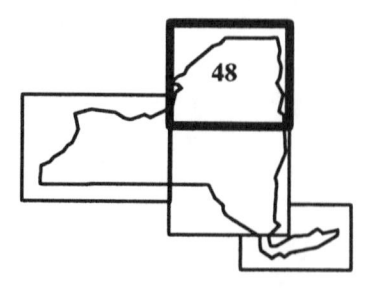

- Located 2 miles west of South Colton off State Route 56
- Open mid–May through Labor Day for camping
- State Park is Open All Year
- 135 Tent & Trailer Sites (43 electric sites, trailer dump)
- 1,250 Acres
- Comfort Station (flush toilets & sink) and Showers
- Potable Water
- Public Telephone
- Pets Allowed
- Handicapped Accessible
- Picnic Area
- Hiking and Nature Trails (within approximately 5 miles)
- Swimming with Sand Beach and Bath House
- Fishing in Raquette River
- Hunting (deer only in designated areas)
- Bicycling on Campground Roads
- Baseball Field, Basketball Court, Horseshoe Pit, and Playground
- Boat Launch
- Cross Country Skiing, Snowshoeing, and Snowmobiling

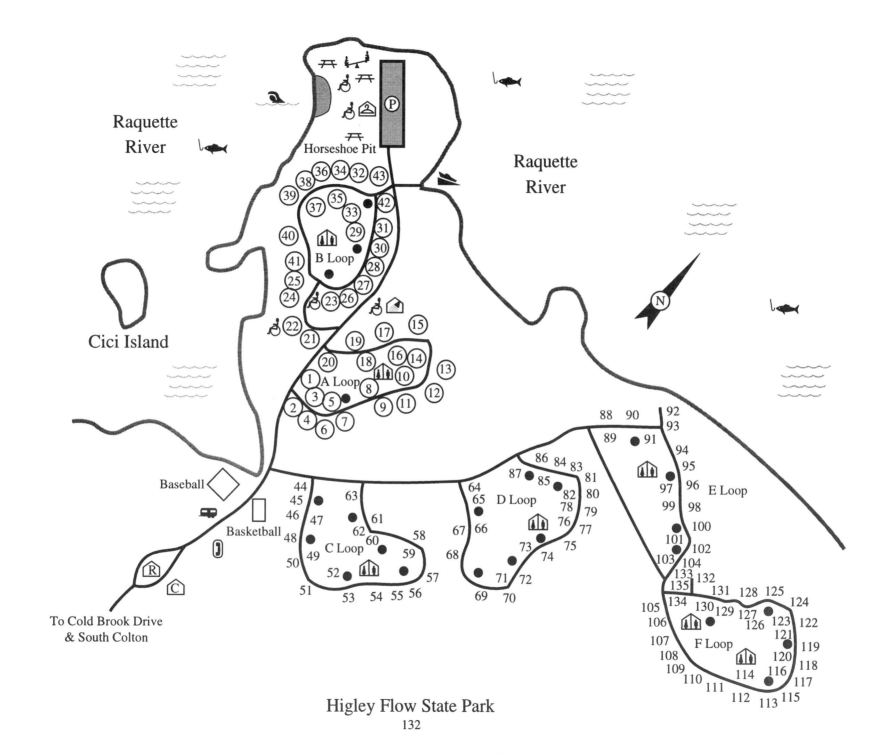

Raquette River

Raquette River

Cici Island

Horseshoe Pit

B Loop

A Loop

Baseball

Basketball

C Loop

D Loop

E Loop

F Loop

To Cold Brook Drive
& South Colton

Higley Flow State Park

132

Hither Hills State Park

50 South Fairview Ave, Montauk, NY 11954

(631) 668–2554

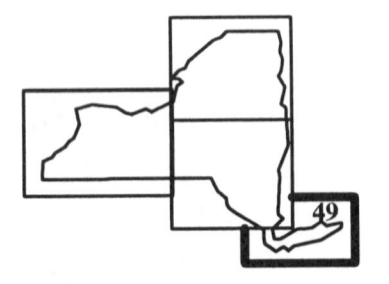

- Located 4 miles southwest of Montauk or 6 miles northeast of Amagansett off State Route 27
- Open mid–April through mid–November for camping
- State Park is Open All Year
- 168 Tent & Trailer Sites (no electric sites, trailer dump)
- 1,755 Acres
- Comfort Station (flush toilets & sink) and Showers
- Potable Water
- Handicapped Accessible
- Picnic Areas
- Recreation Program
- Hiking Trails
- Swimming with Sand Beach and Bath House
- Fishing in Atlantic Ocean, Napeague Bay and Harbor, and Fresh Pond (freshwater)
- Hunting
- Bicycling and Rollerblading on Campground Roads
- Baseball Field, Volleyball Courts, Horseshoe Pits, and Playground
- Cross Country Skiing and Snowshoeing
- General Store

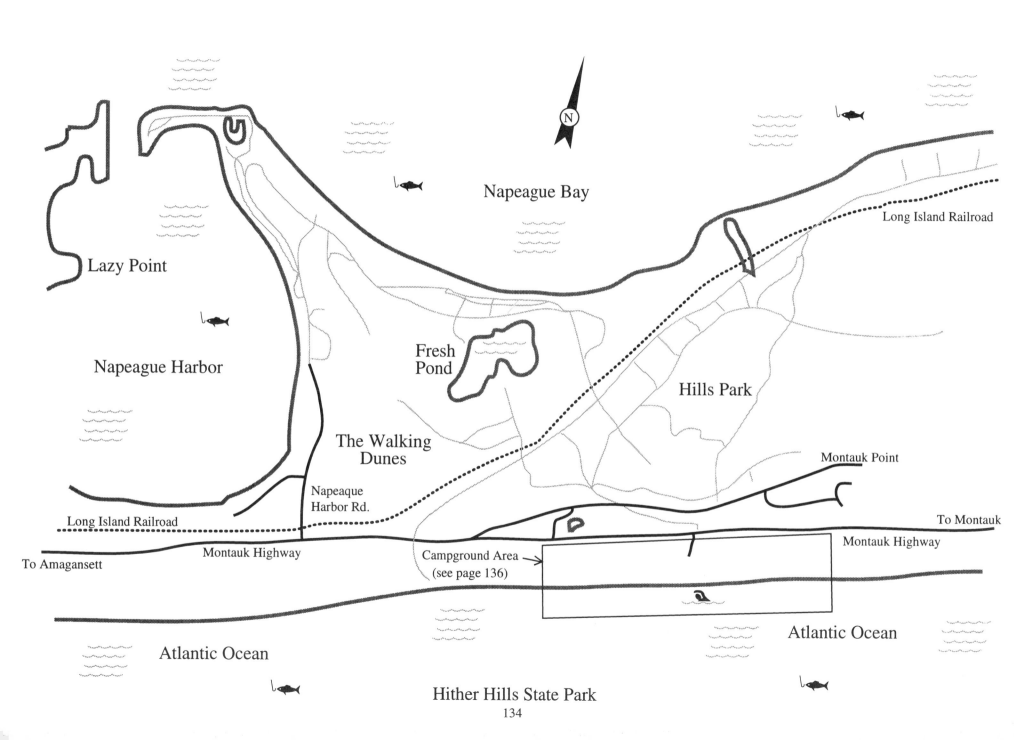

Lazy Point

Napeague Harbor

Napeague Bay

Fresh Pond

Hills Park

The Walking Dunes

Long Island Railroad

Napeaque Harbor Rd.

Montauk Point

Long Island Railroad

Montauk Highway

To Amagansett

Campground Area
(see page 136)

Montauk Highway

To Montauk

Atlantic Ocean

Atlantic Ocean

Hither Hills State Park

Hither Hills State Park

(see page 133 for campground information and main park map)

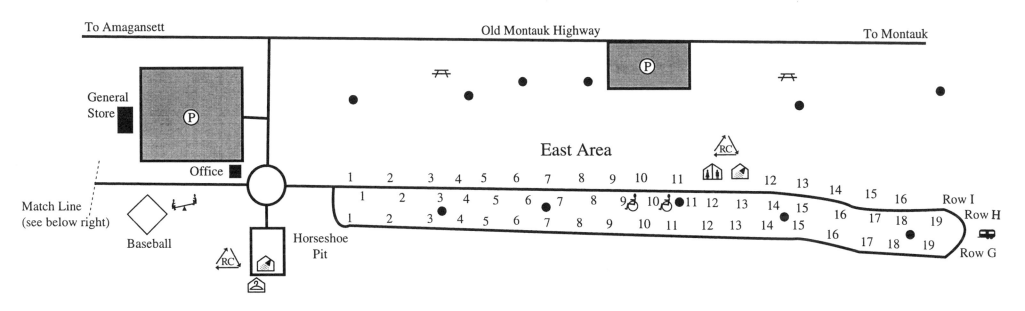

To Amagansett

Old Montauk Highway

To Montauk

General
Store

Office

Match Line
(see below right)

Baseball

Horseshoe
Pit

East Area

Row I
Row H
Row G

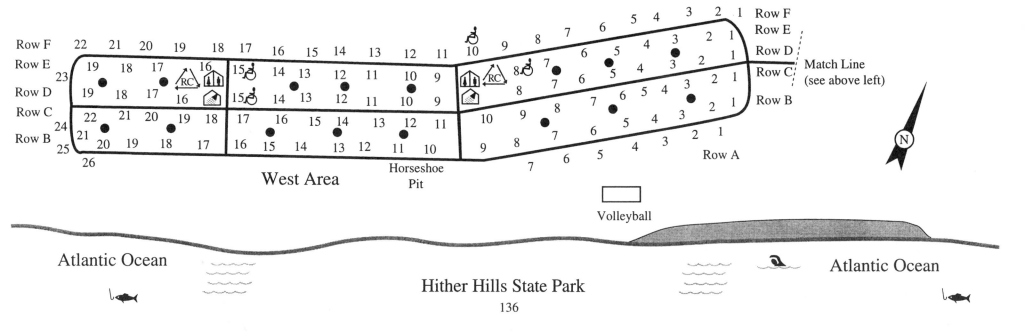

Row F   22   21   20   19   18   17   16   15   14   13   12   11   Row F
Row E   19   18   17   16   15   14   13   12   11   10   9   Row E   Row D   Match Line
Row D   19   18   17   16   15   14   13   12   11   10   9   Row C   (see above left)
Row C   22   21   20   19   18   17   16   15   14   13   12   11   Row B
Row B   21   20   19   18   17   16   15   14   13   12   11   10   Row A

West Area

Horseshoe
Pit

Volleyball

Atlantic Ocean

Hither Hills State Park

Atlantic Ocean

Indian Lake Islands Public Campground

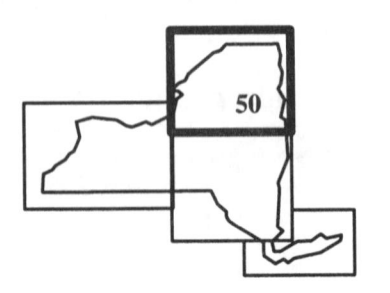

General Delivery, Sabael, NY 12864

(518) 648–5300

- Located 12 miles north of Speculator or 12 miles south of Indian Lake off State Route 30
- Open mid–May through Labor Day for camping
- **Boat Access Only**
- 51 Tent Sites (no electric sites)
- Pit Toilets (at each site)
- No Potable Water
- Pets Allowed
- Picnic Areas (located on islands and shoreline)
- Hiking Trails
- Swimming (no designated area)
- Fishing in Lewey and Indian Lakes
- Boat Launches (on Lewey and Indian Lakes)
- Boat and Canoe Rentals (at Lewey Lake Public Campground)

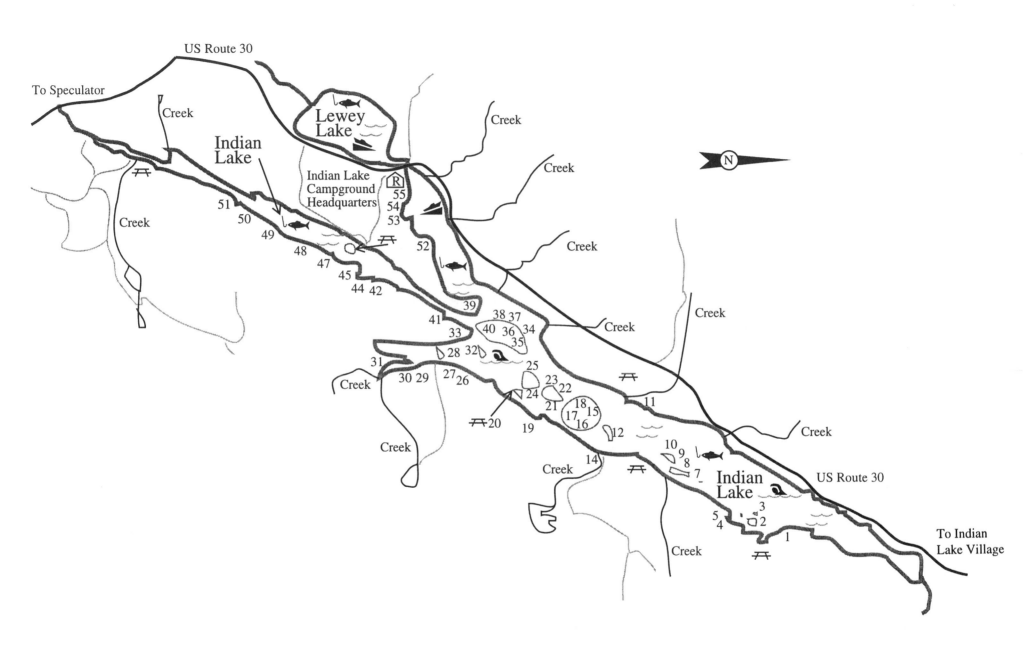

Indian Lake Islands Public Campground

Jacques Cartier State Park

P. O. Box 380, Morristown, NY 13664

(315) 375–6371

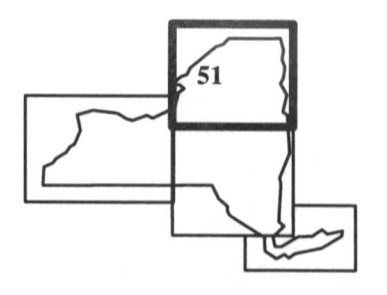

- Located 3 miles west of Morristown off State Route 12
- Open mid–May through mid–October for camping
- State Park is Open All Year
- 94 Tent & Trailer Sites (33 electric sites, trailer dump)
- 463 Acres
- Comfort Station (flush toilets & sink) and Showers
- Potable Water
- Public Telephone
- Pets Allowed
- Handicapped Accessible
- Picnic Area
- Swimming with Sand Beach
- Fishing in St. Lawrence River
- Hunting
- Bicycling on Campground Roads
- Ball and Soccer Field, and Playground
- Boat Launch and Dock
- Marina (2 miles North in Morristown)
- Cross Country Skiing and Ice Fishing
- Concessions

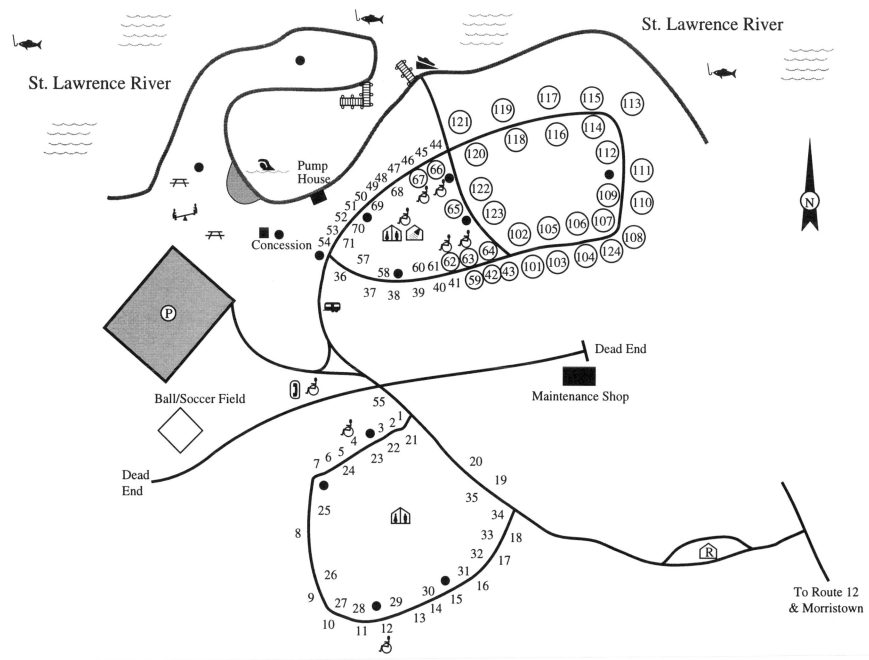

St. Lawrence River

St. Lawrence River

Pump House

Concession

P

Ball/Soccer Field

Dead End

Dead End

Maintenance Shop

N

55

Jacques Cartier State Park

140

To Route 12 & Morristown

Keewaydin State Park

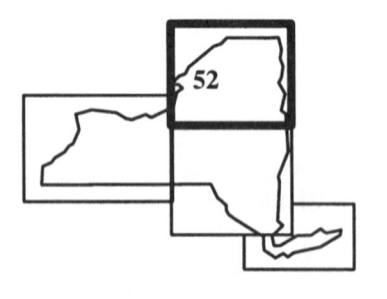

P. O. Box 247, 43165 NYS Route 12, Alexandria Bay, NY 13607

(315) 482–3331

- Located 1 mile southwest of Alexandria Bay or 2 miles northeast of Thousand Islands Bridge off State Route 12
- Open mid–May through Labor Day for camping
- State Park is Open All Year
- 39 Tent & Trailer Sites (no electric sites)
- 179 Acres
- Comfort Station (flush toilets & sink) and Showers
- Potable Water
- Public Telephone
- Pets Allowed
- Handicapped Accessible
- Picnic Area
- Picnic Pavilion (reservable)
- Swimming Pool and Bath House
- Fishing in St. Lawrence River
- Bicycling on Campground Roads
- Playground
- Boat Launch and Marina
- Boat Rental (at marina office)
- Cross Country Skiing, Ice Fishing, and Snowshoeing

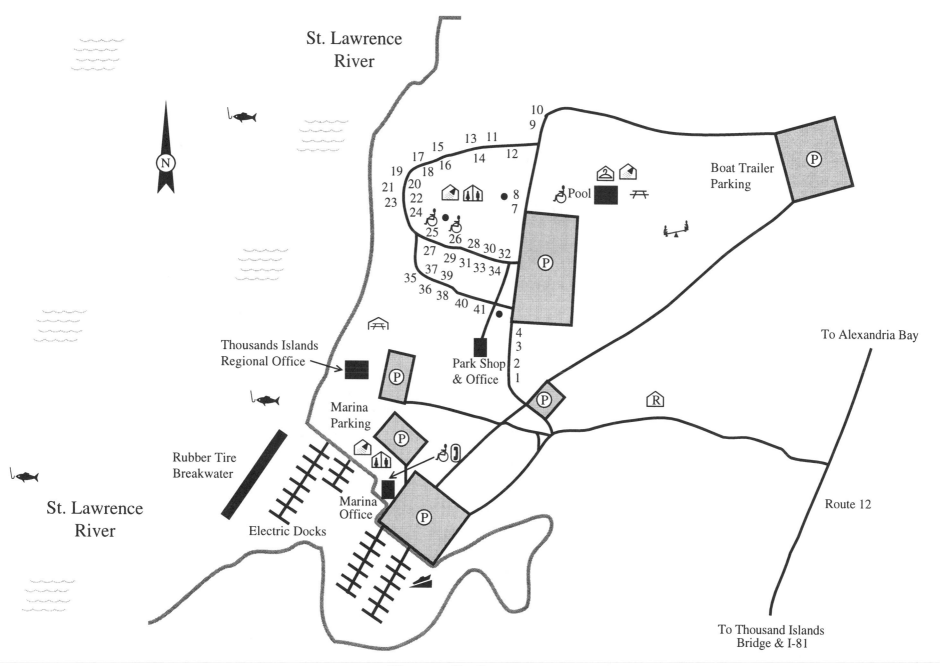

St. Lawrence
River

N

10
9

13 11
15 12
17 14
16
19 18
20
21 22
23 24
25 26 28 30 32
27 29 31 33 34
35 37 39
36 38 40 41
4
3
2
1

8
7

Pool

Boat Trailer
Parking

P

P

P

P

Thousands Islands
Regional Office

Marina
Parking

Rubber Tire
Breakwater

St. Lawrence
River

Electric Docks

Marina
Office

Park Shop
& Office

P

P

R

To Alexandria Bay

Route 12

To Thousand Islands
Bridge & I-81

Keewaydin State Park

Kenneth L. Wilson Public Campground

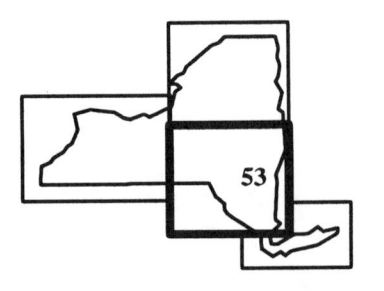

859 Wittenberg Road, Mt. Tremper, NY 12457

(845) 679–7020

- Located 2 miles south of Mt. Tremper off County Road 40
- Open mid–May through mid–October for camping
- 62 Tent & Trailer Sites (no electric sites, trailer dump)
- 125 Acres
- Comfort Station (flush toilets & sink) and Showers
- Potable Water
- Public Telephone
- Handicapped Accessible
- Pets Allowed
- Picnic Area
- Hiking Trails (within approximately 4 miles)
- Swimming with Sand Beach and Bath House
- Fishing in Upper and Lower Ponds
- Bicycling on Campground Roads (mountain bike trail – 7 miles)
- Baseball Field and Volleyball Court
- Boat Launch (no motor boats allowed)
- Canoe Rental

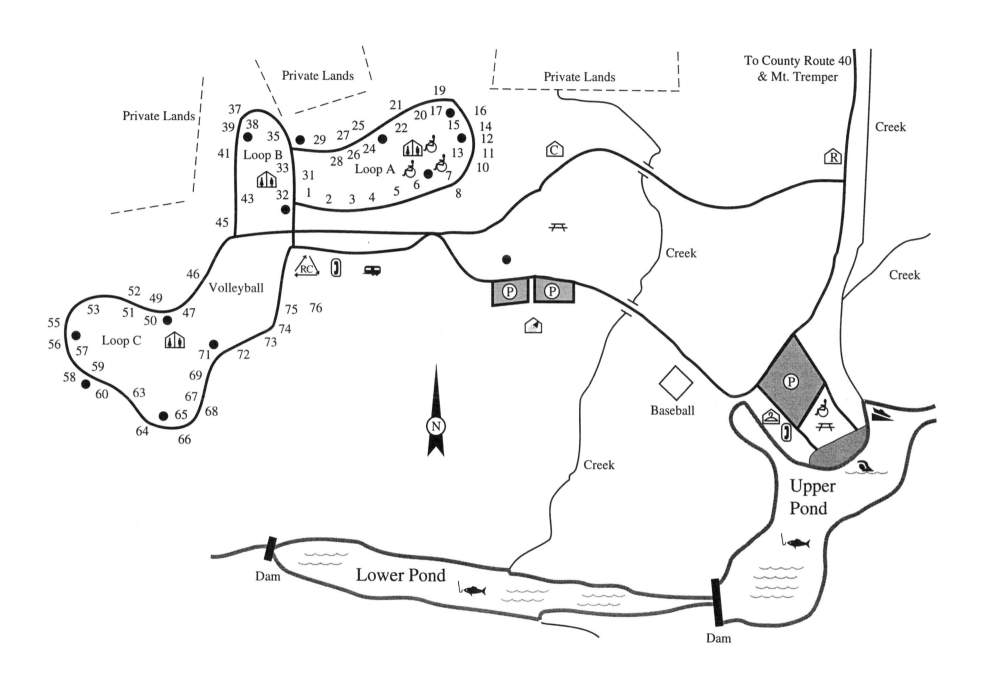

Kenneth L. Wilson Public Campground

144

Keuka Lake State Park

3370 Pepper Road, Keuka Park, NY 14478

(315) 536–3666

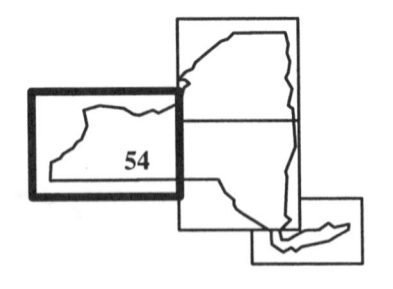

- Located 6 miles southwest of Penn Yan or 2 miles southeast of Branchport off State Route 54A
- Open May through October for camping
- State Park is Open All Year
- 150 Tent & Trailer Sites (53 electric sites, trailer dump)
- 621 Acres
- Comfort Station (flush toilets & sink) and Showers
- Potable Water (throughout campground)
- Public Telephone
- Pets Allowed
- Handicapped Accessible (all sites)
- Picnic Area
- Picnic Pavilion (2 reservable enclosed sections in the same building)
- Hiking Trails
- Swimming (gravel beach) and Bath House
- Fishing in Keuka Lake
- Hunting
- Docks
- Bicycling on Campground Roads
- Volleyball and Playground
- Boat Launch (10 boat slips)
- Cross Country Skiing, Snowshoeing, and Snowmobiling

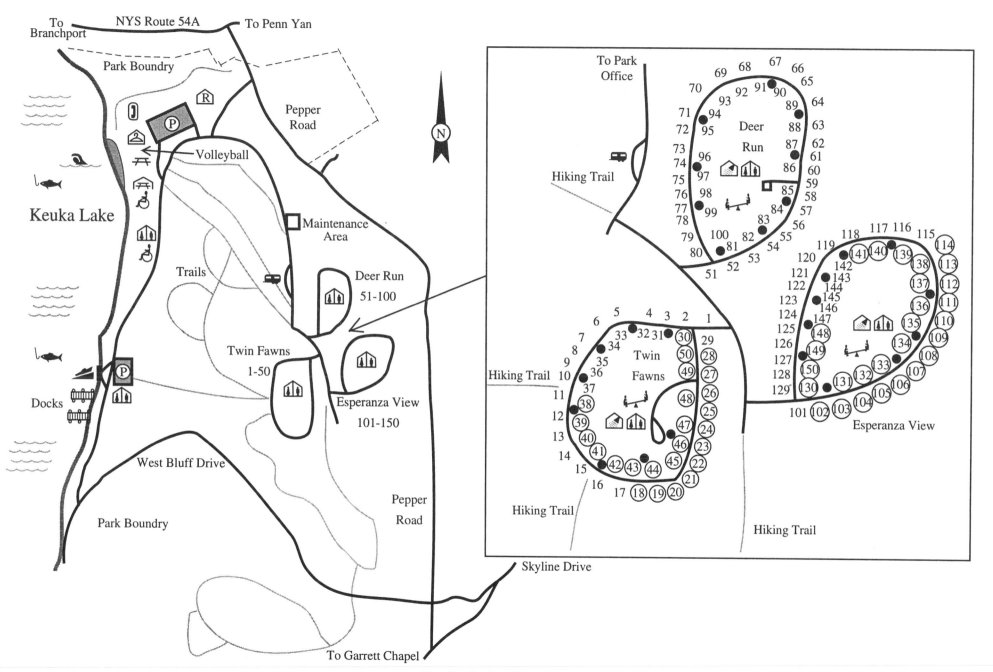

Keuka Lake State Park

146

Kring Point State Park

25950 Kring Point Road, Redwood, NY 13679

(315) 482–2444

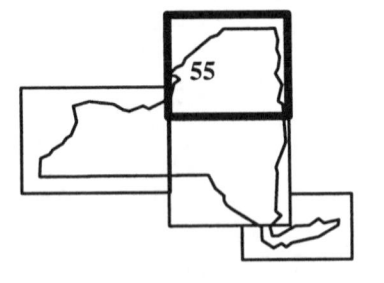

- Located 8 miles northeast of Alexandria Bay off State Route 12
- Open May through mid–October for camping
- 86 Tent & Trailer Sites (30 electric sites, trailer dump)
- 8 Cabins
- 56 Acres
- Comfort Station (flush toilets & sink) and Showers
- Potable Water
- Public Telephone
- Pets Allowed
- Handicapped Accessible
- Picnic Area
- Picnic Pavilion (small pavilion and recreation hall – both reservable)
- Recreation Program
- Swimming with Sand Beach
- Fishing in Goose Bay and St. Lawrence River
- Hunting (waterfowl in season)
- Docks
- Volleyball and Playground
- Boat Launch (approximately 1/2 mile from park)
- Marina (approximately 4 miles south in Alexandria Bay)
- Cross Country Skiing

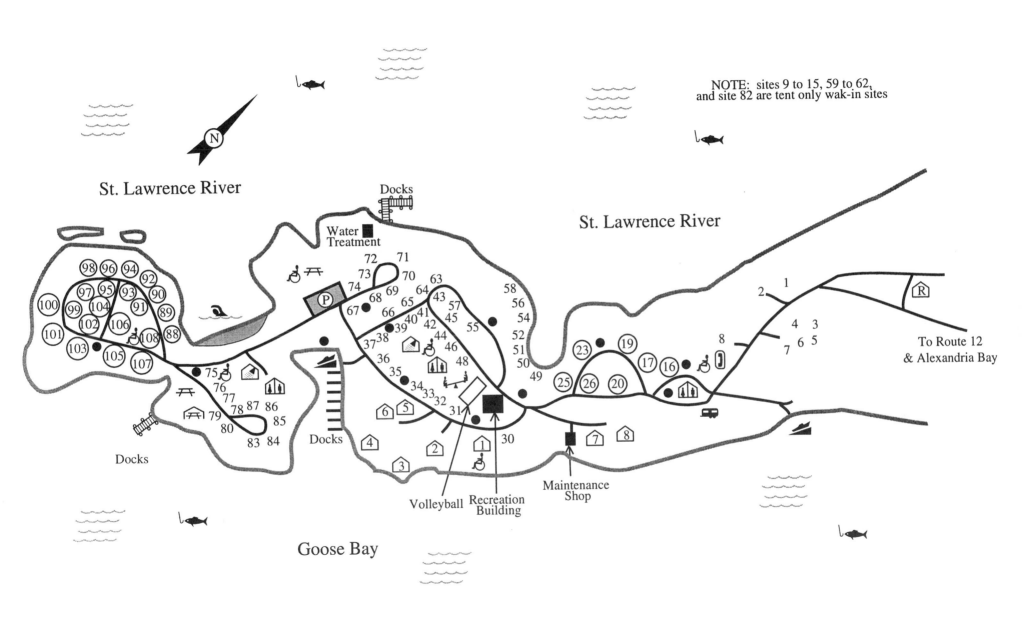

NOTE: sites 9 to 15, 59 to 62, and site 82 are tent only wak-in sites

St. Lawrence River

St. Lawrence River

Docks

Water Treatment

To Route 12 & Alexandria Bay

Volleyball

Recreation Building

Maintenance Shop

Docks

Docks

Goose Bay

Kring Point State Park

Lake Durant Public Campground

Route 28, Blue Mountain Lake, NY 12812

(518) 352-7797

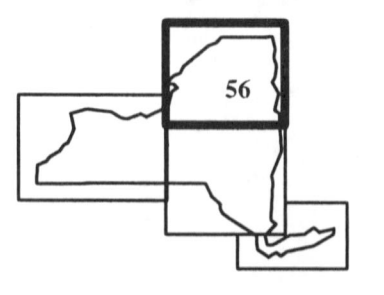

- Located 3 miles east of Blue Mountain Lake or 8 miles west of Indian Lake off State Route 28 & 30
- Open mid–May through mid–October for camping
- 56 Tent & Trailer Sites (no electric sites, trailer dump)
- 25 Acres
- Comfort Station (flush toilets & sink) and Showers
- Potable Water
- Pets Allowed
- Handicapped Accessible
- Picnic Area
- Hiking Trails
- Swimming with Sand Beach and Bath House
- Fishing in Lake Durant
- Dock
- Bicycling on Campground Roads
- Boat Launch
- Boat and Canoe Rental

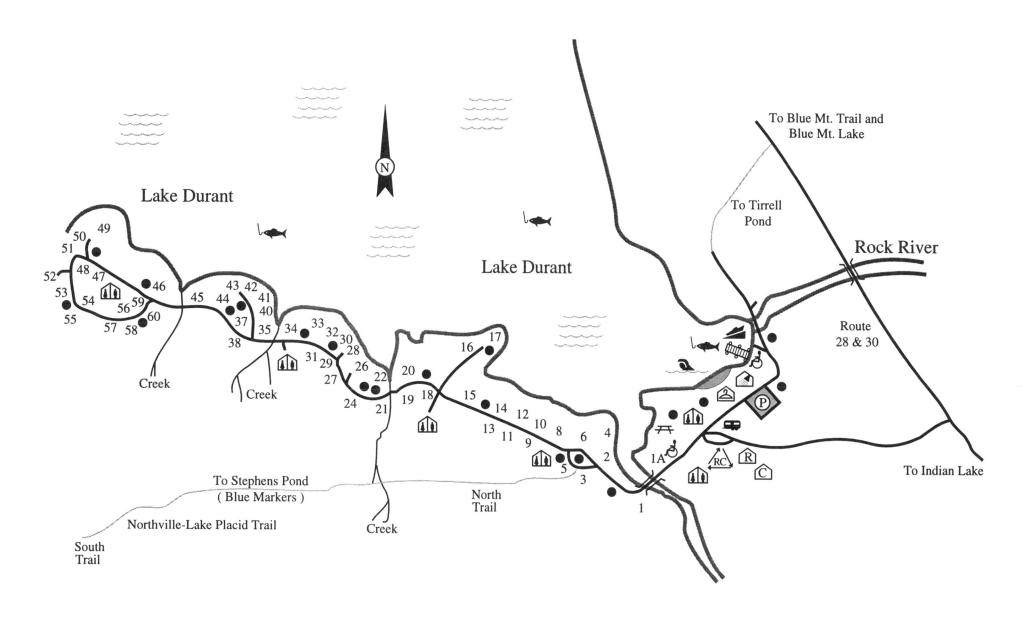

Lake Durant

Lake Durant

To Blue Mt. Trail and
Blue Mt. Lake

To Tirrell
Pond

Rock River

Route
28 & 30

To Indian Lake

To Stephens Pond
(Blue Markers)

Northville-Lake Placid Trail

South
Trail

North
Trail

Creek

Creek

Creek

Creek

Lake Durant Public Campground

Lake Eaton Public Campground

Route 30, Long Lake, NY 12847

(518) 624–2641

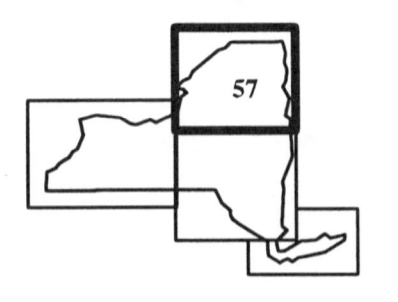

- Located 2 miles northwest of Long Lake off State Route 30
- Open mid–May through mid–October for camping
- 134 Tent & Trailer Sites (no electric sites, trailer dump)
- 30 Acres
- Comfort Station (flush toilets & sink) and Showers
- Potable Water
- Pets Allowed
- Handicapped Accessible
- Picnic Area
- Hiking Trails
- Swimming with Sand Beach and Bath House
- Fishing in Lake Eaton
- Bicycling on Campground Roads
- Boat Launch
- Rowboat and Canoe Rental (at park office)

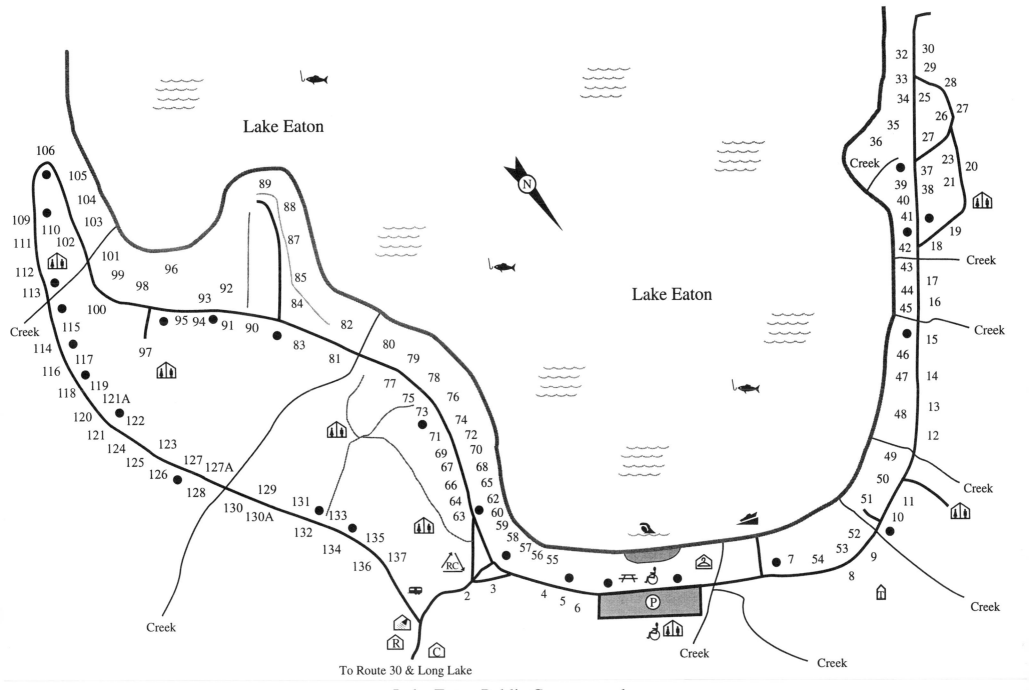

Lake Eaton

Lake Eaton

Creek

Creek

Creek

Creek

Creek

Creek

Creek

Creek

To Route 30 & Long Lake

Lake Eaton Public Campground

Lake Erie State Park

RD #1, Brocton, NY 14716

(716) 792–9214

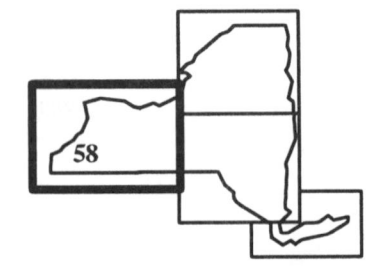

- Located 2 miles northeast of Brocton or 6 miles southwest of Dunkirk off State Route 5
- Open May through mid–October for camping
- State Park is Open All Year
- 102 Tent & Trailer Sites (84 electric sites, trailer dump)
- 10 Cabins
- 355 Acres
- Comfort Station (flush toilets & sink) and Showers
- Potable Water (throughout campground)
- Pets Allowed
- Handicapped Accessible
- Picnic Area
- Picnic Pavilion
- Recreation Program
- Hiking and Nature Trails
- Swimming with Sand Beach and Bath House (concessions)
- Fishing in Lake Erie
- Bicycling on Campground Roads
- Volleyball Court and Playground
- Boat Launch and Marina (in Dunkirk – 6 miles east)
- Cross Country Skiing and Snowmobiling

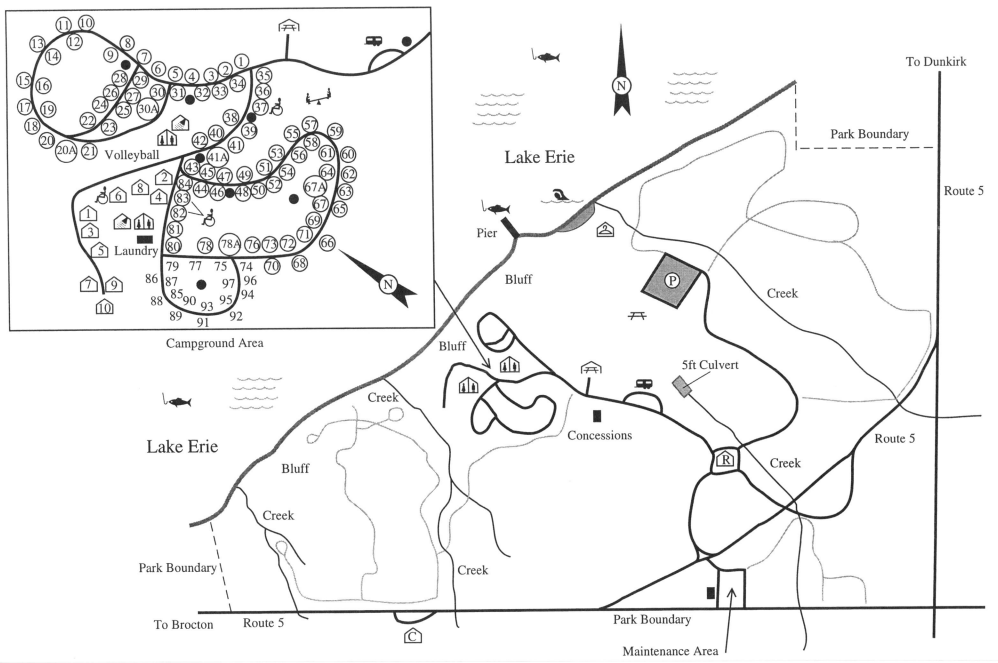

Lake Erie State Park

154

Lake George Battleground Public Campground

US 9, Lake George, NY 12845

(518) 668–3348

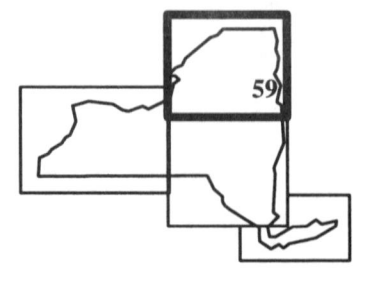

- Located 1/4 mile south of Lake George Village or 6 miles north of Glens Falls off US 9
- Open May through mid–October for camping
- 63 Tent & Trailer Sites (no electric sites, trailer dump, max 40 foot RV)
- 117 Acres
- Comfort Station (flush toilets & sink) and Showers
- Potable Water
- Public Telephone
- Pets Allowed
- Handicapped Accessible
- Picnic Areas (at Lake George Battlefield Park and Lake George Beach)
- Picnic Pavilion (adjacent to campground at Lake George Battlefield Park – reservable)
- Hiking Trails (at Lake George Battlefield Park and within approximately 5 miles)
- Swimming and Bath House (at Lake George Beach Day Use Facility – charge per person)

Note: see section at end of the book for more information on Lake George Battlefield Park and Lake George Beach Day Use Facility

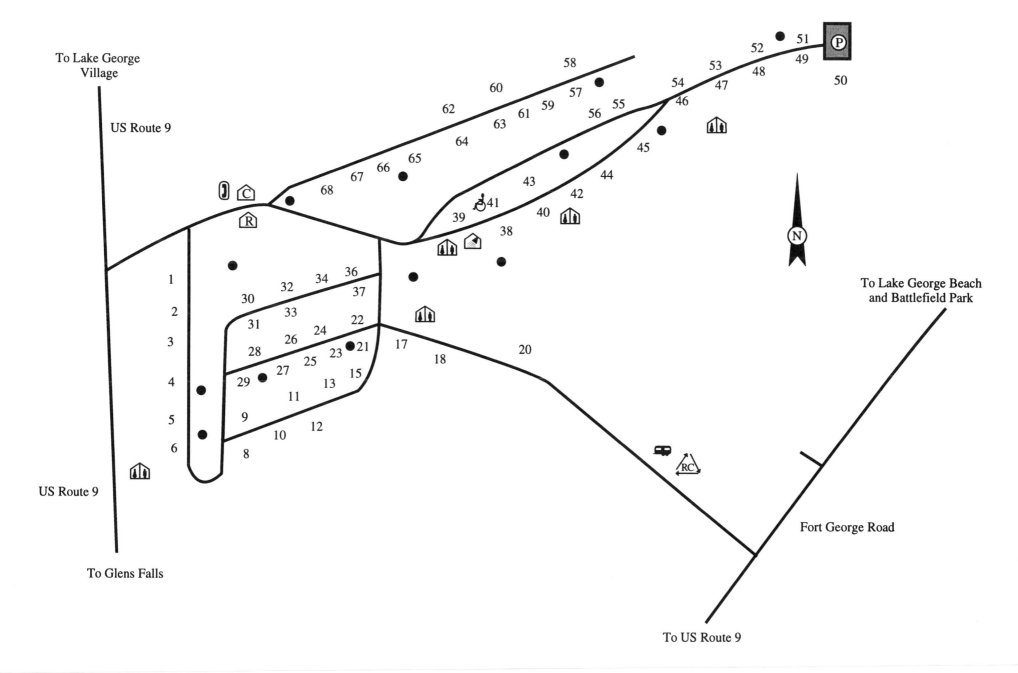

Lake George Battleground Public Campground

156

Lake George Islands Public Campground

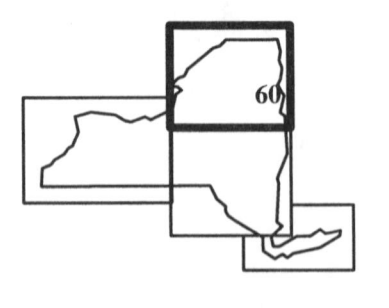

Bolton Landing, NY 12814

Glen Island – Narrows Group (518) 644–9696

Long Island Group (518) 656–9426

Narrow Island – Mother Bunch Group (518) 499–1288

- Located on state owned islands on Lake George
- Open mid–May through mid–October for camping
- **Boat Access Only** (all sites have a dock for at least one boat, all boats
   must be registered with the Lake George Park Commission (518) 668–9347)
- 366 Tent Sites on 47 State Owned Islands (no electric sites)
   - •161 Sites and 40 Cruiser Sites (Red Rock Bay & Log Bay) in the Narrows Group
   - •84 Sites in the Long Island Group
   - •81 Sites in the Mother Bunch Group
- Pit Toilets (at each site)
- No Potable Water
- Picnic Areas (116 day use sites – 8 island and 2 mainland locations, all areas
   have docks and pit toilets, and are accessible only by boat, permit required)
- Picnic Pavilions (9 reservable – one on island #2 and eight on island #6 – reserve pavilion
   at Long Island Ranger Station located at the south end of the lake)
- Hiking Trails (trails to many of the surrounding mountains)
- Swimming (no designated area)
- Fishing in Lake George
- Boat Launch (Lake George Village, Rogers Rock Public Campground, Mossy Point,
   and cartop launch at Northwest Bay)

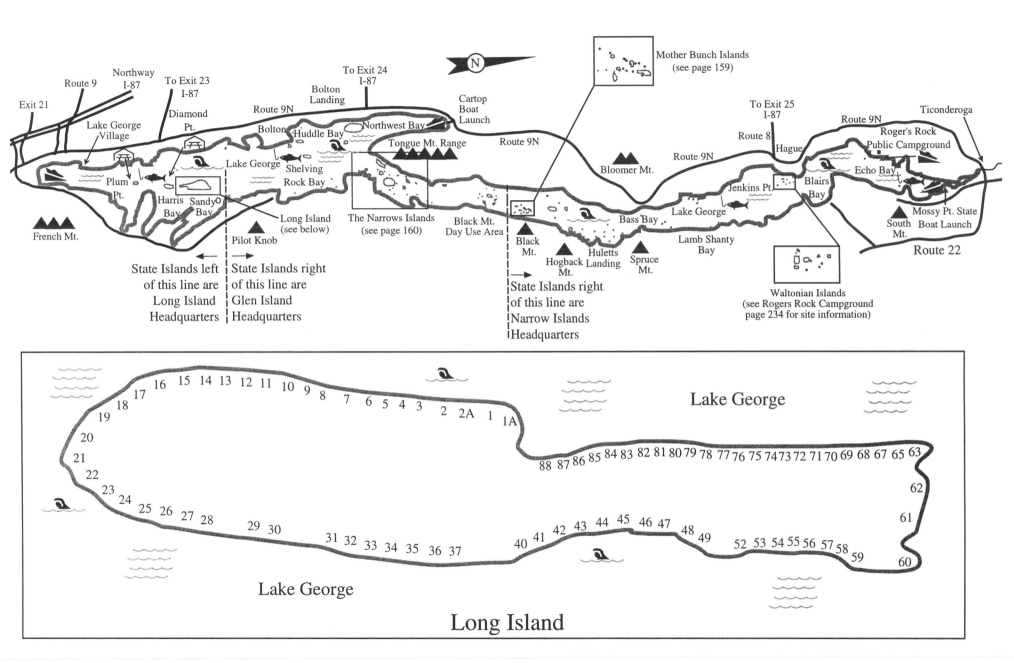

Lake George Islands Public Campground

Lake George Islands Public Campground

(see page 157 for campground information and main park map)

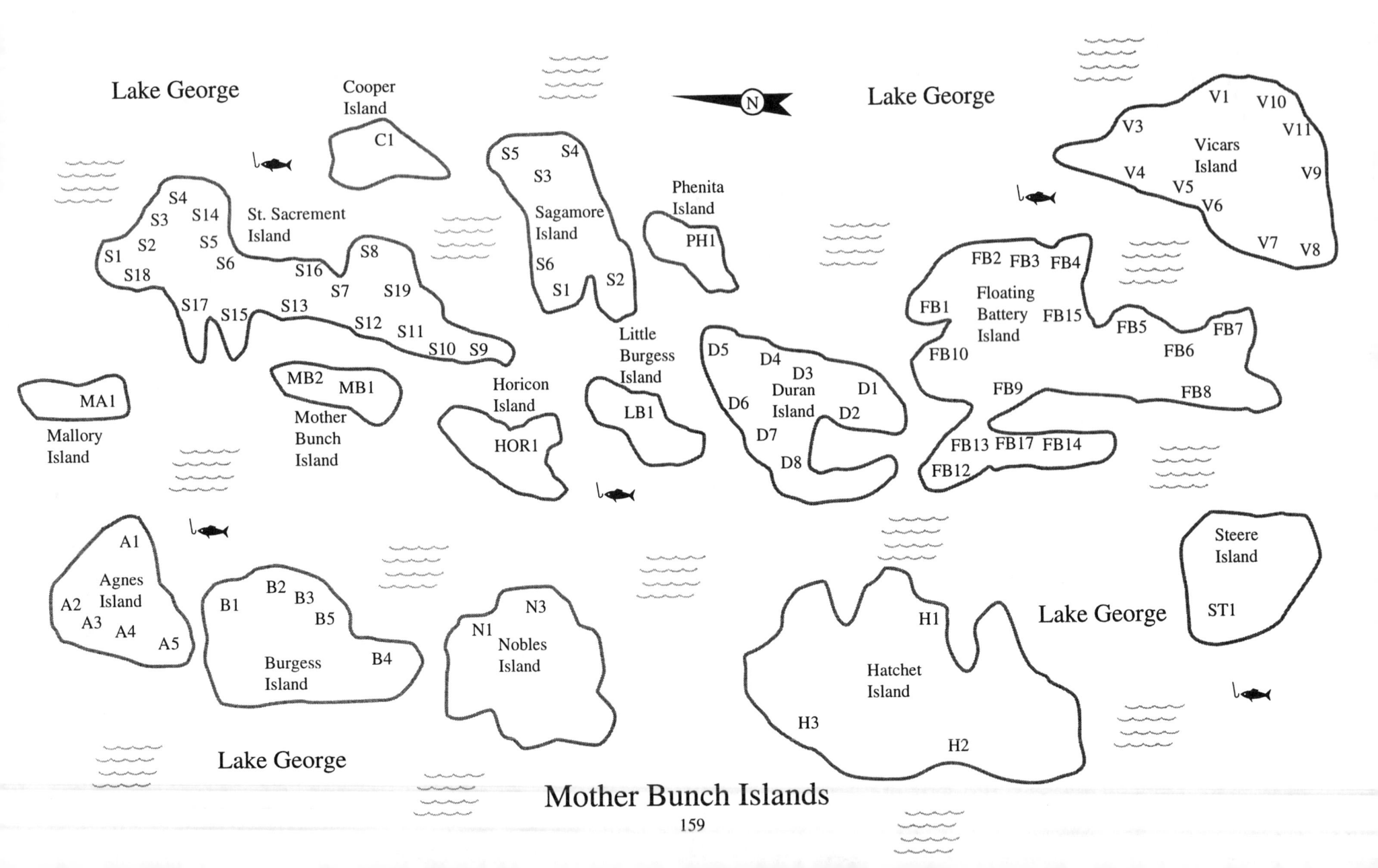

Lake George

Cooper Island
C1

Lake George

N

V1 V10
V3 V11
V4 Vicars Island V9
V5 V6 V7 V8

S5 S4
S3
Sagamore Island

Phenita Island
PH1

S4
S3 S14
S2 S5
S1 S18 S6
S17 S15 S13

St. Sacrement Island

S8
S16 S7 S19
S12 S11
S10 S9

S6
S1 S2

FB2 FB3 FB4
FB1 Floating Battery Island FB15 FB5 FB7
FB10 FB6
FB9 FB8
FB13 FB17 FB14
FB12

Little Burgess Island
LB1

D5 D4 D3 D1
D6 Duran Island D2
D7 D8

MA1
Mallory Island

MB2 MB1
Mother Bunch Island

Horicon Island
HOR1

Steere Island
ST1

A1
Agnes Island
A2
A3 A4 A5

B2 B3
B1 B5
Burgess Island B4

N3
N1 Nobles Island

H1
Hatchet Island
H3 H2

Lake George

Lake George

Mother Bunch Islands

159

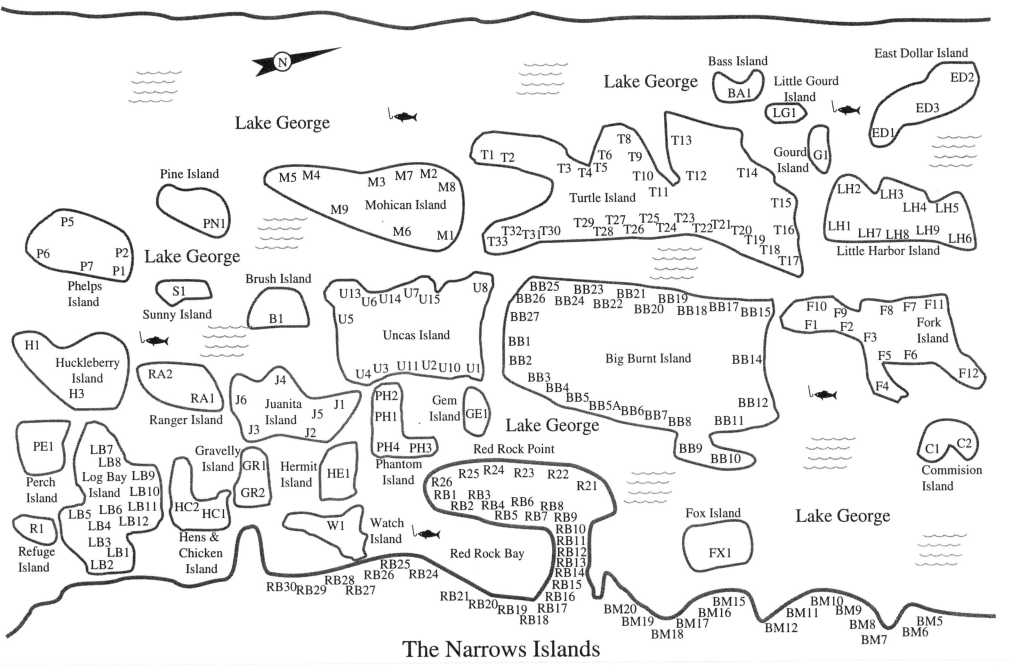

The Narrows Islands

Lake George Islands Public Campground

Lake Harris Public Campground

Campsite Road, Newcomb, NY 12852

(518) 582–2503

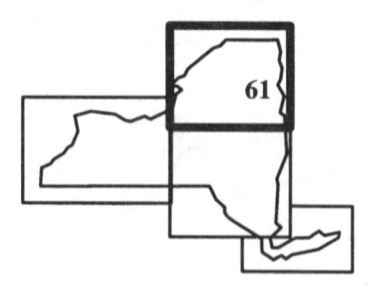

- Located 3 miles northeast of Newcomb off State Route 28N
- Open mid–May through mid–September for camping
- 88 Tent & Trailer Sites (no electric sites, trailer dump, max 40 foot RV)
- 275 Acres
- Comfort Station (flush toilets & sink) and Showers
- Potable Water
- Pets Allowed
- Handicapped Accessible
- Picnic Areas
- Hiking Trails (within approximately 3 miles)
- Swimming with Sand Beach and Bath House
- Fishing in Lake Harris
- Bicycling on Campground Roads
- Boat Launch (cartop)
- Rowboat and Canoe Rental (at park office)

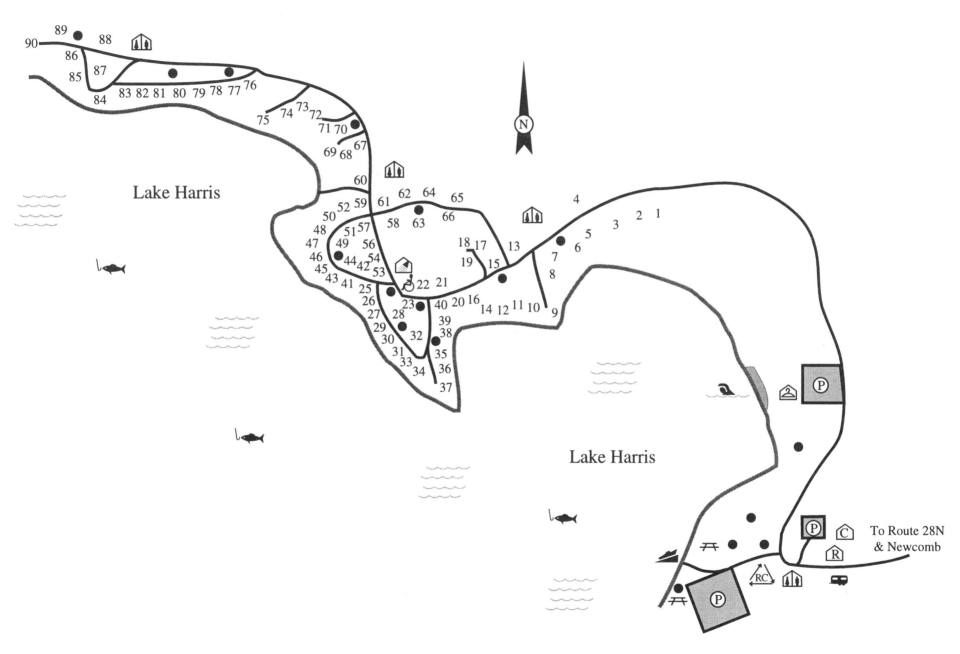

Lake Harris

Lake Harris

To Route 28N
& Newcomb

Lake Harris Public Campground

Lake Taghkanic State Park

1528 State Route 82, Ancram, NY 12502

(518) 851–3631

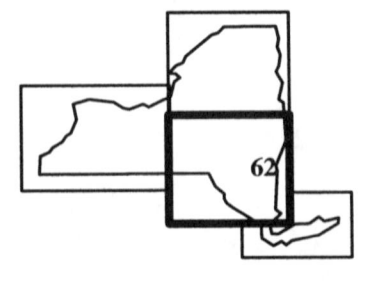

- Located 12 miles southeast of Hudson off State Route 82
- Open mid–May through October for camping
- State Park is Open All Year
- 61 Tent & Trailer Sites (no electric sites, 32 tent platforms)
- 15 Cabins and 17 Cottages (cottages are all on the lake and have bathrooms)
- 1,604 Acres
- Comfort Station (flush toilets & sink) and Showers
- Potable Water
- Handicapped Accessible
- Picnic Areas
- Picnic Pavilion (2 reservable)
- Recreation Program
- Nature Program and Center
- Hiking Trails (within approximately 5 miles)
- Swimming with Sand Beach and Bath House (2 locations)
- Fishing in Lake Taghkanic
- Bicycling on Campground Roads, Baseball, Basketball, Volleyball and Playground
- Bow Hunting for deer (mid–October through mid–November)
- Boat Launch (no gas motors, cartop launch, boat launch 8 miles northwest at Copake Lake)
- Rowboat Rental (at west beach area boat house)
- Cross Country Skiing, Ice Fishing, Ice Skating, and Snowmobiling
- Concessions

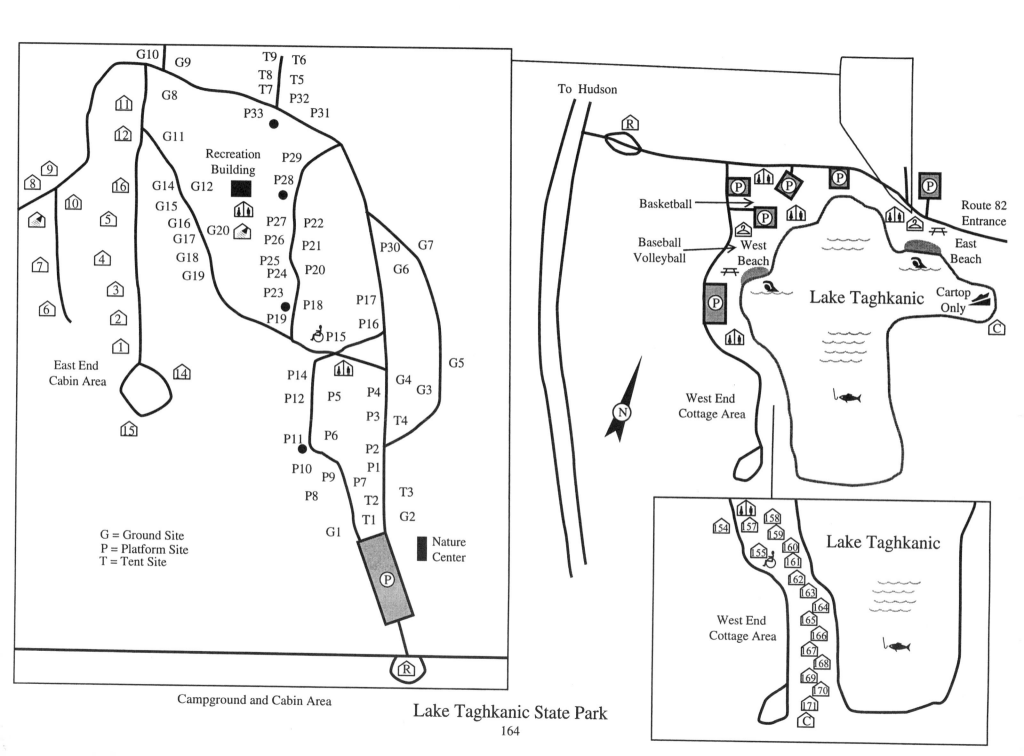

Lake Taghkanic State Park

164

Campground and Cabin Area

G = Ground Site
P = Platform Site
T = Tent Site

Nature Center

Recreation Building

East End Cabin Area

West End Cottage Area

Lake Taghkanic

West Beach

East Beach

Basketball

Baseball Volleyball

Cartop Only

To Hudson

Route 82 Entrance

N

West End Cottage Area

Lakeside Beach State Park

Route 18, Waterport, NY 14571

(845) 682–4888

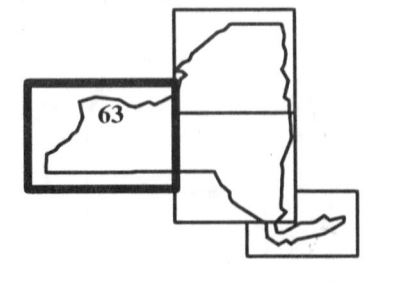

- Located 4 miles west of Point Breeze or 10 miles north of Albion off Lake Ontario State Parkway
- Open May through November for camping
- State Park is Open All Year
- 274 Tent & Trailer Sites (274 electric sites, trailer dump)
- 743 Acres
- Comfort Station (flush toilets & sink) and Showers
- Potable Water
- Pets Allowed (E, F, and G loops only)
- Handicapped Accessible
- Picnic Area
- Picnic Pavilion (1 reservable)
- Hiking Trails (on campground roads)
- Recreation Program and Hall
- Fishing in Lake Ontario
- Hunting (waterfowl only in season)
- Bicycling and Rollerblading on Campground Roads
- Baseball Field, Basketball Court, Horseshoe Pits (near recreation building), and Playground
- Boat Launch (at Point Breeze – approximately 2 miles east)
- Cross Country Skiing and Snowmobiling
- Store and Laundry

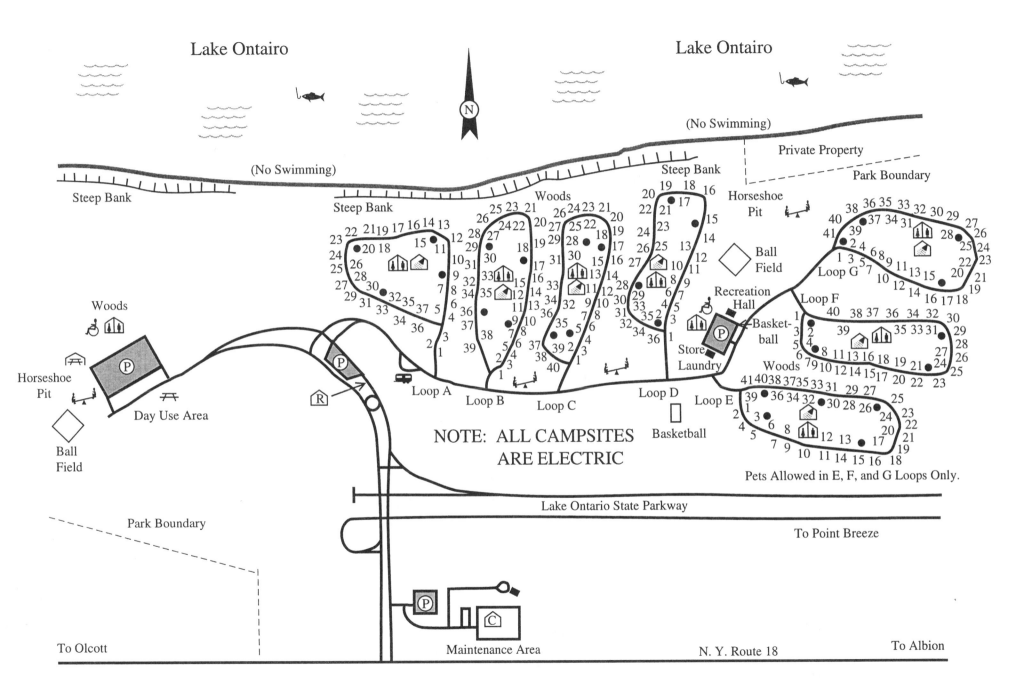

Lake Ontairo

Lake Ontairo

(No Swimming)

Private Property

Park Boundary

Steep Bank

(No Swimming)

Steep Bank

Steep Bank

Woods

Horseshoe Pit

Ball Field

Woods

Loop G

Loop F

Recreation Hall

Basket-ball

Store

Laundry

Woods

Loop A

Loop B

Loop C

Loop D

Loop E

Basketball

NOTE: ALL CAMPSITES ARE ELECTRIC

Pets Allowed in E, F, and G Loops Only.

Woods

Horseshoe Pit

Day Use Area

Ball Field

Lake Ontario State Parkway

To Point Breeze

Park Boundary

Maintenance Area

To Olcott

N. Y. Route 18

To Albion

Lakeside Beach State Park

166

Letchworth State Park

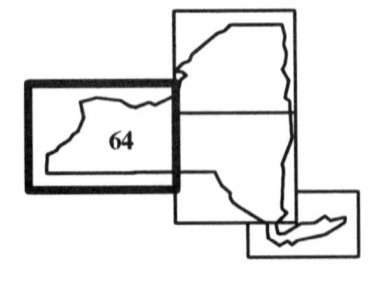

1 Letchworth State Park, Castile, NY 14427

(845) 273–3303

- Located 6 miles south of the Mount Morris or 3 miles east of Perry off Main Park Road
- Open mid–May through October for camping
- State Park is Open All Year
- 270 Tent & Trailer Sites (270 electric sites, trailer dump)
- 85 Cabins (areas A, B, C, D, and E)
- 14,350 Acres
- Comfort Station (flush toilets & sink) and Showers
- Potable Water (throughout campground)
- Public Telephone
- Pets Allowed (camping loops 100–143, 200–249, and 700–743 only)
- Handicapped Accessible
- Picnic Areas
- Picnic Pavilions (reservable)
- Recreation Program, Interpretive Program and Summer Performing Arts Series
- Hiking Trails and Bridle Paths (throughout the park)
- Swimming Pools (open late June till Labor Day)
- Fishing in Genesee River (St. Helena area)
- Hunting
- Bicycling on Campground Roads
- Basketball Court and Playground
- Cross Country Skiing, Ice Skating, Snowshoeing, Snowmobiling, and Snowtubing
- Recreation Hall, Store, and Laundry

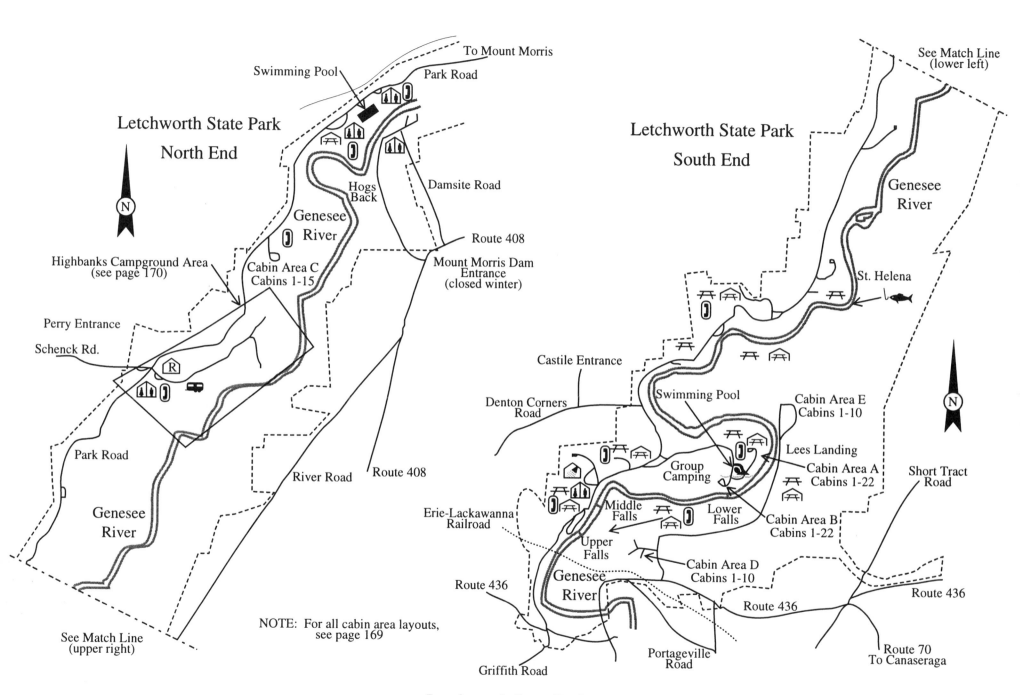

Swimming Pool

To Mount Morris

Park Road

Letchworth State Park
North End

N

Hogs Back

Damsite Road

Genesee River

Route 408

Highbanks Campground Area
(see page 170)

Cabin Area C
Cabins 1-15

Mount Morris Dam
Entrance
(closed winter)

Perry Entrance

Schenck Rd.

R

Park Road

Genesee River

River Road

Route 408

See Match Line
(upper right)

NOTE: For all cabin area layouts,
see page 169

See Match Line
(lower left)

Letchworth State Park
South End

Genesee River

St. Helena

Castile Entrance

N

Swimming Pool

Cabin Area E
Cabins 1-10

Denton Corners
Road

Lees Landing

Group Camping

Cabin Area A
Cabins 1-22

Short Tract
Road

Erie-Lackawanna
Railroad

Middle Falls

Lower Falls

Cabin Area B
Cabins 1-22

Upper Falls

Cabin Area D
Cabins 1-10

Route 436

Genesee River

Route 436

Route 436

Griffith Road

Portageville Road

Route 70
To Canaseraga

Letchworth State Park

Letchworth State Park

(see page 167 for campground information and main park map)

NOTE: No pets allowed in the cabins

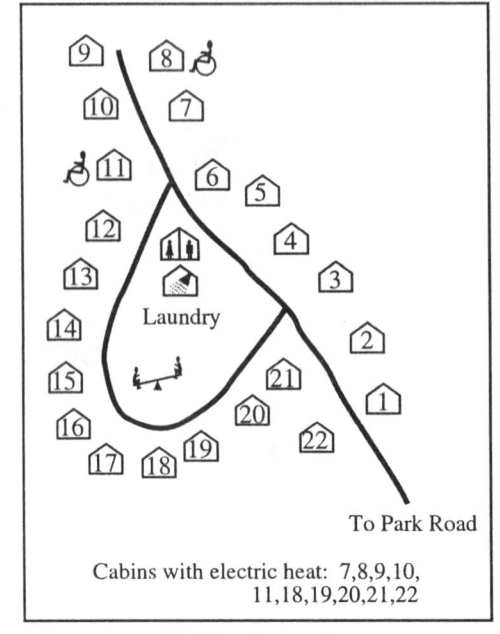

Cabins with electric heat: 7,8,9,10, 11,18,19,20,21,22

Cabin Area A

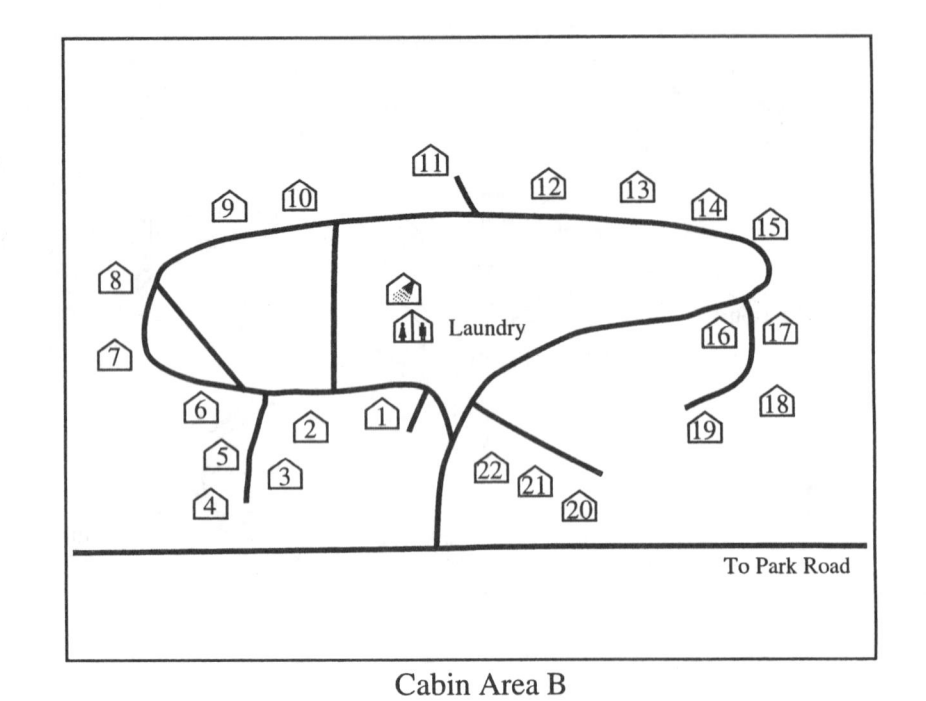

To Park Road

Cabin Area B

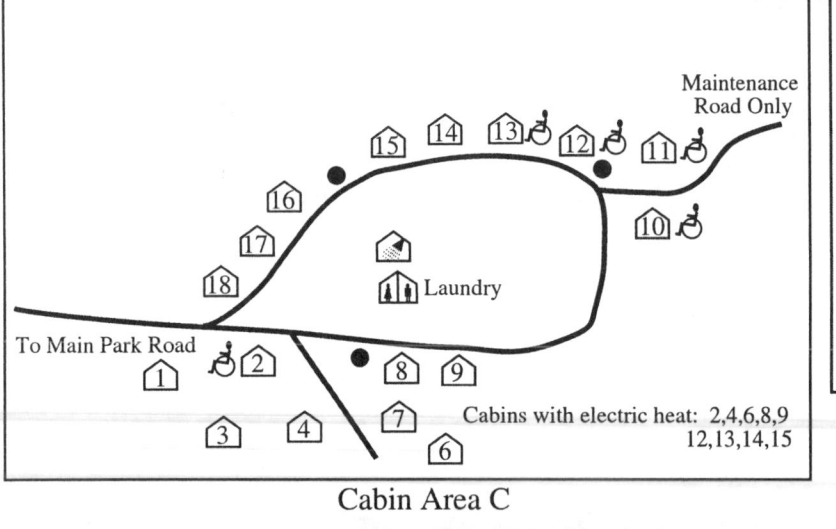

To Main Park Road

Cabins with electric heat: 2,4,6,8,9 12,13,14,15

Cabin Area C

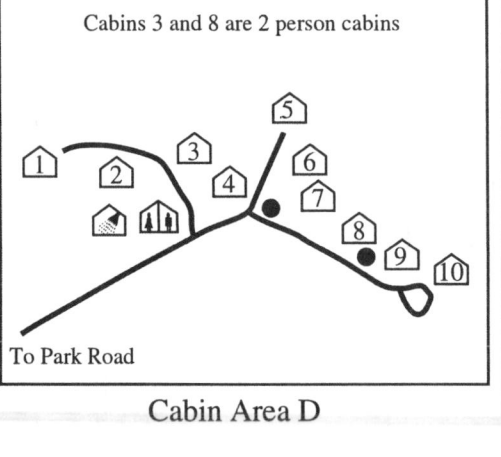

Cabins 3 and 8 are 2 person cabins

To Park Road

Cabin Area D

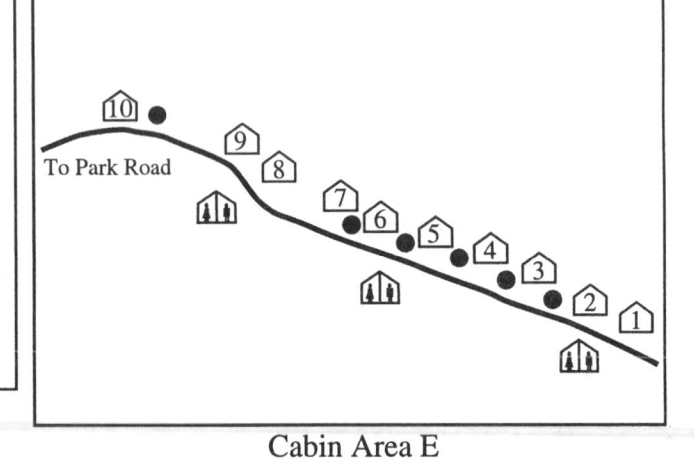

To Park Road

Cabin Area E

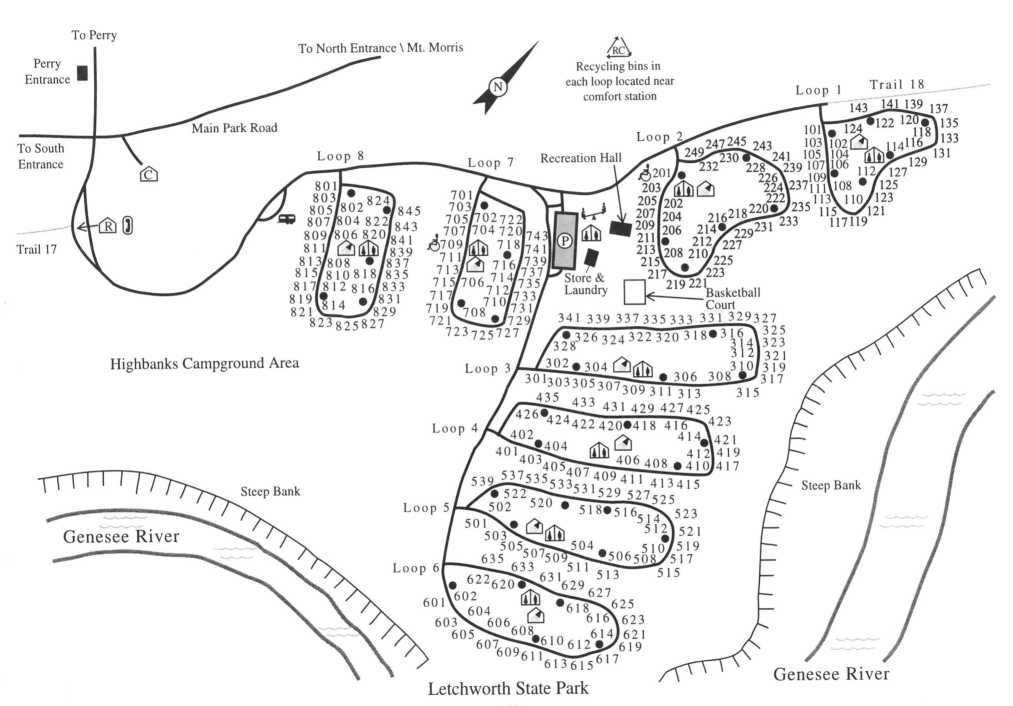

To Perry

Perry Entrance

To North Entrance \ Mt. Morris

Recycling bins in each loop located near comfort station

RC

N

Main Park Road

To South Entrance

Trail 17

C

R

Loop 8

801 803 805 807 809 811 813 815 817 819 821 823
802 804 806 808 810 812 814
824 822 820 818 816 825
845 843 841 839 837 835 833 831 829 827

Highbanks Campground Area

Loop 7

701 703 705 707 709 711 713 715 717 719 721
702 704 706 708 710 712 714 716 718 720 722
743 741 739 737 735 733 731 729 727
723 725

Recreation Hall

Store & Laundry

P

Loop 2

201 203 205 207 209 211 213 215 217
202 204 206 208 210 212 214 216 218 220 222
219 221 223 225 227 229 231 233 235 237 239 241 243 245 247 249
228 226 224 230 232

Basketball Court

Loop 1

Trail 18

101 103 105 107 109 111 113 115 117 119
102 104 106 108 110 112 114 116
121 123 125 127 129 131 133 135 137 139 141 143
122 124 120 118

Loop 3

341 339 337 335 333 331 329 327
328 326 324 322 320 318 316 325 314 323 312 321 310 319 317 315
302 304 306 308
301 303 305 307 309 311 313

Loop 4

435 433 431 429 427 425
426 424 422 420 418 416 423
402 404 406 408 414 421 412 419 410 417
401 403 405 407 409 411 413 415

Loop 5

539 537 535 533 531 529 527 525
522 520 518 516 514 523
502 504 506 508 512 521 510 519 517 515
501 503 505 507 509 511 513
635 633 631 629 627 625

Loop 6

622 620 618 616 623
601 602 604 606 608 610 612 614 621
603 605 607 609 611 613 615 617 619

Steep Bank

Genesee River

Steep Bank

Genesee River

Letchworth State Park

170

Lewey Lake Public Campground

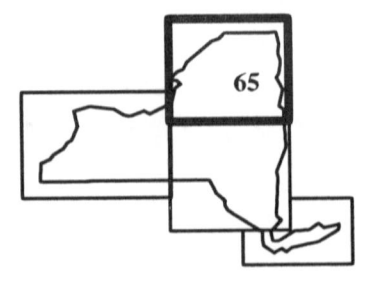

General Delivery, Sabael, NY 12864

(518) 648–5266

- Located 12 miles south of Indian Lake or 12 miles north of Speculator off State Route 30
- Open mid–May through mid–October for camping
- 209 Tent & Trailer Sites (no electric sites, trailer dump, max 40 foot RV)
- 40 Acres
- Comfort Station (flush toilets & sink) and Showers
- Potable Water
- Public Telephone
- Pets Allowed
- Handicapped Accessible
- Picnic Area (at Lewey Lake near bathhouse)
- Hiking Trail
- Swimming with Sand Beach and Bath House
- Fishing in Indian and Lewey Lakes
- Bicycling and Rollerblading on Campground Roads
- Boat Launch (on Lewey and Indian Lakes)
- Rowboat and Canoe Rental (private vendor at campground)

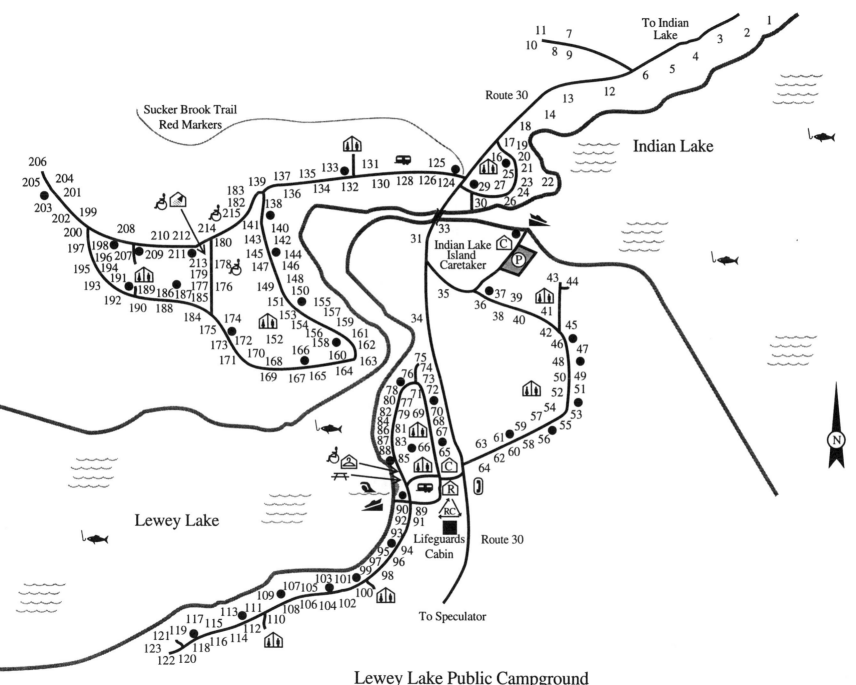

Lewey Lake Public Campground

172

Limekiln Lake Public Campground

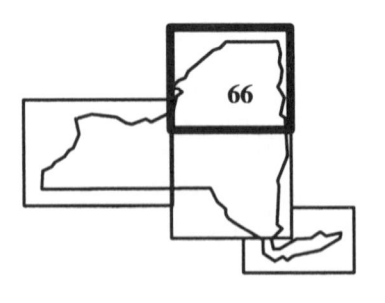

Limekiln Lake Road, Inlet, NY 13360

(315) 357–4401

- Located 3 miles south of Inlet off State Route 28
- Open mid–May through Labor Day for camping
- 254 Tent & Trailer Sites (no electric sites, trailer dump)
- Food Lockers at each site
- 50 Acres
- Comfort Station (flush toilets & sink) and Showers
- Potable Water
- Pets Allowed
- Handicapped Accessible
- Picnic Area
- Picnic Pavilion
- Hiking and Nature Trails
- Swimming with Sand Beach and Bath House
- Fishing in Limekiln Lake
- Bicycling on Campground Roads
- Boat Launch
- Rowboat and Canoe Rental (near boat launch)

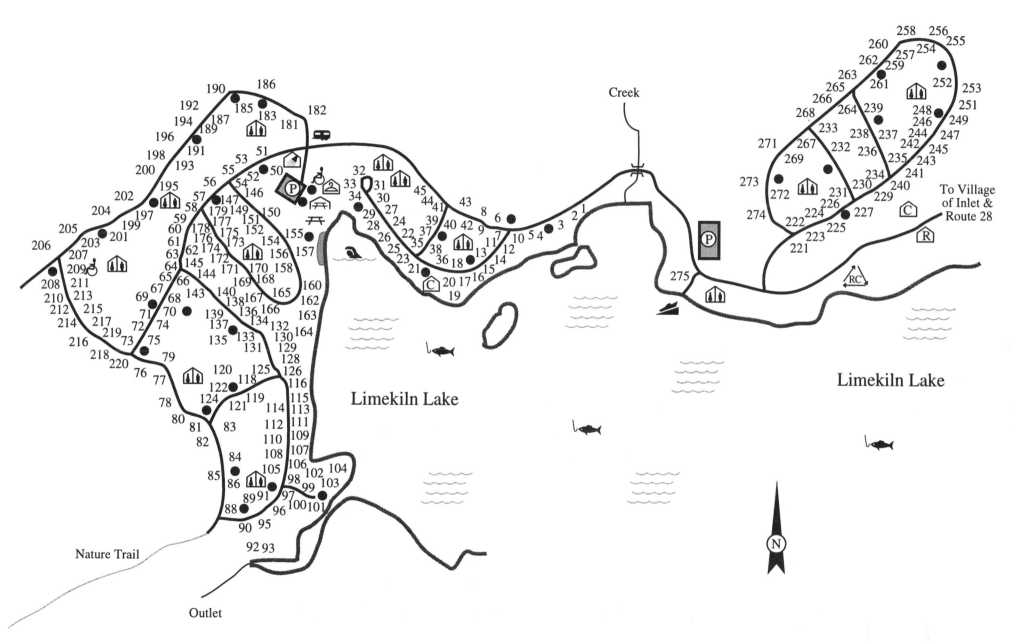

Creek

To Village
of Inlet &
Route 28

Limekiln Lake

Limekiln Lake

Nature Trail

Outlet

N

Limekiln Lake Public Campground

Lincoln Pond Public Campground

County Route 7, Elizabethtown, NY 12932

(518) 942–5292

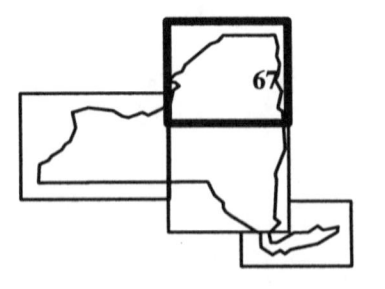

- Located 6 miles south of Elizabethtown or 4 miles northwest of Mineville off County Road 7
- Open mid–May through Labor Day for camping
- 35 Tent & Trailer Sites (no electric sites, trailer dump)
- 10 Interior sites in remote areas and do not have potable water or flush toilets (sites I4, I5, &I6 are accessible only by boat)
- 105 Acres
- Comfort Station (flush toilets & sink) and Showers
- Potable Water
- Public Telephone
- Pets Allowed
- Handicapped Accessible
- Picnic Area
- Hiking Trails (within approximately 4 miles)
- Swimming with Sand Beach and Bath House
- Fishing in Lincoln Pond
- Rowboat and Canoe Rental (at park office)
- Boat Launch (cartop only)

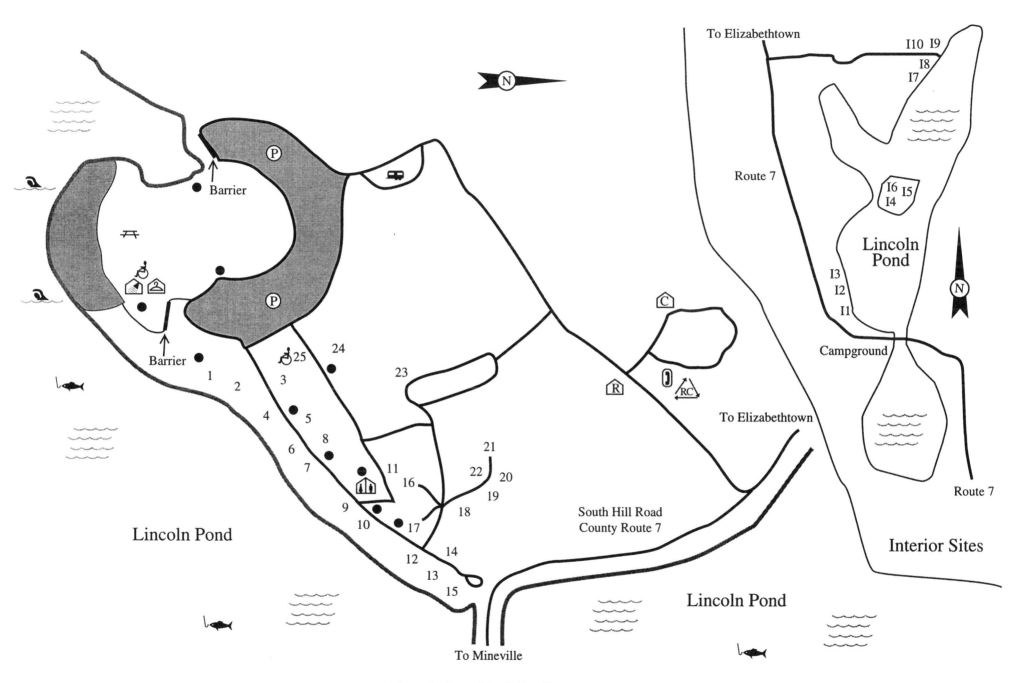

Lincoln Pond Public Campground

176

Little Pond Public Campground

Barkaboom Road, Livingston Manor, NY 12758

(845) 439–5480

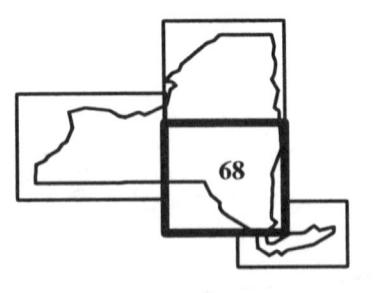

- Located 14 miles north of Livingston Manor off State Route 54
- Open mid–May through mid–October for camping
- 68 Tent & Trailer Sites (no electric sites, trailer dump)
- 46 Acres
- Vault & Pit Toilets
- Showers
- Potable Water
- Public Telephone
- Pets Allowed
- Handicapped Accessible
- Picnic Pavilion (reservable)
- Hiking Trails
- Swimming with Sand Beach and Bath House
- Fishing in Little Pond
- Boat Launch (no motor boats)
- Rowboat and Canoe Rental

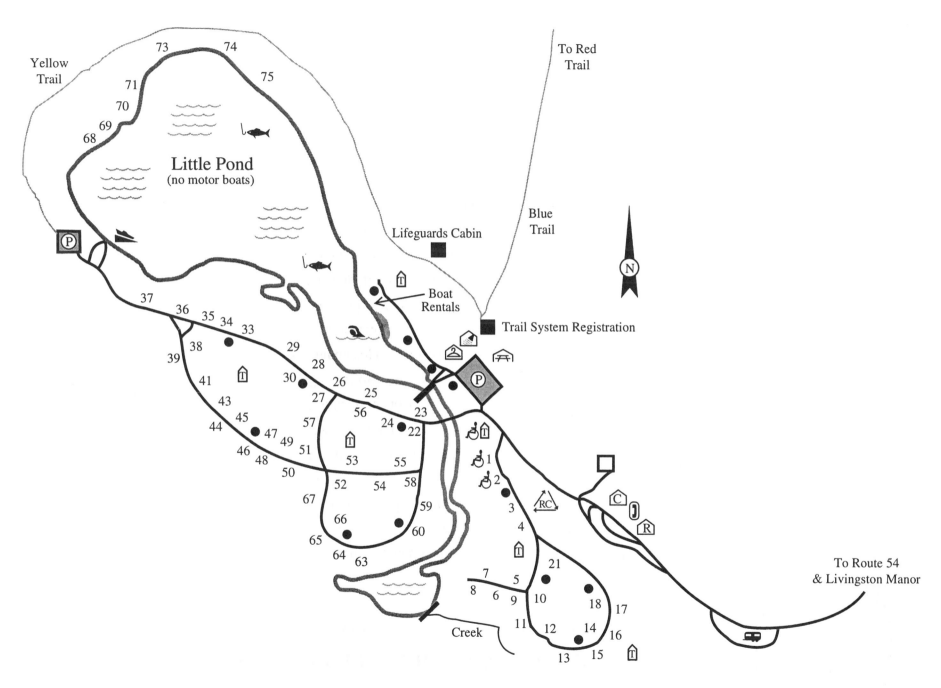

Little Pond Public Campground

Little Sand Point Public Campground

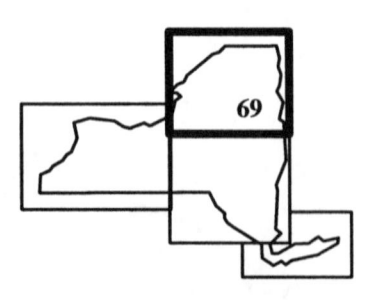

Old Piseco Road, Piseco, NY 12139

(518) 548–7585

- Located 12 miles southwest of Speculator off Old Piseco Road
- Open mid–May through Labor Day for camping
- 76 Tent & Trailer Sites (no electric sites, trailer dump)
- 20 Acres
- Comfort Station (flush toilets & sink)
- Potable Water
- Public Telephone
- Pets Allowed
- Handicapped Accessible
- Hiking Trails
- Swimming with Sand Beach
- Fishing in Piseco Lake
- Bicycling on Campground Roads
- Boat Launch
- Rowboat and Canoe Rental (Piseco Lake Lodge)

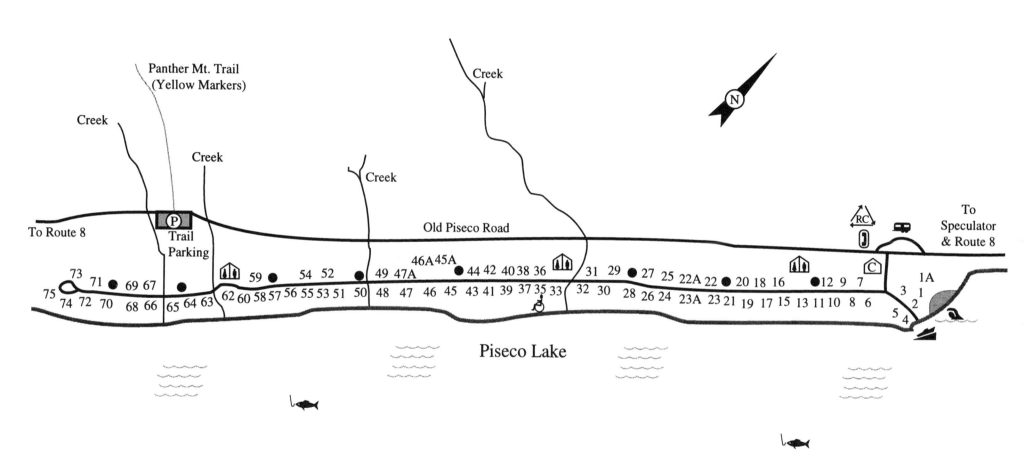

Panther Mt. Trail
(Yellow Markers)

Creek

Creek

Creek

Creek

Creek

N

To Route 8

P

Trail
Parking

Old Piseco Road

RC

To
Speculator
& Route 8

C

73   71   69 67   59   54 52   49 47A   46A 45A   44 42 40 38 36   31 29   27 25   22A 22   20 18 16   12 9   7   1A
75   3   1
74 72 70   68 66   65 64 63   62 60 58 57 56 55 53 51 50   48   47   46 45 43 41 39 37 35 33   32 30   28 26 24   23A 23 21 19 17 15 13 11 10 8 6   2
                                                                                                                                                        5 4

Piseco Lake

Little Sand Point Public Campground

Long Point State Park

7495 State Park Road, Three Mile Bay, NY 13693

(315) 649–5258

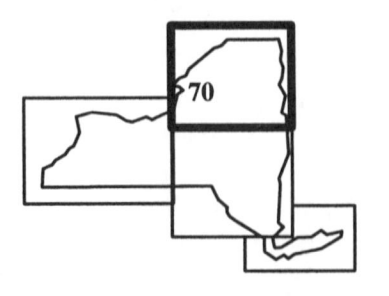

- Located 9 miles south of Three Mile Bay off State Route 12E
- Open mid–May through mid–October for camping
- 86 Tent & Trailer Sites (19 electric sites, trailer dump)
- 22 Acres
- Comfort Station (flush toilets & sink) and Showers
- Potable Water
- Pets Allowed
- Handicapped Accessible
- Picnic Areas
- Picnic Pavilion (reservable)
- Fishing in Chaumont Bay and Long Bay
- Rollerblading on Campground Roads
- Hunting
- Boat Launch and Marina (docks with 32 slips)

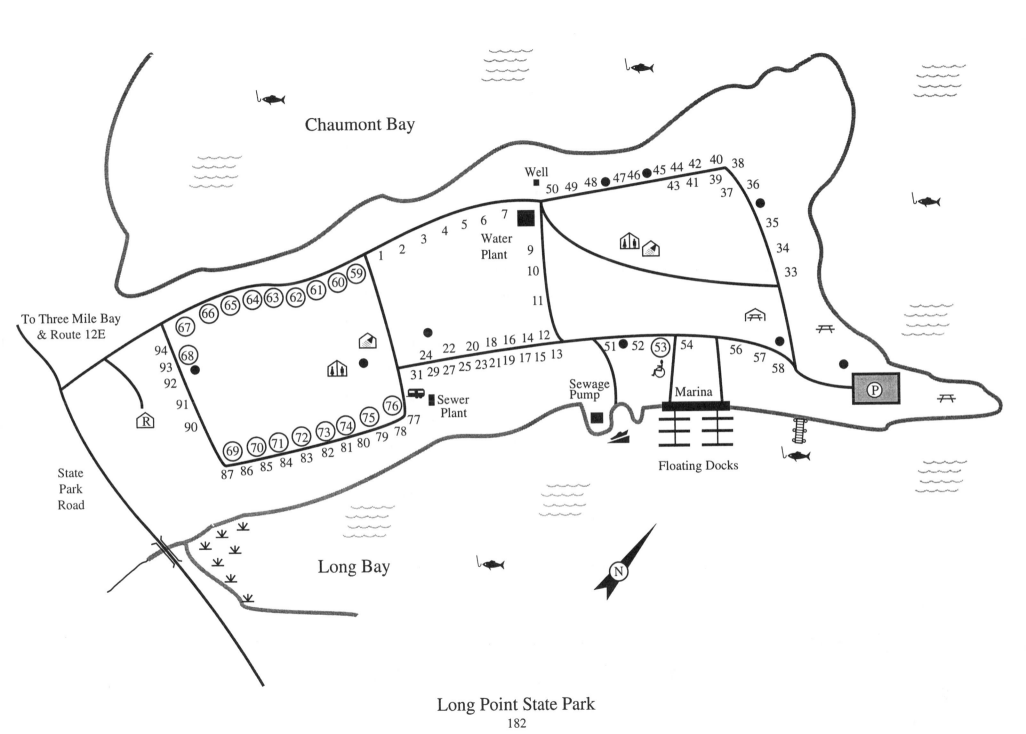

Chaumont Bay

Well

Water
Plant

To Three Mile Bay
& Route 12E

Sewer
Plant

Sewage
Pump

Marina

Floating Docks

State
Park
Road

Long Bay

N

Long Point State Park
182

Luzerne Public Campground

Route 9N, 892 Lake Ave, Lake Luzerne, NY 12846

(518) 696–2031

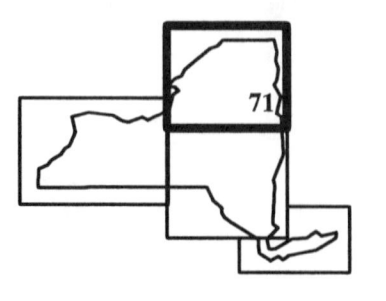

- Located 8 miles southwest of Lake George Village or 4 miles north of Lake Luzerne off State Route 9N
- Open mid–May through mid–September for camping
- 166 Tent & Trailer Sites (no electric sites, trailer dump, max 40 foot RV)
- 721 Acres
- Comfort Station (flush toilets & sink) and Showers
- Potable Water
- Public Telephone
- Pets Allowed
- Handicapped Accessible
- Picnic Area
- Hiking Trails (within approximately 2 miles)
- Swimming with Sand Beach (2 areas) and Bath House (day use area only)
- Fishing in Fourth Lake
- Bicycling on Campground Roads
- Volleyball, Horseshoe Pit (day use area) and Playground
- Horse Shelters and Horse Barn (22 paddocks & 2 corrals)
- Bridle Trails (5 miles of state trails and 60 miles of private trails)
- Boat Launch (cartop launch, no motor boats)
- Rowboat and Canoe Rental (at park office)

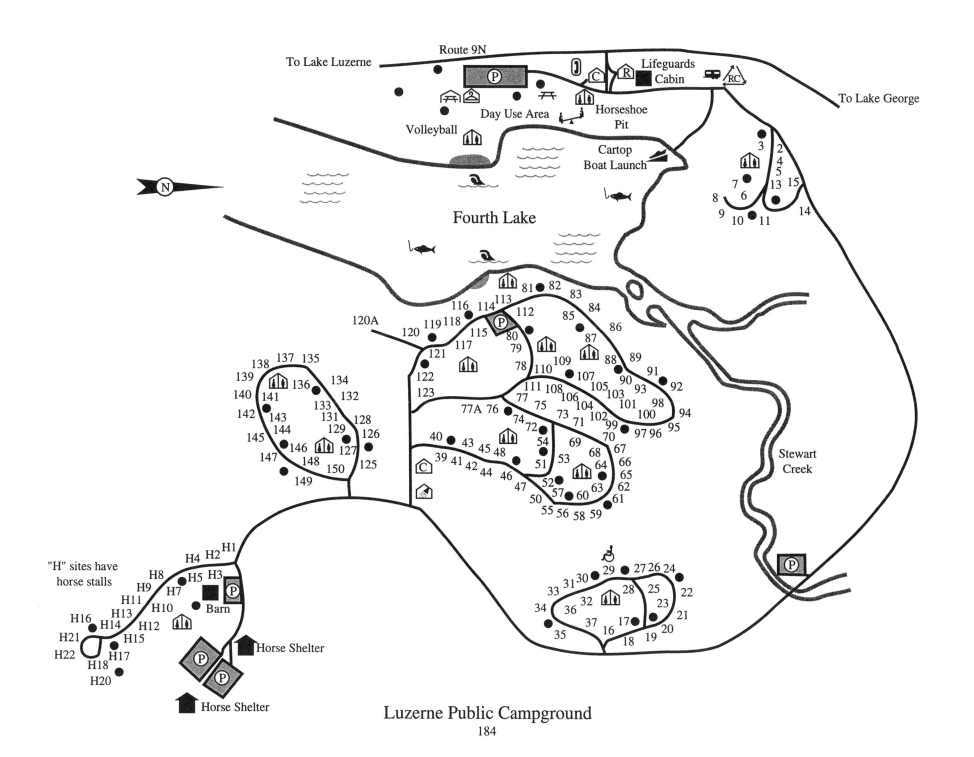

Route 9N

To Lake Luzerne

To Lake George

Lifeguards Cabin

Day Use Area

Horseshoe Pit

Volleyball

Cartop Boat Launch

Fourth Lake

N

3 2
4
5
7 6 13 15
8
9 14
10 11

81 82
83
116 114 113 84
119 118 112 85
120 115 86
120A 117 80 79 87
121 78 110 109 88 89
122 111 108 107 105 90 91
123 77A 76 77 106 104 103 101 92
75 73 102 100 98
74 72 71 99 97 96 94
138 137 135 40 54 69 70 95
139 136 134 43 48 51 53 68 67
140 141 133 132 39 41 42 45 46 47 52 64 66 65
142 131 44 50 57 60 63 62
143 129 128 55 56 58 59 61
145 144 146 127 126
147 148 150 125
149

Stewart Creek

"H" sites have horse stalls

H4 H2 H1
H8 H5 H3
H9 H7
H11 H10 Barn
H13 H12
H16 H14
H21 H15
H22 H17
H18
H20

P
P
P

Horse Shelter

Horse Shelter

29 27 26 24
31 30 28 25
33 32 23 22
34 36 37 16 17 21
35 18 19 20

Luzerne Public Campground

184

Macomb Reservation State Park

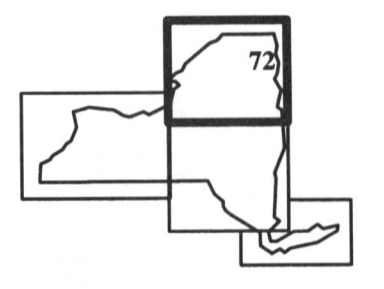

201 Campsite Road, Schuyler Falls, NY 12985

(518) 643–9952

- Located 3 miles west of Schuyler Falls off Norrisville Road
- Open mid–May through Labor Day for camping
- State Park is Open All Year
- 170 Tent & Trailer Sites (no electric sites, trailer dump)
- 600 Acres
- Comfort Station (flush toilets & sink) and Showers
- Potable Water (throughout campground)
- Public Telephone
- Pets Allowed
- Handicapped Accessible
- Picnic Areas
- Picnic Pavilions (2 reservable)
- Recreation Program
- Hiking Trails (within approximately 5 miles)
- Swimming with Sand Beach and Bath House
- Fishing in Salmon River and Davis Pond
- Dock
- Bicycling on Campground Roads
- Baseball Fields and Playground
- Boat Launch (no boat motors, cartop launch)
- Cross Country Skiing, Ice Skating, Snowshoeing, and Snowmobiling
- Recreation Hall

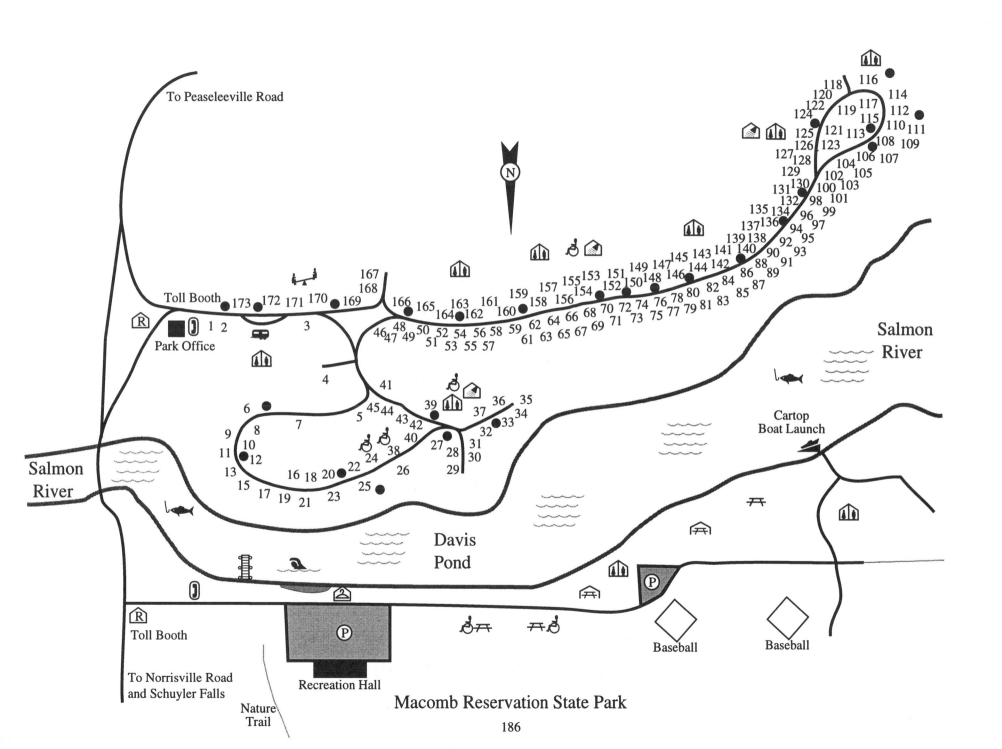

To Peaseleeville Road

Salmon River

Toll Booth
Park Office
R

Salmon River

Davis Pond

Cartop Boat Launch

Baseball   Baseball

Toll Booth
R

To Norrisville Road and Schuyler Falls

Recreation Hall

Nature Trail

Macomb Reservation State Park

186

Mary Island State Park

c/o Cedar Point State Park, 36661 Cedar Point State Park Drive, Clayton, NY 13624

(315) 654–2522

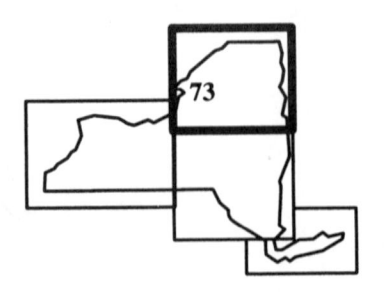

- Located 2 miles north of Alexandria Bay
- Open mid–May through mid–September for camping
- **Boat Access Only**
- 12 Tent Sites (no electric sites)
- 12 Acres
- Comfort Station (flush toilets & sink)
- Potable Water
- Picnic Area
- Hiking Trail (limited to island)
- Fishing in St. Lawrence River
- Boat Dock

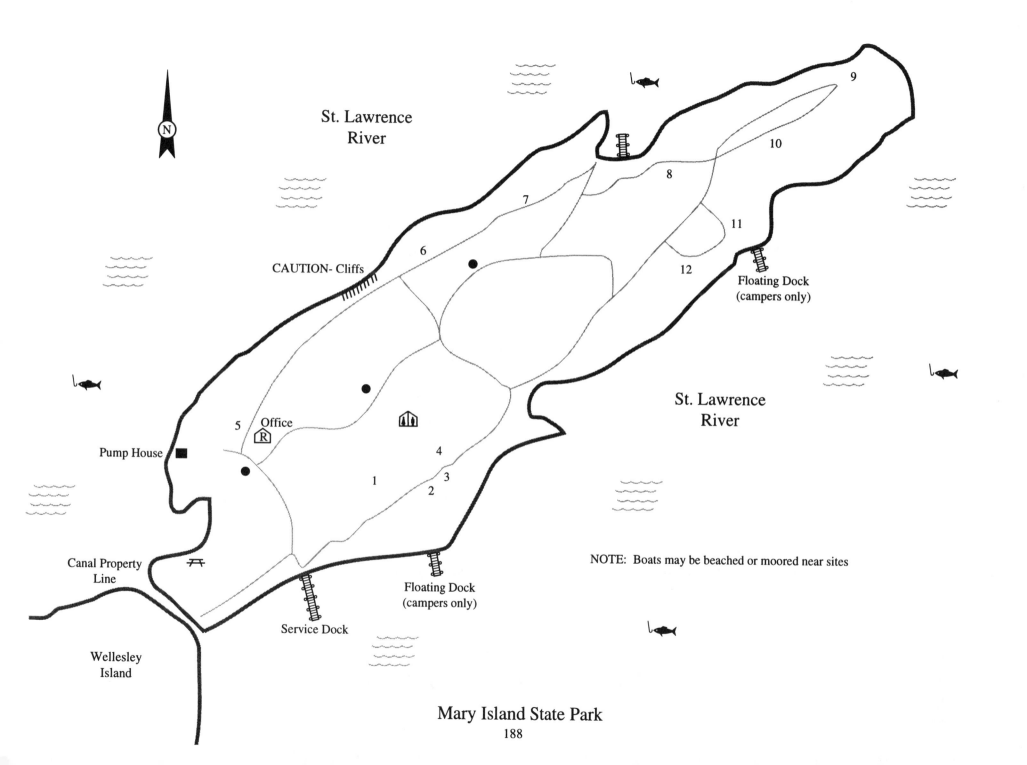

St. Lawrence
River

N

St. Lawrence
River

9

10

8

7

11

6

12

Floating Dock
(campers only)

CAUTION- Cliffs

5

Office
R

4

Pump House

1

3

2

NOTE: Boats may be beached or moored near sites

Canal Property
Line

Wellesley
Island

Service Dock

Floating Dock
(campers only)

Mary Island State Park

Max V. Shaul State Park

P. O. Box 23, Fultonham, NY 12071

(518) 827–4711

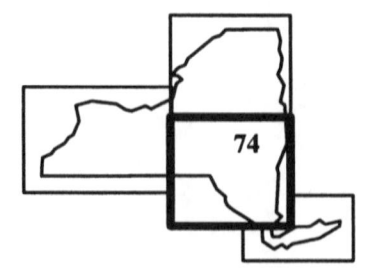

- Located 6 miles southwest of Middleburgh or 8 miles north of Mine Kill State Park off State Route 30
- Open mid–May through mid–October for camping
- 29 Tent & Trailer Sites (no electric sites)
- 54 Acres
- Comfort Station (flush toilets & sink) and Showers
- Potable Water
- Public Telephone
- Pets Allowed
- Handicapped Accessible
- Picnic Area
- Picnic Pavilion (reservable)
- Hiking Trails (within approximately 2 miles and at Mine Kill State Park)
- Swimming Pool (at Mine Kill State Park – approximately 9 miles south)
- Fishing in Panther Creek
- Softball Field, Basketball Court, Horseshoe Pits, and Playground
- Cross Country Skiing

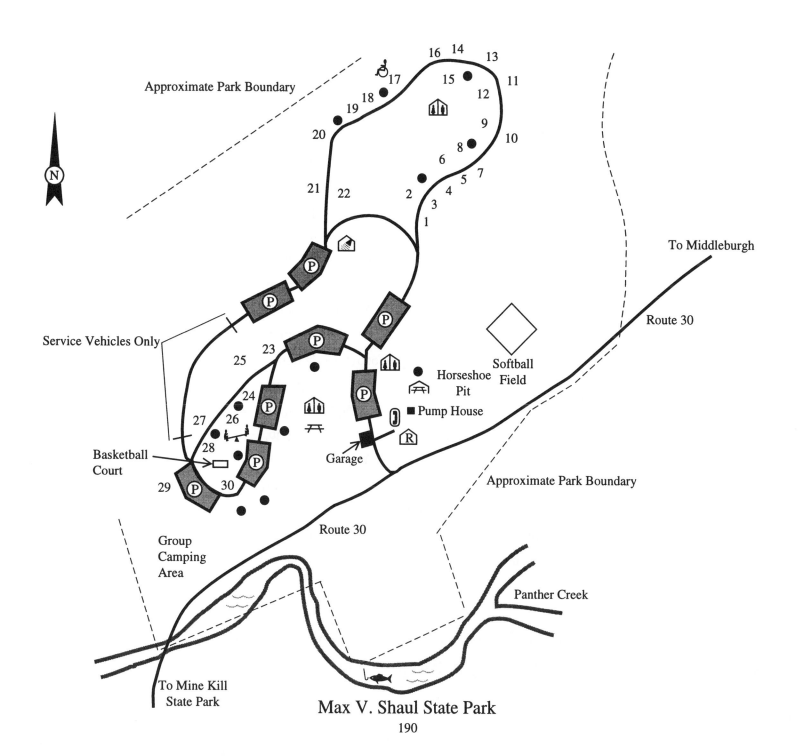

Approximate Park Boundary

N

To Middleburgh

Route 30

Route 30

Softball
Field

Horseshoe
Pit

Pump House

Service Vehicles Only

Garage

Basketball
Court

Approximate Park Boundary

Group
Camping
Area

Panther Creek

To Mine Kill
State Park

Max V. Shaul State Park

190

Meacham Lake Public Campground

P. O. Box 29A, State Route 30, Paul Smiths, NY 12970

(518) 483–5116

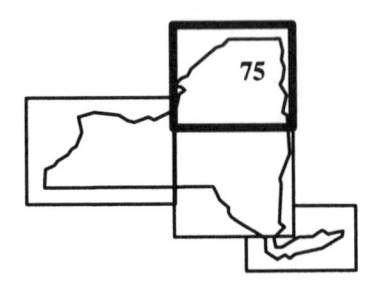

- Located 19 miles south of Malone or 10 miles north of Paul Smiths off State Route 30
- Open mid–May through mid–October for camping
- 224 Tent & Trailer Sites (no electric sites, trailer dump)
- 100 Acres
- Comfort Station (flush toilets & sink) and Showers
- Potable Water
- Public Telephone
- Pets Allowed
- Handicapped Accessible
- Picnic Areas
- Picnic Pavilions (reservable)
- Recreation Program
- Hiking Trails (within approximately 1 mile)
- Swimming with Sand Beach and Bath House
- Fishing in Meacham Lake
- Bicycling on Campground Roads
- Playground
- Boat Launch
- Rowboat and Canoe Rental (at park office)
- Amphitheater

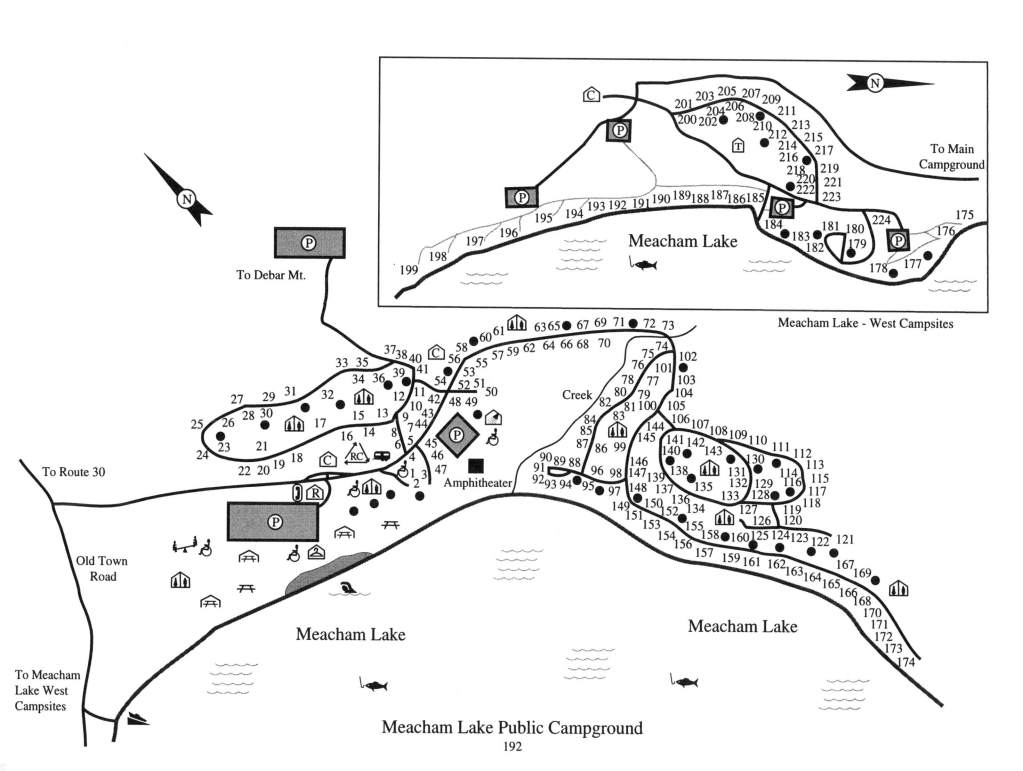

Meacham Lake - West Campsites

Creek

Meacham Lake

Meacham Lake

Amphitheater

To Debar Mt.

To Route 30

Old Town Road

To Meacham Lake West Campsites

To Main Campground

Meacham Lake Public Campground

192

Meadowbrook Public Campground

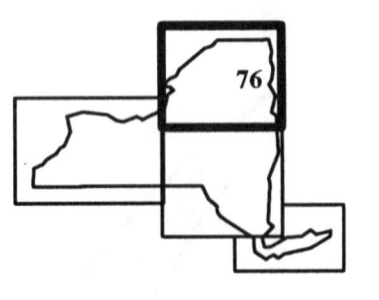

State Route 86, Box 296 (Operations), Ray Brook, NY 12977

(518) 891–4351

- Located 4 miles east of Saranac Lake or 5 miles west of Lake Placid off State Route 86
- Open mid–May through Labor Day for camping
- 62 Tent & Trailer Sites (no electric sites, trailer dump)
- 13 Acres
- Comfort Station (flush toilets & sink) and Showers
- Potable Water
- Public Telephone
- Pets Allowed
- Handicapped Accessible
- Picnic Area
- Picnic Pavilion (reservable)
- Hiking Trails
- Bicycling on Campground Roads

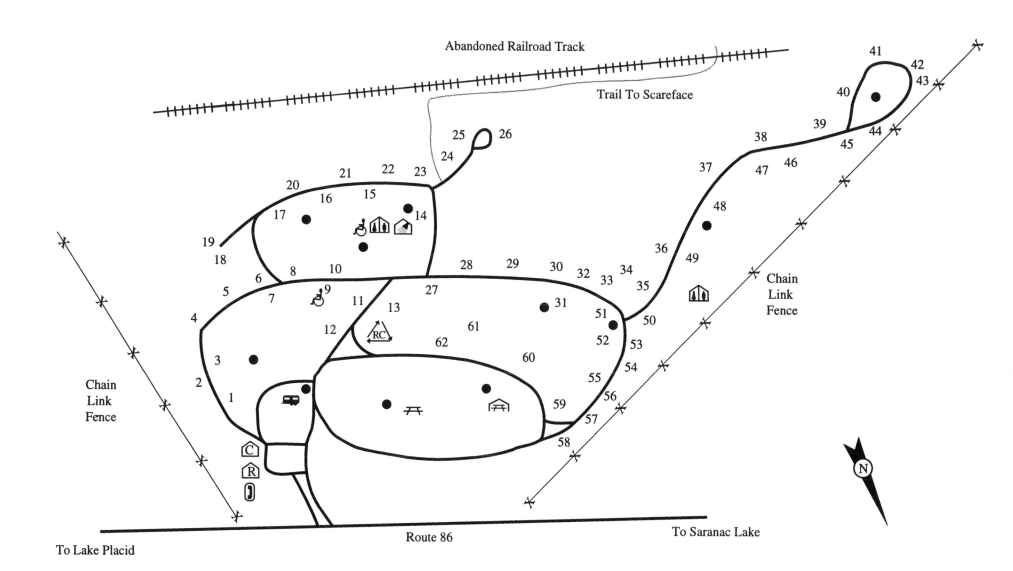

Abandoned Railroad Track

Trail To Scareface

41
42
40　　　　　43
39
38　　　　44
37　　47　46　　45

25　26
24
20　21　22　23
16　15
17　　　14
36
48
49

19
18
6　8　10
5　7　9　11　13　28　29　30　32　33　34　35　50
4　　　12　27　　　31　51　53
RC　　61　52　54
3　　62　60　55
2　　　　56
1　　59　57
58

Chain
Link
Fence

Chain
Link
Fence

C
R

N

Route 86

To Lake Placid

To Saranac Lake

Meadowbrook Public Campground
194

Mills – Norrie State Park

Old Post Road, P. O. Box 308, Staatsburg, NY 12580

(845) 889–4646

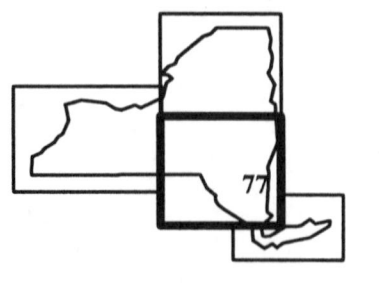

- Located 5 miles north of Hyde Park or 5 mile south of Rhinebeck off US 9
- Open mid–May through October for camping
- State Park is Open All Year
- 51 Tent & Trailer Sites (no electric sites, trailer dump)
- 10 Cabins
- 1,000 Acres
- Comfort Station (flush toilets & sink) and Showers
- Potable Water (throughout campground)
- Handicapped Accessible
- Picnic Areas
- Recreation Program
- Hiking and Nature Trails
- Bridle Paths (within state park)
- Fishing in Hudson River
- Bicycling on Campground Roads
- Boat Launch and Marina (at Norrie Marina)
- Two 9–hole Golf Courses and Clubhouse
- Cross Country Skiing, Sledding Hills, and Snowmobiling
- Mills Mansion

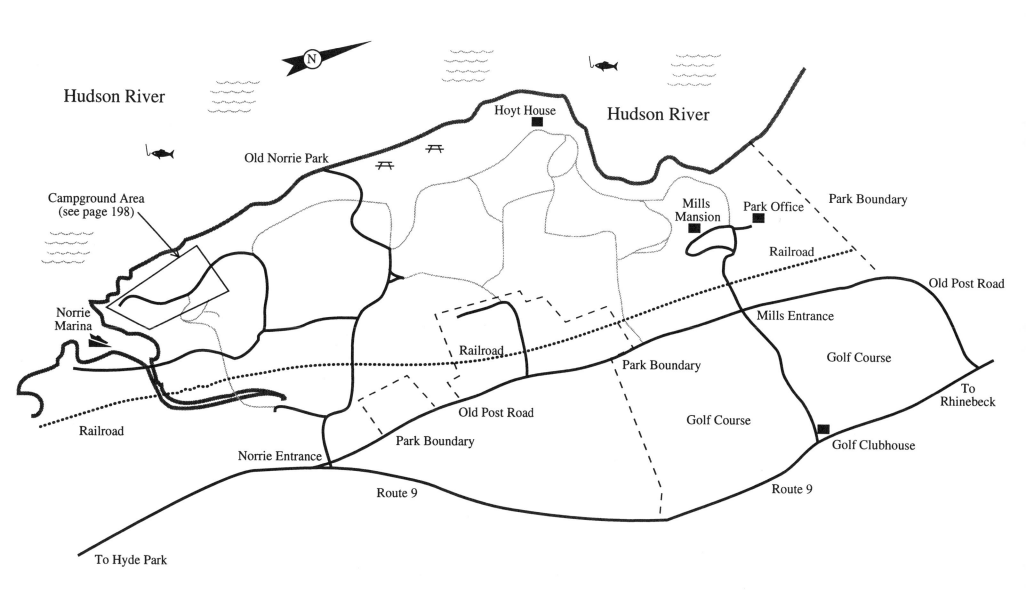

Hudson River

N

Hudson River

Hoyt House

Old Norrie Park

Mills Mansion

Park Office

Park Boundary

Campground Area
(see page 198)

Railroad

Old Post Road

Norrie Marina

Mills Entrance

Railroad

Golf Course

Railroad

Park Boundary

To Rhinebeck

Old Post Road

Golf Course

Park Boundary

Golf Clubhouse

Norrie Entrance

Railroad

Route 9

Route 9

To Hyde Park

Mills - Norrie State Park

Mills – Norrie State Park

(see page 195 for campground information and main park map)

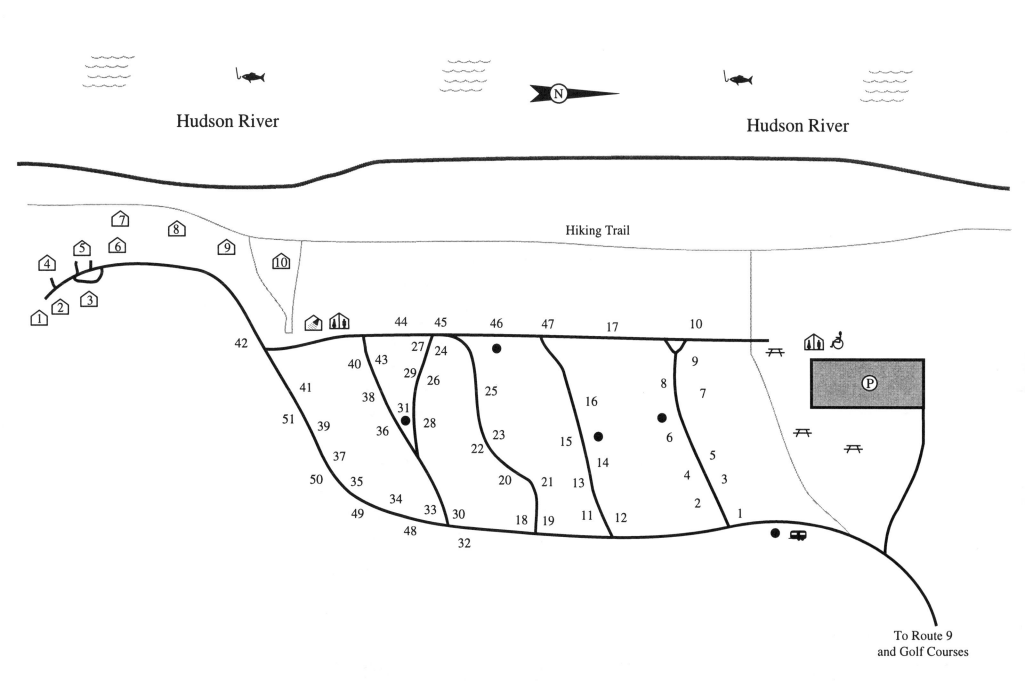

Hudson River

Hudson River

Hiking Trail

Mills - Norrie State Park

Moffitt Beach Public Campground

Page Street, Speculator, NY 12164

(518) 548–7102

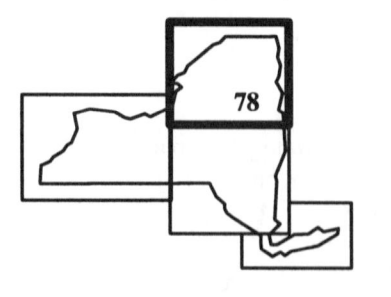

- Located 2 miles west of Speculator off State Route 8
- Open mid–May through mid–October for camping
- 253 Tent & Trailer Sites (no electric sites, trailer dump)
- 75 Acres
- Comfort Station (flush toilets & sink) and Showers
- Potable Water
- Pets Allowed
- Handicapped Accessible
- Picnic Area
- Picnic Pavilion (reservable)
- Recreation Program
- Nature Trail
- Swimming with Sand Beach and Bath House
- Fishing in Sacandaga Lake
- Bicycling on Campground Roads
- Playground
- Boat Launch (2 locations)
- Rowboat and Canoe Rental (at privately owned store in campground)

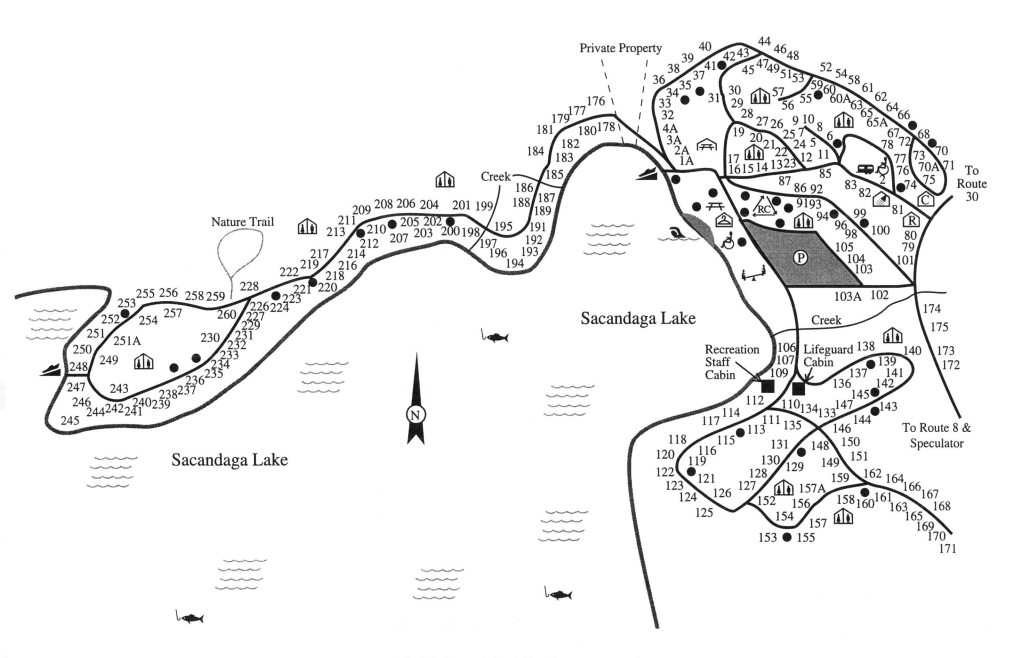

Moffit Beach Public Campground

200

Mongaup Pond Public Campground

RR 1, Box 231, Livingston Manor, NY 12758

(845) 439–4233

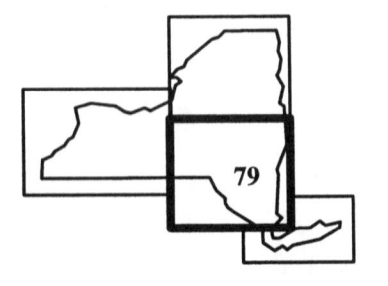

- Located 9 miles northeast of Livingston Manor off Mongaup Road
- Open mid–May through mid–October for camping
- 142 Tent & Trailer Sites (no electric sites, trailer dump)
- 275 Acres
- Comfort Station (flush toilets & sink) and Showers
- Potable Water
- Public Telephone
- Pets Allowed
- Handicapped Accessible
- Picnic Area
- Picnic Pavilion (reservable)
- Recreation Program
- Hiking Trails
- Swimming with Sand Beach and Bath House
- Fishing in Mongaup Pond
- Dock
- Bicycling on Campground Roads
- Boat Launch (no motor boats)
- Rowboat and Canoe Rental (at park office)
- Snowmobile Trail

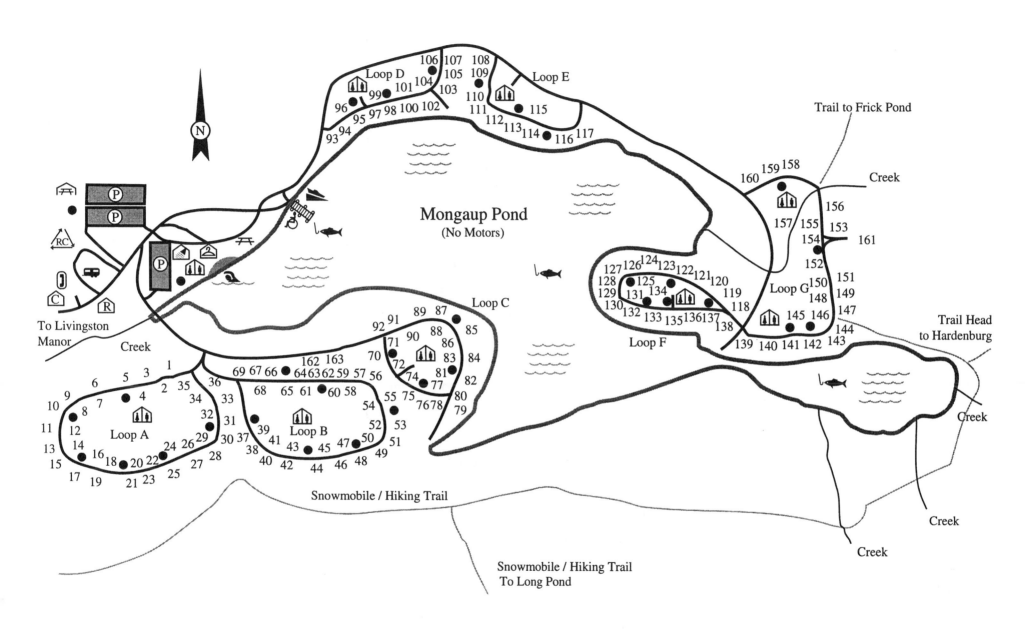

Mongaup Pond Public Campground

202

Moreau Lake State Park

605 Old Saratoga Road, Gansevoort, NY 12831

(518) 793–0511

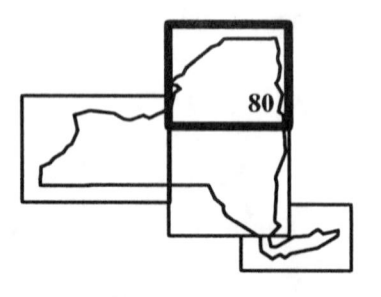

- Located 10 mile north of Saratoga Springs or 6 miles south of Glens Falls off US 9
- Open mid–May through mid–October for camping
- State Park is Open All Year
- 148 Tent & Trailer Sites (no electric sites, trailer dump)
- 740 Acres
- Comfort Station (flush toilets & sink) and Showers
- Potable Water
- Public Telephone
- Pets Allowed
- Handicapped Accessible
- Picnic Areas
- Picnic Pavilions
- Recreation Program
- Hiking Trail, Nature Trail and Nature Center
- Swimming with Sand Beach and Bath House
- Fishing in Moreau Lake
- Hunting
- Bicycling on Campground Roads, Volleyball and Playground
- Boat Launch and Dock (no motor boats, cartop launch)
- Rowboat Rental
- Cross Country Skiing, Ice Fishing, and Snowshoeing
- Walk In Camping Area

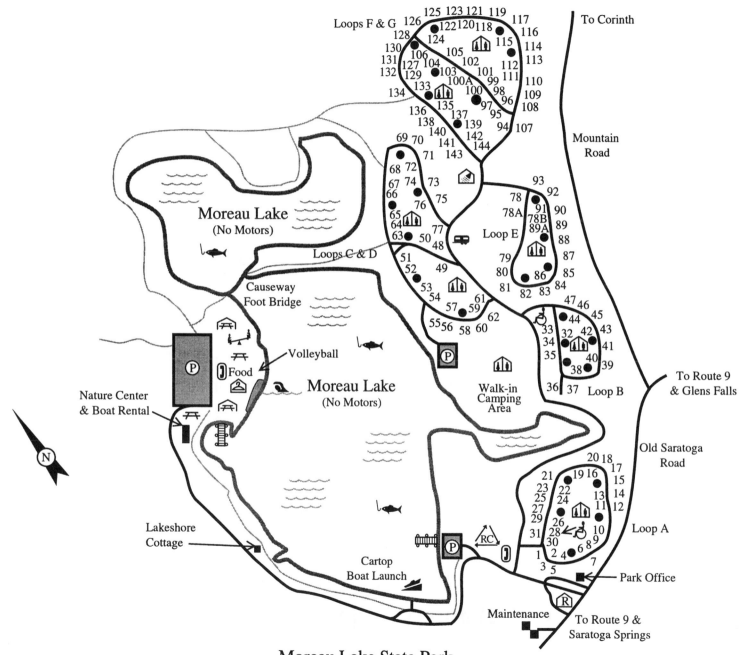

Loops F & G

125 123 121 119
126 122 120 118 117
128 124 116
130 106 105 115 114
131 127 104 102 113
132 129 103 101 112
134 133 100A 99 111 110
135 100 98 109
136 137 95 96 108
138 139 94 107
140 142
141 144
143

69 70
71
68 72
67 74 73
66 75
65 76
64 77
63 50 48
51
52 49
53
54
57 61
55 56 58 59
60 62

93 92
78 91 90
78A 78B 89
Loop E 89A 88
79 87
80 86 85
81 82 83 84

47 46
44 45
33 32 42 43
34 41
35 40
38 39
36 37 Loop B

Walk-in
Camping
Area

To Corinth

Mountain
Road

To Route 9
& Glens Falls

Old Saratoga
Road

20 18
21 19 16 17
23 22 15
25 24 13 14
27 11 12
29 26
31 28 10
30 6 9
1 2 4 8 7
3 5

Loop A

RC

Moreau Lake
(No Motors)

Moreau Lake
(No Motors)

Loops C & D

Causeway
Foot Bridge

Volleyball

Food

Nature Center
& Boat Rental

N

Lakeshore
Cottage

Cartop
Boat Launch

Maintenance

R

Park Office

To Route 9 &
Saratoga Springs

Moreau Lake State Park

204

Nicks Lake Public Campground

Bisby Lake Road, Old Forge, NY 13420

(315) 369–3314

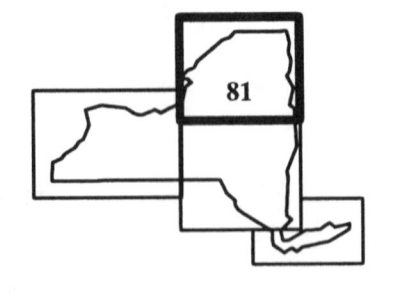

- Located 2 miles south of Old Forge off State Route 28
- Open mid–April through October for camping
- 104 Tent & Trailer Sites (no electric sites, trailer dump, max 40 foot RV)
- 200 Acres
- Comfort Station (flush toilets & sink) and Showers
- Potable Water (throughout campground)
- Public Telephone
- Pets Allowed
- Handicapped Accessible
- Picnic Areas
- Picnic Pavilion (reservable)
- Recreation Program
- Hiking and Nature Trails
- Swimming with Sand Beach and Bath House
- Fishing in Nicks Lake
- Bicycling and Rollerblading on Campground Roads
- Baseball Field, Basketball Court, Volleyball Courts, Horseshoe Pits, and Playground
- Boat Launch (no motor boats, cartop launch)
- Boat / Canoe Rental (locally in Old Forge – approximately 2 miles north)
- Interpreters Cabin

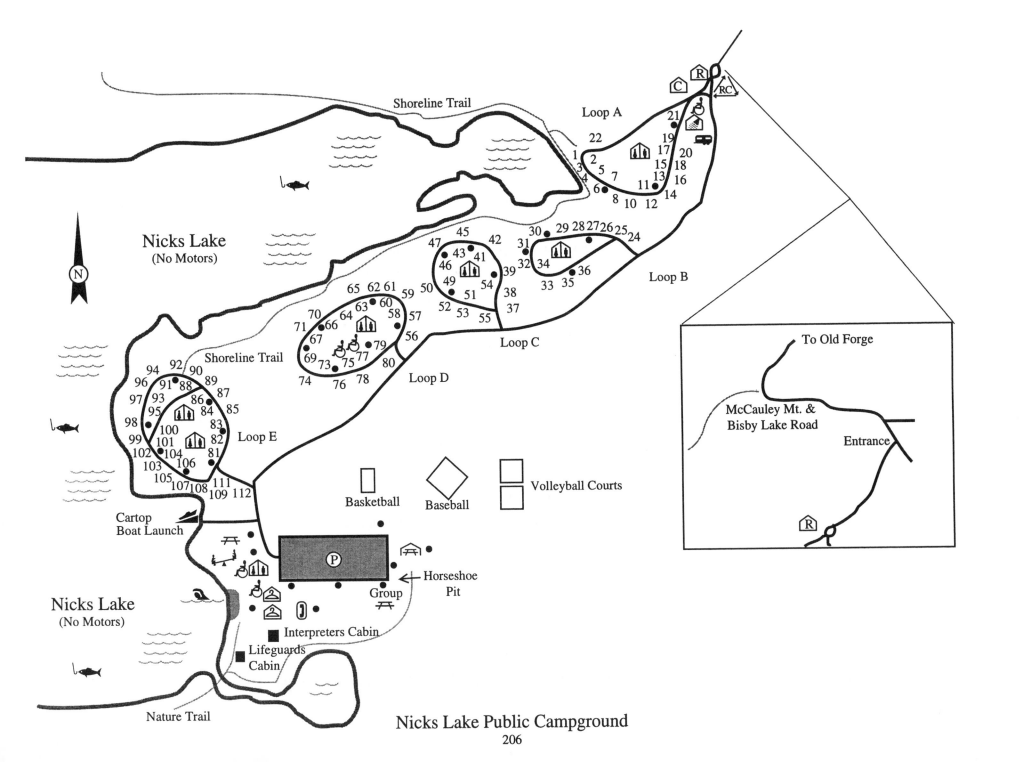

Nicks Lake Public Campground

206

Northampton Beach Public Campground

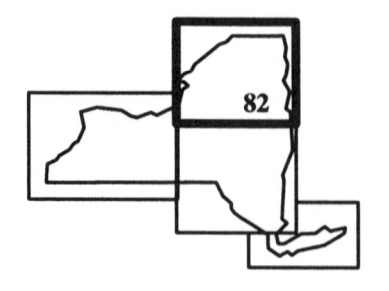

Houseman Street, Mayfield, NY 12117

(518) 863–6000

- Located 3 miles south of Northville or 13 miles northeast of Gloversville off State Route 30
- Open late–April through mid–October for camping
- 223 Tent & Trailer Sites (no electric sites, trailer dump, max 40 foot RV)
- 60 Acres
- Comfort Station (flush toilets & sink) and Showers
- Potable Water
- Public Telephone
- Pets Allowed
- Handicapped Accessible
- Picnic Areas
- Picnic Pavilion (reservable)
- Hiking Trails (within approximately 8 miles)
- Swimming with Sand Beach and Bath House
- Fishing in Great Sacandaga Lake
- Bicycling on Campground Roads
- Playground
- Boat Launch
- Boat Rental (nearby marina – approximately 1/4 mile north)

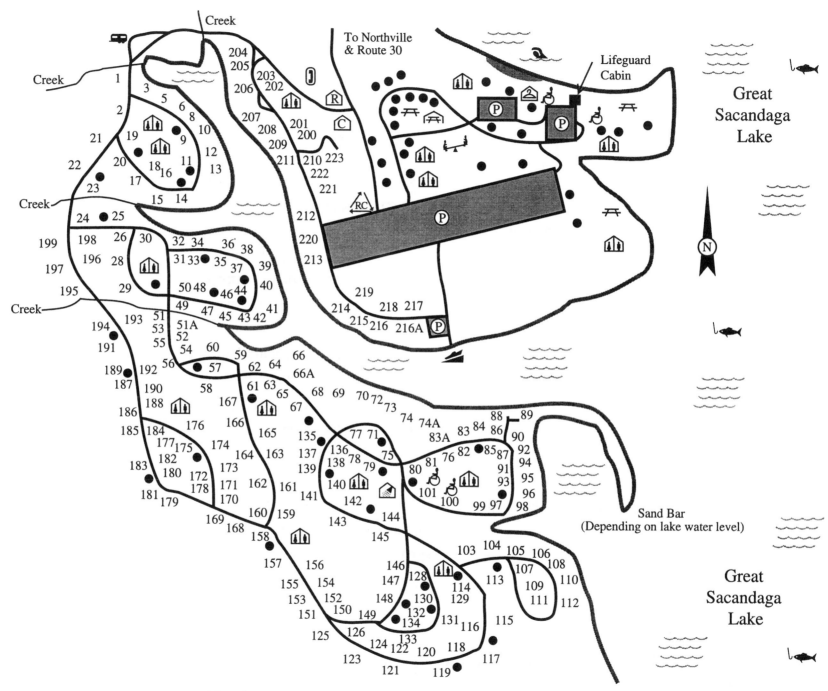

Northampton Beach Public Campground

208

North – South Lake Public Campground

P. O. Box 347, Haines Falls, NY 12436

(518) 589–5058

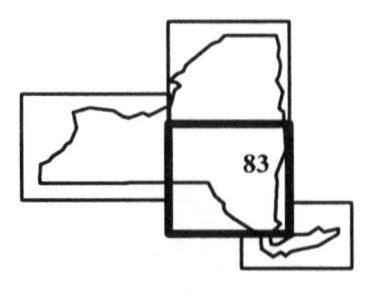

- Located 3 miles east of Haines Falls off Route 23A
- Open May through mid–October for camping
- 202 Tent & Trailer Sites (no electric sites, trailer dump, max 40 foot RV)
- 128 Acres
- Comfort Station (flush toilets & sink) and Showers
- Potable Water (throughout campground)
- Public Telephone
- Pets Allowed
- Handicapped Accessible
- Picnic Areas
- Picnic Pavilions (2 reservable)
- Recreation Program
- Hiking and Nature Trails
- Swimming with Sand Beach and Bath House (2 locations)
- Fishing in North and South Lakes
- Bicycling on Campground Roads
- Boat Launch (no motor boats)
- Rowboat and Canoe Rental

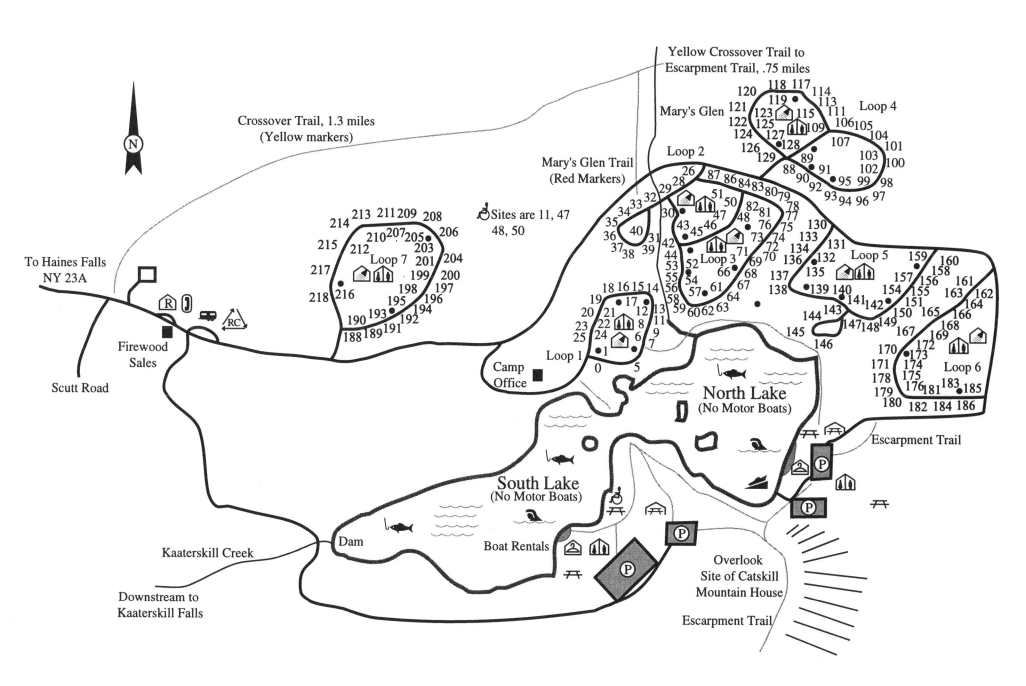

North-South Lake Public Campground

210

Oquaga Creek State Park

5995 City Highway 20, Bainbridge, NY 13733

(607) 467–4160

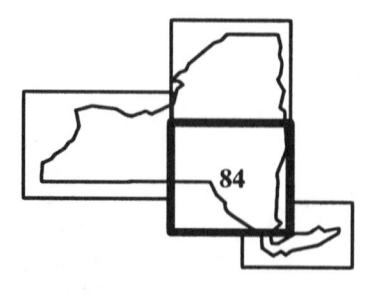

- Located 9 miles southeast of Bainbridge or 8 miles north of Deposit off State Route 20
- Open mid–May through mid–October for camping
- State Park is Open All Year
- 95 Tent & Trailer Sites (no electric sites, trailer dump), 1 Cottage
- 1,481 Acres
- Comfort Station (flush toilets & sink) and Showers
- Potable Water (throughout campground)
- Public Telephone
- Pets Allowed
- Handicapped Accessible
- Picnic Area
- Picnic Pavilion (reservable)
- Recreation Program (limited)
- Hiking and Nature Trails
- Swimming with Sand Beach and Bath House
- Fishing in Lake Artic
- Bicycling on Campground Roads
- Hunting (in season)
- Baseball Field, Frisbee–Disc Golf Course (near beach area) and Playgrounds
- Boat Launch (cartop launch, permit required)
- Rowboat Rental (at snackbar)
- Cross Country Skiing, Ice Skating and Sledding Hills

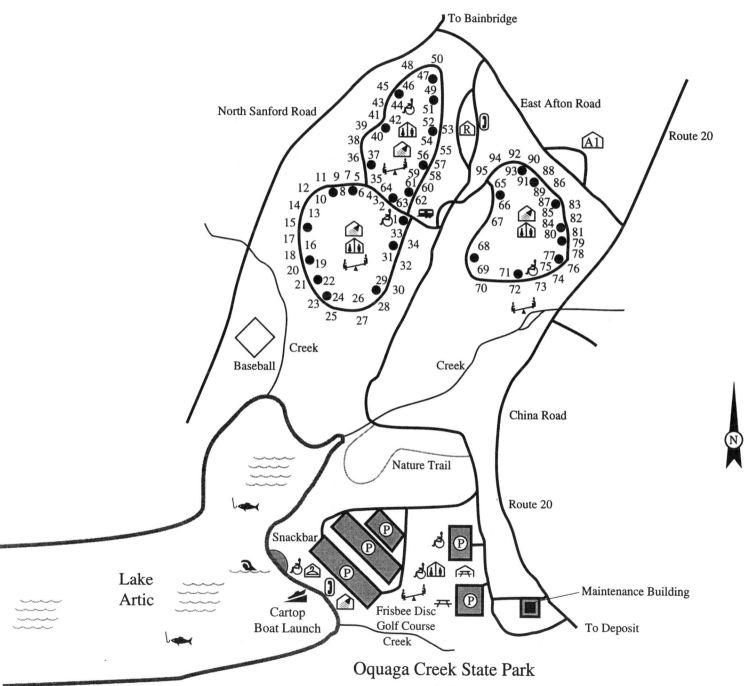

To Bainbridge

North Sanford Road

East Afton Road

Route 20

R

A1

Creek

Baseball

Creek

China Road

N

Nature Trail

Route 20

Snackbar

Lake
Artic

Cartop
Boat Launch

Frisbee Disc
Golf Course
Creek

Maintenance Building

To Deposit

Oquaga Creek State Park

212

Paradox Lake Public Campground

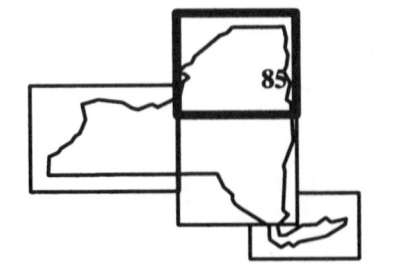

State Route 74, Severance, NY 12872

(518) 532–7451

- Located 2 miles east of Severance off State Route 74
- Open mid–May through mid–October for camping
- State Park is Open All Year
- 58 Tent & Trailer Sites (no electric sites, trailer dump, max 30 foot RV)
- 6 Acres
- Comfort Station (flush toilets & sink) and Showers
- Potable Water
- Public Telephone
- Pets Allowed
- Handicapped Accessible
- Picnic Area
- Picnic Pavilion (reservable)
- Hiking Trails (within approximately 3 miles)
- Swimming with Sand Beach and Bath House
- Fishing in Paradox Lake
- Bicycling on Campground Roads
- Boat Launch
- Rowboat and Canoe Rental (at park office)
- Cross Country Skiing and Ice Fishing

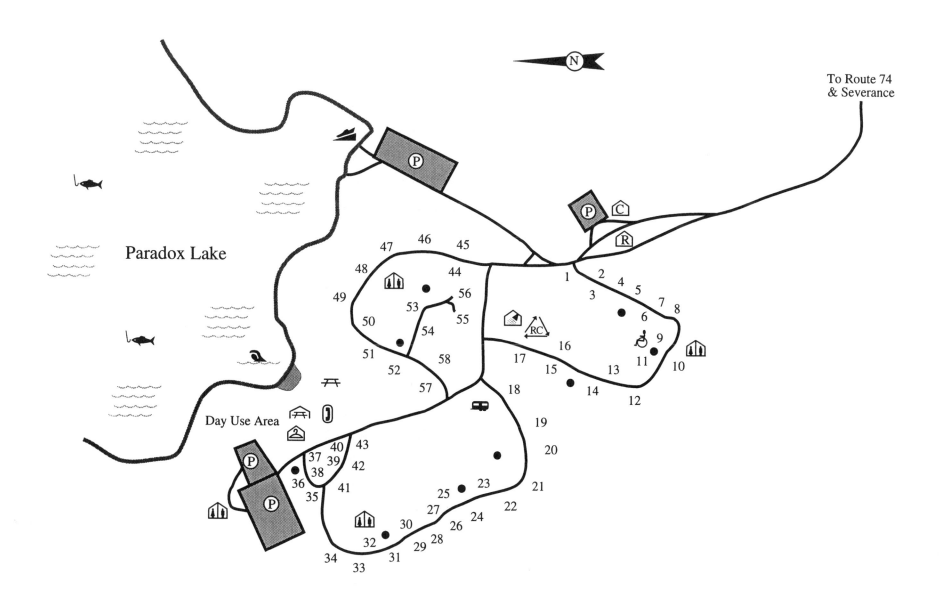

Paradox Lake Public Campground

Pixley Falls State Park

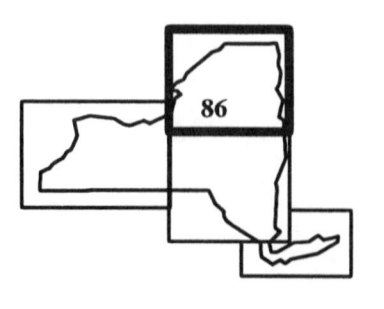

11430 State Route 46, Boonville, NY 13309

(315) 942–4713

- Located 6 miles south of Boonville or 15 miles north of Rome off State Route 46
- Open mid–May through Labor Day for camping
- State Park is Open All Year
- 22 Tent & Trailer Sites (no electric sites)
- 375 Acres
- Comfort Station (flush toilets & sink)
- Potable Water
- Public Telephone
- Pets Allowed
- Handicapped Accessible
- Picnic Areas
- Picnic Pavilion
- Hiking Trails, Winter Sky Trail, and Summer Nature Trail
- Fishing in Lansing Kill
- Hunting
- Bridle Paths and Mountain Biking (Black River Canal Trail)
- Softball Field and Horseshoe Pit
- Cross Country Skiing and Snowshoeing

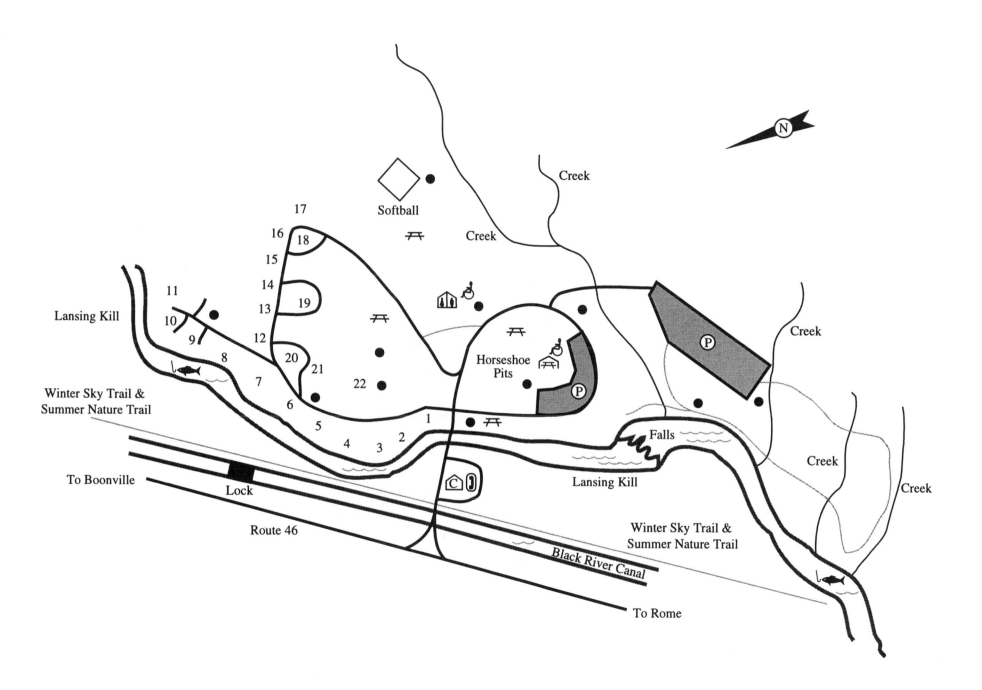

Pixley Falls State Park

216

Point Comfort Public Campground

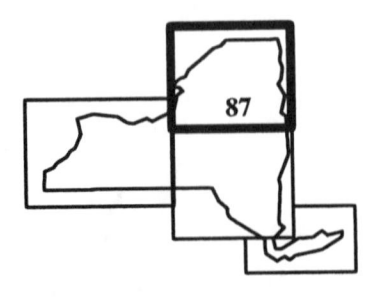

Old Piseco Road, Piseco, NY 12139

(518) 548–7586

- Located 4 miles southwest of Piseco or 6 miles east of Hoffmeister off State Route 8
- Open mid–May through mid–October for camping
- 65 Tent & Trailer Sites (no electric sites, recycling and trailer dump at Little Sand Point Campground – 2 miles northeast)
- 15 Acres
- Vault Toilets (composting)
- Potable Water
- Pets Allowed
- Handicapped Accessible
- Picnic Area
- Hiking Trails (within approximately 5 miles)
- Swimming with Sand Beach and Bath House
- Fishing in Piseco Lake
- Boat Launch
- Rowboat and Canoe Rental (Piseco Lake Lodge)

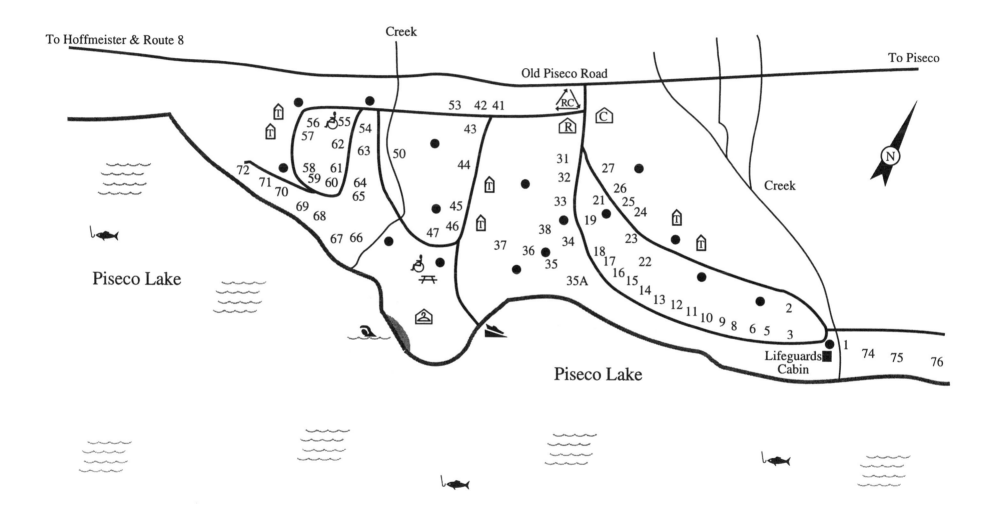

Point Comfort Public Campground

Poke–O–Moonshine Public Campground

Box 163B, Keeseville, NY 12944

(518) 834–9045

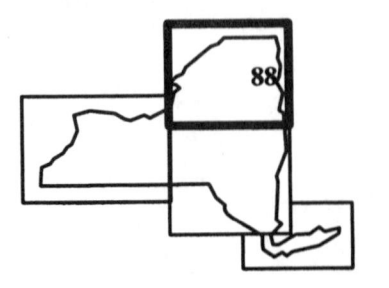

- Located 6 miles south of Keeseville or 13 miles north of Elizabethtown off US 9
- Open mid–May through Labor Day for camping
- 25 Tent & Trailer Sites (no electric sites)
- 3 Acres
- Comfort Station (flush toilets & sink) and Showers
- Potable Water
- Pets Allowed
- Picnic Area
- Hiking Trail (rock climbing for advanced climbers only)

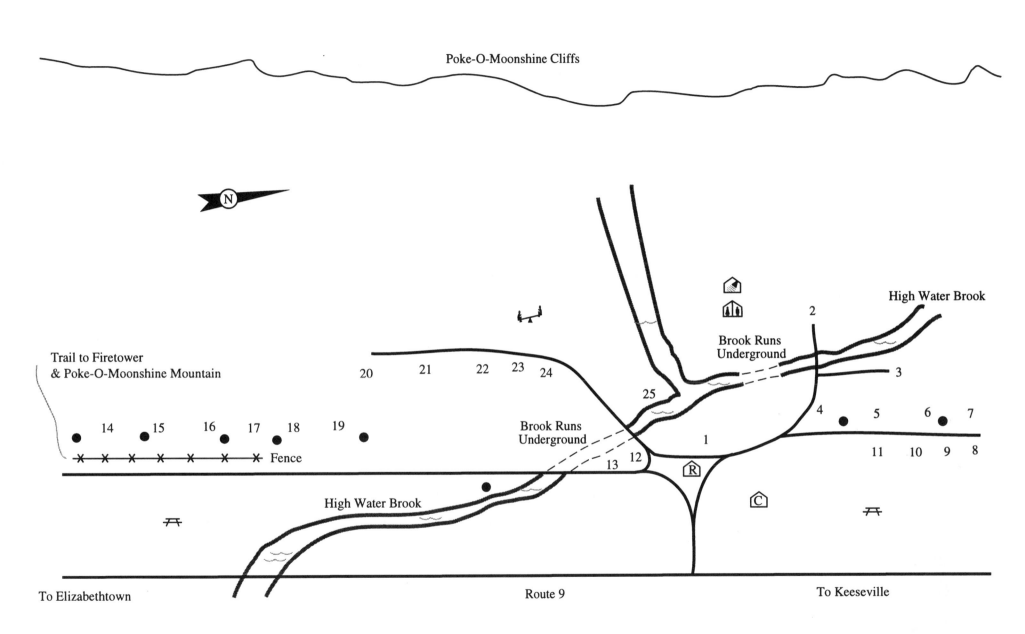

Poke-O-Moonshine Cliffs

N

High Water Brook

Brook Runs
Underground

2

3

Trail to Firetower
& Poke-O-Moonshine Mountain

20   21   22   23   24

25

4   5   6   7

14   15   16   17   18   19

Brook Runs
Underground

1

11   10   9   8

13   12

R

C

Fence

High Water Brook

To Elizabethtown

Route 9

To Keeseville

Poke-O-Moonshine Public Campground

Poplar Point Public Campground

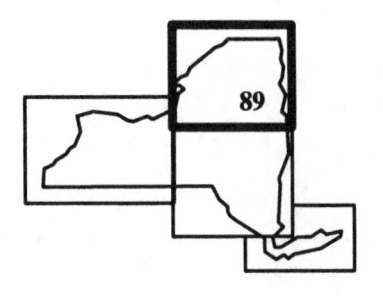

Old Piseco Road, Piseco, NY 12139

(518) 548–8031

- Located 2 miles southwest of Piseco or 10 miles east of Hoffmeister off State Route 8
- Open mid–May through Labor Day for camping
- 21 Tent & Trailer Sites (no electric sites)
- 15 Acres
- Vault Toilets
- Potable Water
- Pets Allowed
- Handicapped Accessible
- Picnic Area
- Hiking Trail
- Swimming with Sand Beach and Bath House
- Fishing in Piseco Lake
- Boat Launch
- Rowboat and Canoe Rental (Piseco Lake Lodge)

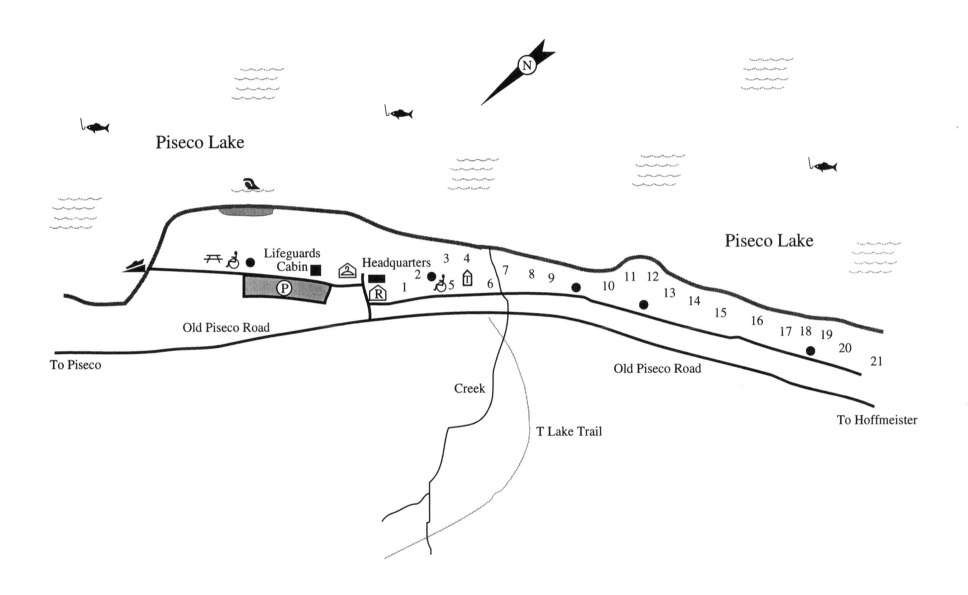

Piseco Lake

Piseco Lake

Lifeguards
Cabin

Headquarters

3   4

2

1   5

6

7

8   9

10

11   12

13

14

15

16

17   18   19

20

21

Old Piseco Road

To Piseco

Creek

T Lake Trail

Old Piseco Road

To Hoffmeister

Poplar Point Public Campground

Putnam Pond Public Campground

Rural Delivery, Chilson, NY 12818

(518) 585–7280

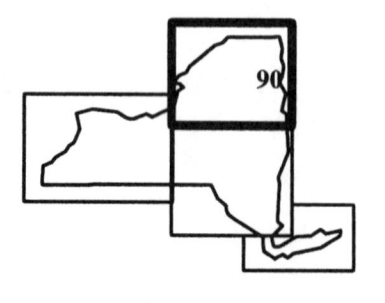

- Located 6 miles west of Ticonderoga off State Route 74
- Open mid–May through Labor Day for camping
- 63 Tent & Trailer Sites (no electric sites, trailer dump)
- 9 Interior Sites (boat and canoe access only, no potable water)
- 30 Acres
- Comfort Station (flush toilets & sink) and Showers
- Potable Water
- Public Telephone
- Pets Allowed
- Handicapped Accessible
- Picnic Areas
- Picnic Pavilion (reservable)
- Hiking Trails
- Swimming with Sand Beach and Bath House
- Fishing in Putnam Pond
- Bicycling and Rollerblading on Campground Roads
- Boat Launch
- Boat and Canoe Rental
- Day Use Area

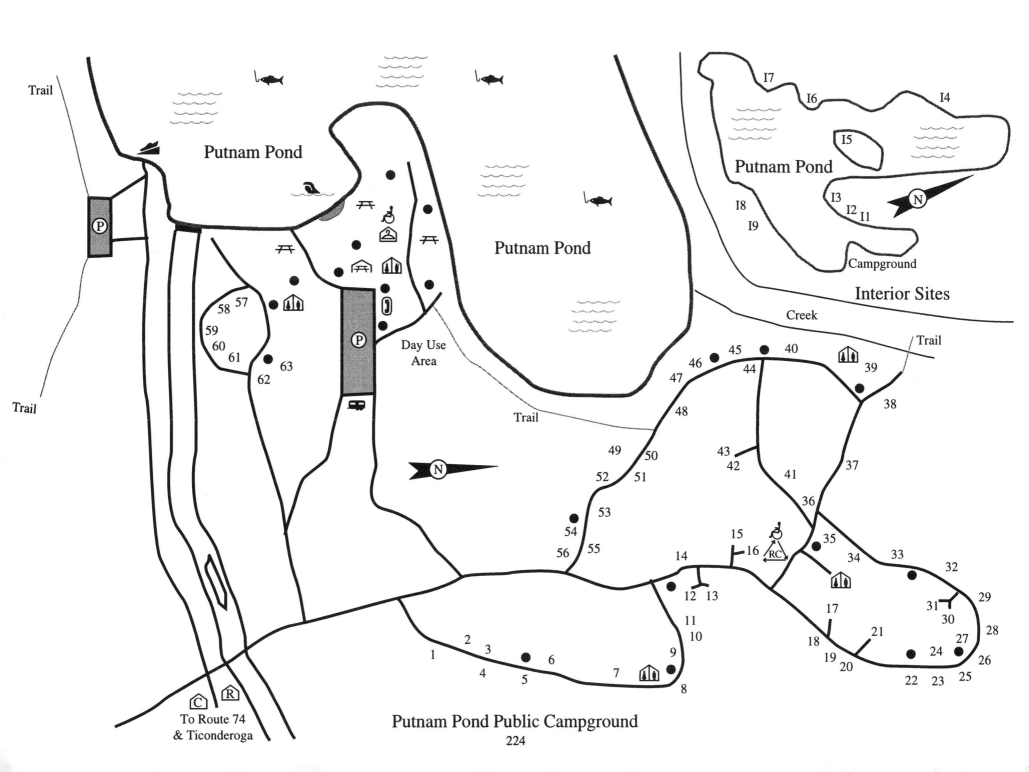

Putnam Pond Public Campground

224

Robert Moses State Park

P.O. Box 548, Massena, NY 13662

(315) 769–8663

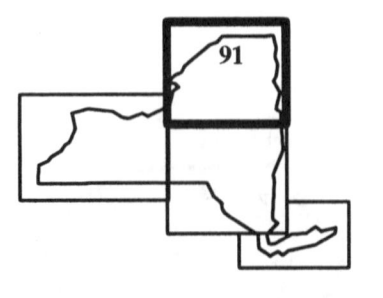

- Located 4 miles northeast of Massena off State Route 37
- Open mid–May through mid–October for camping
- State Park is Open All Year
- 168 Tent & Trailer Sites (38 electric sites, trailer dump)
- 15 Cabins (pets allowed in Cabins #8–15)
- 2,322 Acres
- Comfort Station (flush toilets & sink) and Showers
- Potable Water
- Public Telephone
- Pets Allowed
- Handicapped Accessible
- Picnic Areas and Pavilions (3 reservable)
- Recreation Program
- Hiking and Nature Trails (starting at Nature Center)
- Swimming with Sand Beach and Bath House
- Fishing in St. Lawrence River and Lake St. Lawrence
- Bicycling on Campground Roads
- Softball, Volleyball, 9–Hole Mini–Golf, Horseshoe Pits, Tennis Court, and Playground
- Boat Launch and Marina
- Boat Rental (at marina)
- Cross Country Skiing, Ice Skating, Ice Fishing, Snowshoeing, and Snowmobiling
- Eisenhower Lock, Visitors Information Center and Observation Deck

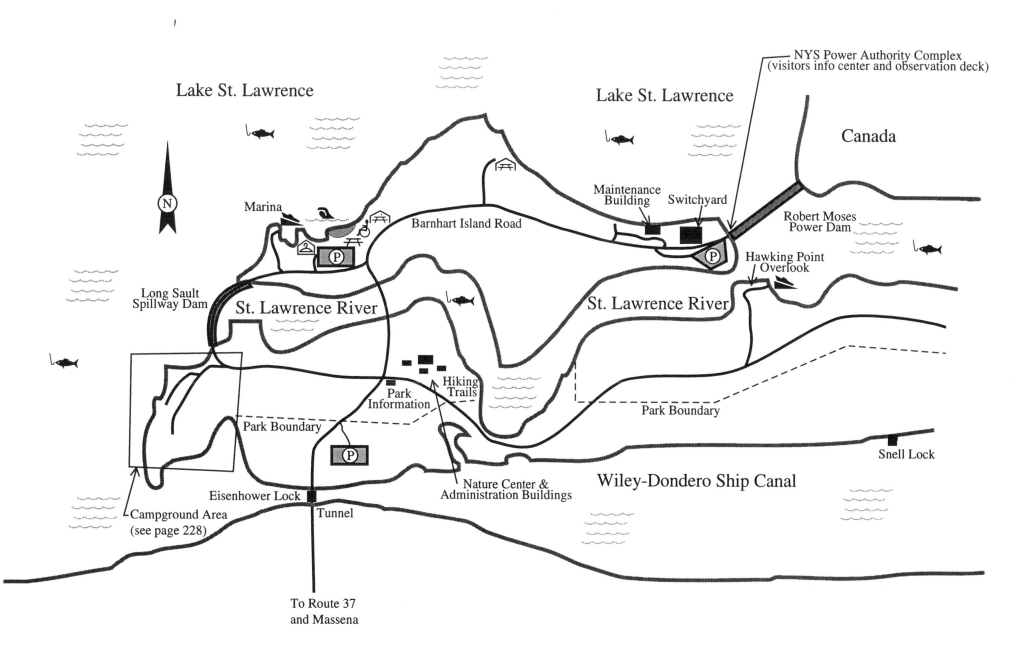

Lake St. Lawrence

Lake St. Lawrence

NYS Power Authority Complex
(visitors info center and observation deck)

Canada

N

Marina

Maintenance
Building

Switchyard

Barnhart Island Road

Robert Moses
Power Dam

P

Hawking Point
Overlook

Long Sault
Spillway Dam

St. Lawrence River

St. Lawrence River

P

Hiking
Trails

Park
Information

Park Boundary

Snell Lock

Park Boundary

P

Wiley-Dondero Ship Canal

Nature Center &
Administration Buildings

Campground Area
(see page 228)

Eisenhower Lock

Tunnel

To Route 37
and Massena

Robert Moses State Park

226

Robert Moses State Park

(see page 225 for campground information and main park map)

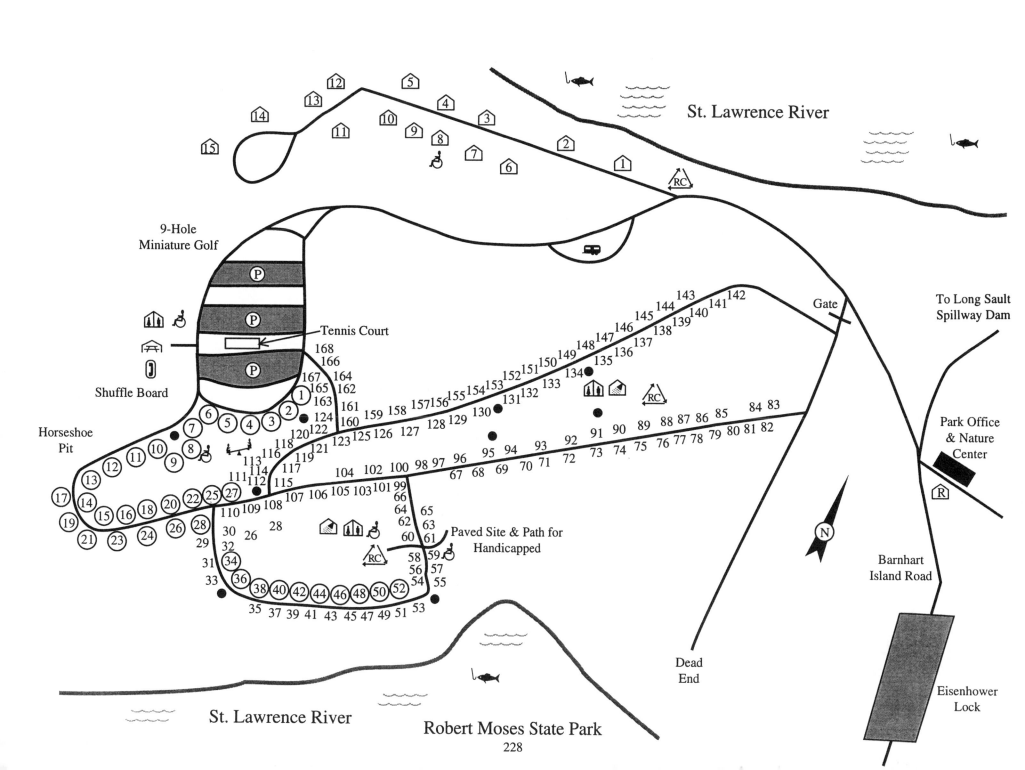

St. Lawrence River

9-Hole Miniature Golf

Tennis Court

Horseshoe Pit

Shuffle Board

Paved Site & Path for Handicapped

Dead End

Gate

To Long Sault Spillway Dam

Park Office & Nature Center

Barnhart Island Road

Eisenhower Lock

N

St. Lawrence River

Robert Moses State Park

228

Robert H. Treman State Park

RD #10, Ithaca, NY 14850

(607) 273–3440

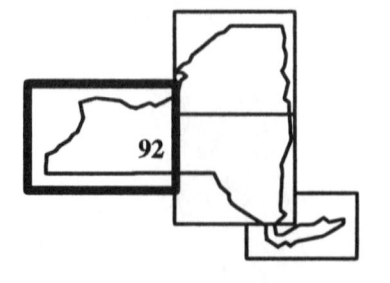

- Located 5 miles south of Ithaca or 24 miles northeast of Elmira off State Route 13
- Open mid–May through November for camping
- State Park is Open All Year
- 72 Tent & Trailer Sites (11 electric sites, trailer dump)
- 14 Cabins
- 1025 Acres
- Comfort Station (flush toilets & sink) and Showers
- Potable Water (throughout campground)
- Pets Allowed
- Handicapped Accessible
- Picnic Area
- Picnic Pavilions (2 reservable)
- Recreation Program
- Hiking Trails (all gorge trails closed mid–November)
- Swimming in Stream–fed Lifeguarded Pool, Bath House (concessions)
- Fishing in Enfield Creek
- Hunting (fall archery)
- Bicycling on Campground Roads
- Playground
- Cross Country Skiing (limited)

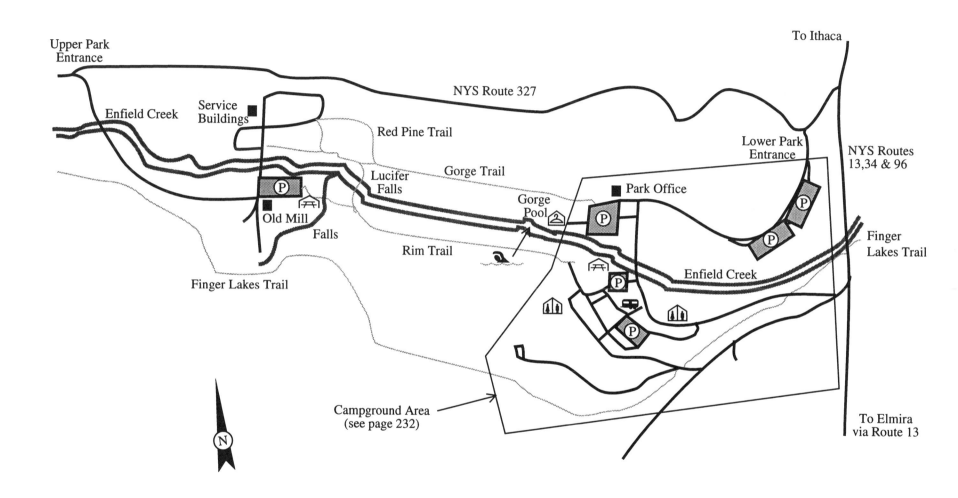

Upper Park
Entrance

Service
Buildings

Enfield Creek

NYS Route 327

Red Pine Trail

Gorge Trail

Lucifer
Falls

Rim Trail

Old Mill

Falls

Finger Lakes Trail

To Ithaca

Lower Park
Entrance

NYS Routes
13, 34 & 96

Gorge
Pool

Park Office

Finger
Lakes Trail

Enfield Creek

Campground Area
(see page 232)

To Elmira
via Route 13

N

Robert H. Treman State Park

Robert H. Treman State Park

(see page 229 for campground information and main park map)

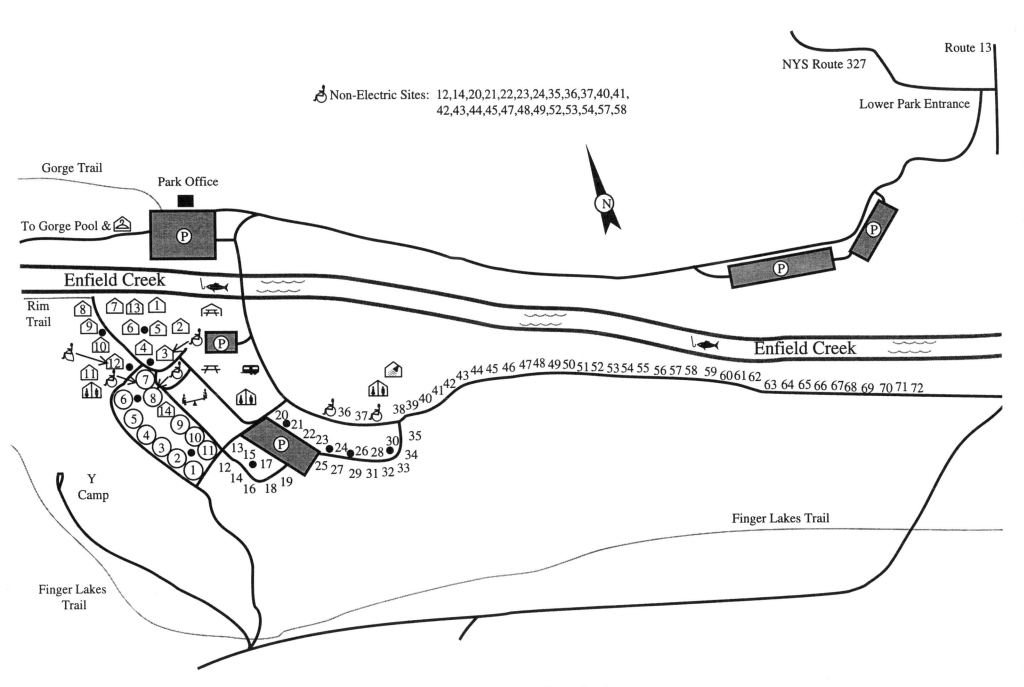

Non-Electric Sites: 12,14,20,21,22,23,24,35,36,37,40,41,
42,43,44,45,47,48,49,52,53,54,57,58

NYS Route 327

Route 13

Lower Park Entrance

Gorge Trail

Park Office

To Gorge Pool &

N

Enfield Creek

Rim
Trail

Enfield Creek

Y
Camp

Finger Lakes Trail

Finger Lakes
Trail

Robert H. Treman State Park

Rogers Rock Public Campground

State Route 9N, Hague, NY 12836

(518) 585–6746

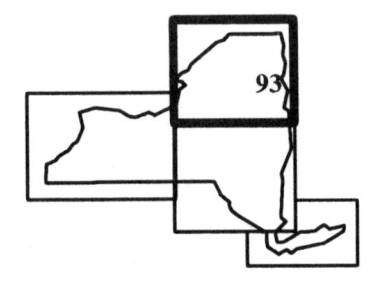

- Located 3 miles north of Hague or 5 miles south of Ticonderoga off State Route 9N
- Open May through mid–October for camping
- 299 Tent & Trailer Sites (no electric sites, 246 trailer sites, trailer dump, max 40 foot RV)
- 10 Island Sites (boat access only, no potable water)
- 186 Acres
- Comfort Station (flush toilets & sink) and Showers
- Potable Water
- Public Telephone
- Pets Allowed
- Handicapped Accessible
- Picnic Area
- Hiking Trails (within approximately 4 miles)
- Swimming with Sand Beach and Bath House
- Fishing in Lake George
- Bicycling on Campground Roads
- Volleyball Court and Horseshoe Pit (near recycling center)
- Boat Launch (30 boat moorings)
- Cross Country Skiing

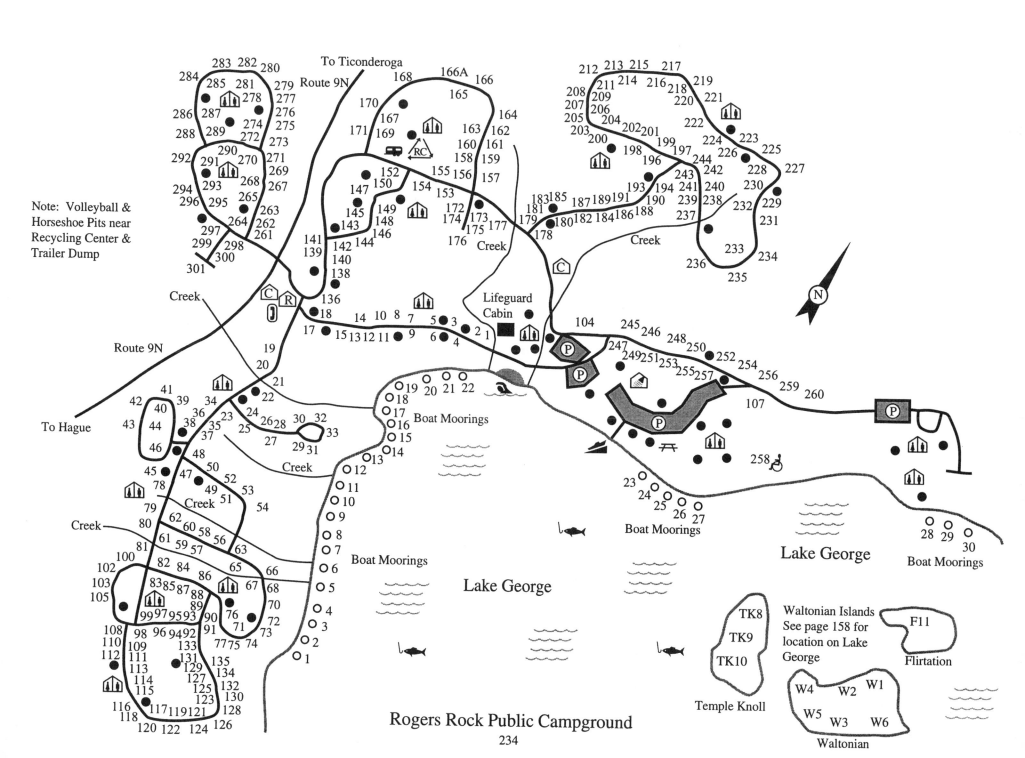

Rogers Rock Public Campground

234

Rollins Pond Public Campground

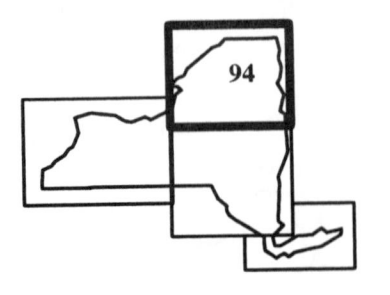

Star Route Box 75, Saranac Lake, NY 12983

(518) 891–3239

- Located 12 miles northeast of Tupper Lake off State Route 30
- Open mid–May through Labor Day for camping
- 288 Tent & Trailer Sites (no electric sites, trailer dump, max 40 foot RV)
- 95 Acres
- Comfort Station (flush toilets & sink) and Showers
- Potable Water
- Public Telephone
- Pets Allowed
- Handicapped Accessible
- Hiking Trails (within approximately 2 miles)
- Swimming (no designated area – sand beach 1 mile east at Fish Creek
  Pond Public Campground)
- Fishing in Rollins Pond
- Bicycling on Campground Roads
- Boat Launch (under 25 hp and cartop boat launch)
- Rowboat and Canoe Rental

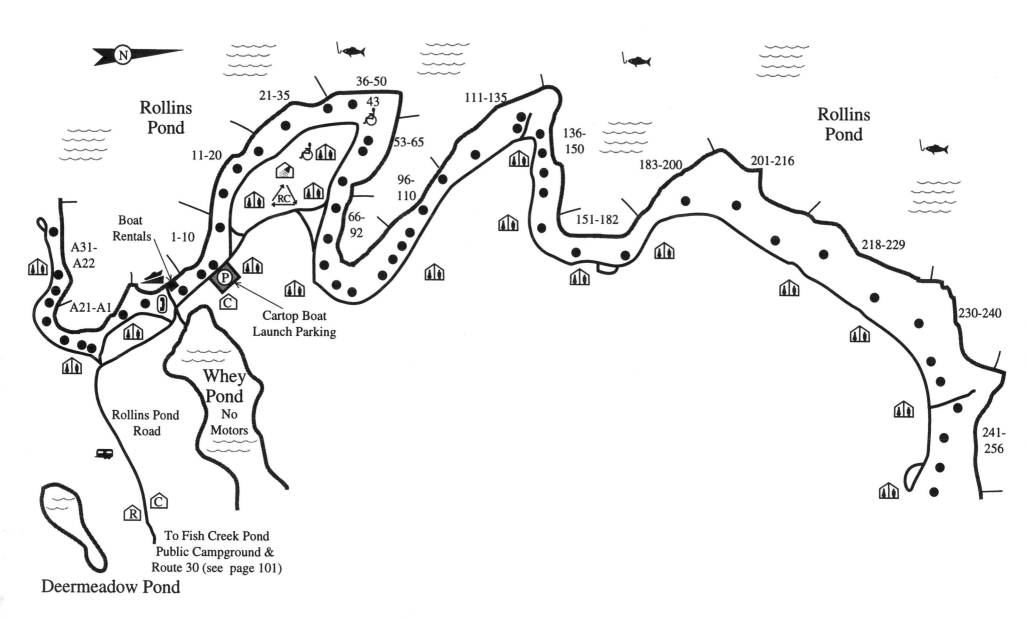

Rollins Pond

Rollins
Pond

21-35
36-50
43
11-20
53-65
96-110
66-92
111-135
136-150
183-200
201-216
151-182
218-229
230-240
241-256

N

Boat Rentals
1-10
Cartop Boat Launch Parking

A31-A22
A21-A1

Whey Pond
No Motors

Rollins Pond Road

Deermeadow Pond

To Fish Creek Pond Public Campground & Route 30 (see page 101)

Rollins Pond Public Campground

Sacandaga Public Campground

HC–01, Star Route 30, Box 104, Northville, NY 12134

(518) 924–4121

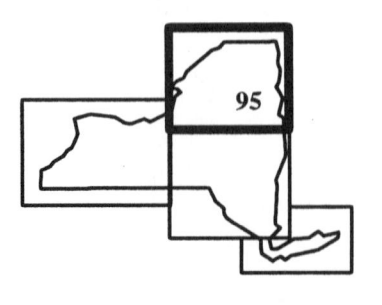

- Located 3 miles south of Wells or 11 miles north of Northville off State Route 30
- Open mid–May through Labor Day for camping
- 137 Tent & Trailer Sites (no electric sites, trailer dump)
- 125 Acres
- Comfort Station (flush toilets & sink) and Showers
- Potable Water
- Public Telephone
- Pets Allowed
- Handicapped Accessible
- Picnic Area
- Hiking Trails (within approximately 4 miles)
- Fishing in Sacandaga River and Lake Algonquin
- Bicycling and Rollerblading on Campground Roads
- Tubing Allowed in River
- Boat Launch (on the backside of Lake Algonquin in the town of Wells – 3 miles north)

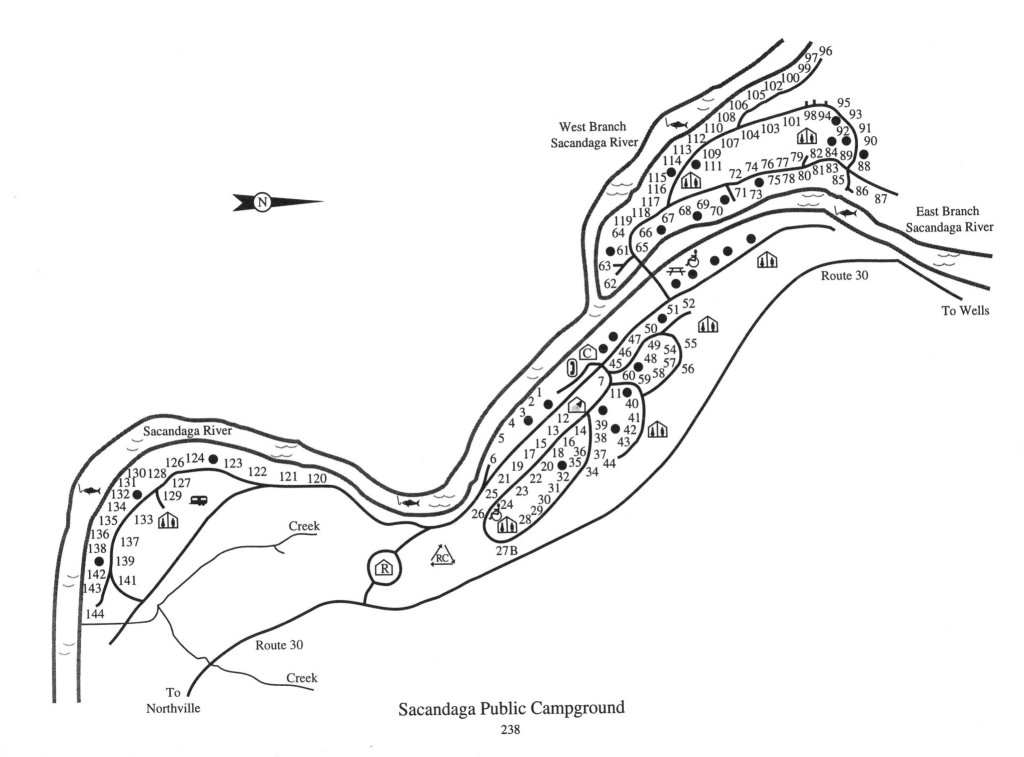

West Branch
Sacandaga River

East Branch
Sacandaga River

Route 30

To Wells

N

Sacandaga River

Creek

Route 30

Creek

To
Northville

Sacandaga Public Campground

238

Sampson State Park

6096 Route 96A, Romulus, NY 14541

(315) 585–6392

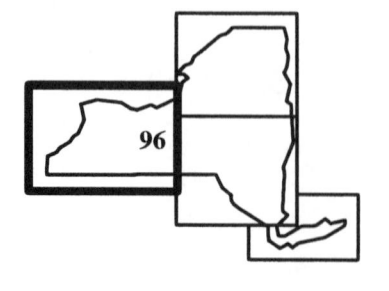

- Located 11 miles south of Geneva or 6 miles northwest of Ovid off State Route 96A
- Open May through October for camping
- State Park is Open All Year
- 344 Tent & Trailer Sites (245 electric sites, trailer dump)
- 1,852 Acres
- Comfort Station (flush toilets & sink) and Showers
- Potable Water
- Public Telephone
- Pets Allowed
- Handicapped Accessible
- Picnic Areas
- Picnic Pavilions (1 of 3 reservable)
- Recreation Program and Building
- Hiking and Nature Trails
- Swimming with Sand Beach and Bath House
- Fishing in Seneca Lake
- Hunting (deer, waterfowl and small game)
- Bicycling on Campground Roads
- Baseball Field, Tennis and Basketball Courts, Horseshoe Pits, and Playground
- Boat Launch and Marina
- Cross Country Skiing, Snowshoeing, Snowmobiling, and, Sledding Hills
- Navy Museum, Sampson Sailor Memorial, and Snack Bar

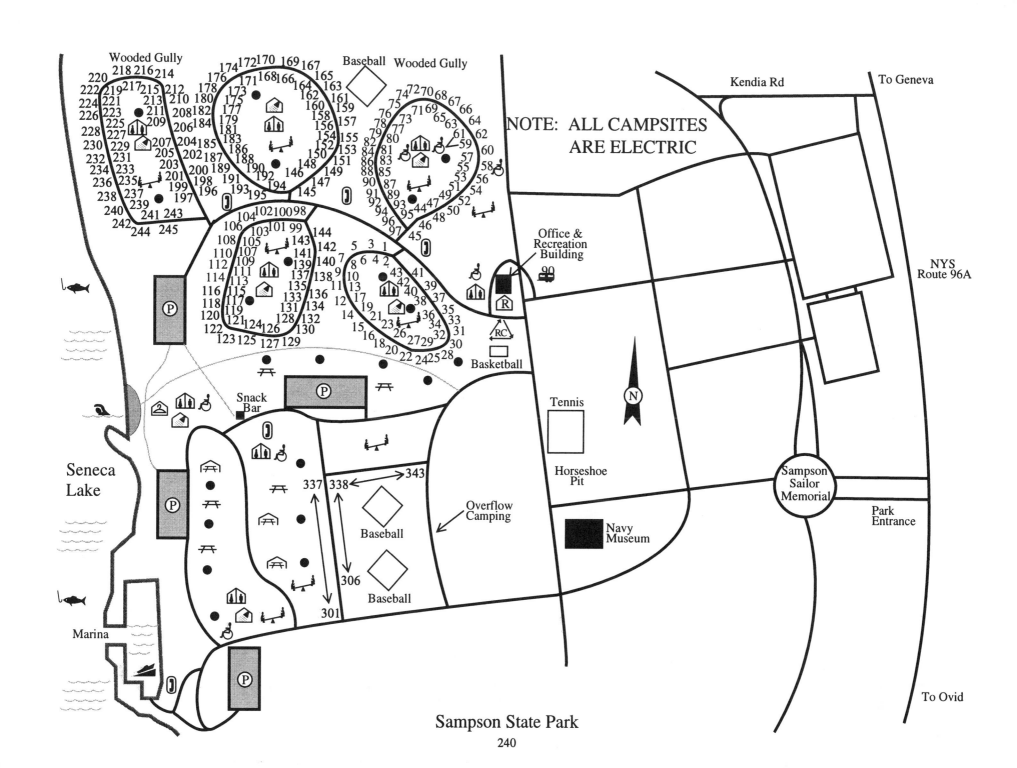

Sampson State Park

240

Saranac Lake Islands Public Campground

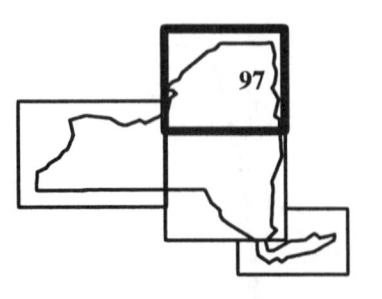

Ampersand Bay Road, Box 24 Saranac Lake, NY 12983

(518) 891–2841

- Located 3 miles southwest of Saranac Lake Village or 15 miles east of Tupper Lake off State Route 3
- Open mid–May through Labor Day for camping
- **Boat Access Only** (no docks at the sites – tie boat to shoreline)
- 79 Tent Sites (no electric sites)
- 5,056 Acres
- Vault Toilets (at each site)
- No Potable Water
- Pets Allowed
- Picnic Areas (Bluff Island and near sites 55 and 67)
- Hiking Trails (around islands and campsites)
- Swimming (no designated area)
- Fishing in Lower, Middle, and Upper Saranac Lakes
- Boat Launch (at Second Pond) and Cartop Boat Launch (at Ampersand Bay)

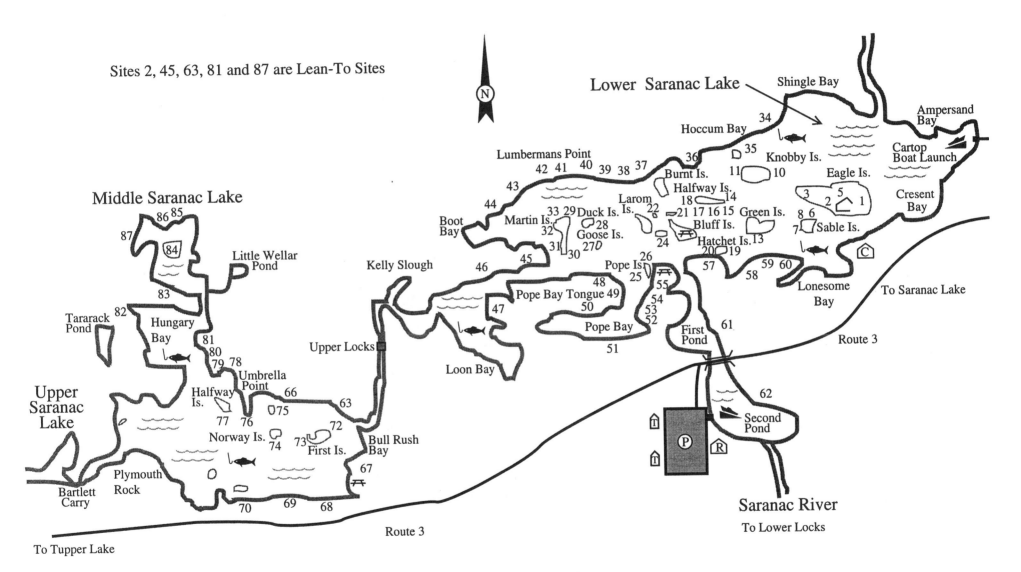

Sites 2, 45, 63, 81 and 87 are Lean-To Sites

Lower Saranac Lake

Shingle Bay

Ampersand Bay

Hoccum Bay

34

Cartop Boat Launch

Lumbermans Point

36

35 Knobby Is.

11 10

Eagle Is.

42 41 40 39 38 37

Burnt Is.

Middle Saranac Lake

43

Halfway Is. 14

3 5

Cresent Bay

86 85

44

Larom 18 22

2 1

87

Is. 21 17 16 15 Green Is.

8 6

84

Boot Bay

33 29 Duck Is.

6

7 Sable Is.

Little Wellar Pond

Martin Is. 32

28

Bluff Is.

24

Hatchet Is. 13

Kelly Slough

83

31 30 27

20 19

Tararack Pond

82

Goose Is.

Pope Is. 26

57

59 60

58

Lonesome Bay

To Saranac Lake

Hungary Bay

81

46

45

25

55

80

Pope Bay Tongue 49

54

First Pond

61

Route 3

Upper Saranac Lake

79 78

48

53 52

Umbrella Point

47

50

Halfway Is.

66

Pope Bay

63

Upper Locks

51

77 76 75

Norway Is.

72

Loon Bay

Second Pond

62

73

74 First Is.

Bull Rush Bay

Plymouth Rock

67

P

R

Bartlett Carry

Saranac River

70 69 68

To Lower Locks

To Tupper Lake

Route 3

Saranac Lake Islands Public Campground

242

Selkirk Shores State Park

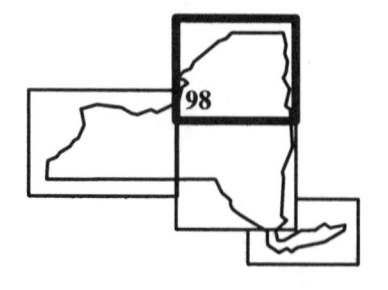

7101 State Route 3, Pulaski, NY 13142

(315) 298–5737

- Located 3 miles west of Pulaski or 6 miles north of Mexico off State Route 3
- Open May through October for camping
- State Park is Open All Year
- 148 Tent & Trailer Sites (87 electric sites, trailer dump)
- 26 Cabins
- 980 Acres
- Comfort Station (flush toilets & sink) and Showers
- Potable Water
- Public Telephone
- Pets Allowed
- Handicapped Accessible
- Picnic Area
- Picnic Pavilions (2 reservable)
- Recreation Program and Hall
- Hiking Trails
- Swimming with Sand Beach and Bath House
- Fishing in Lake Ontario and Salmon River
- Playground
- Bicycling on Campground Roads
- Boat Launches (launch at Salmon River and at nearby Mexico Point approximately 4 miles)
- Cross Country Skiing and Snowmobiling
- Store

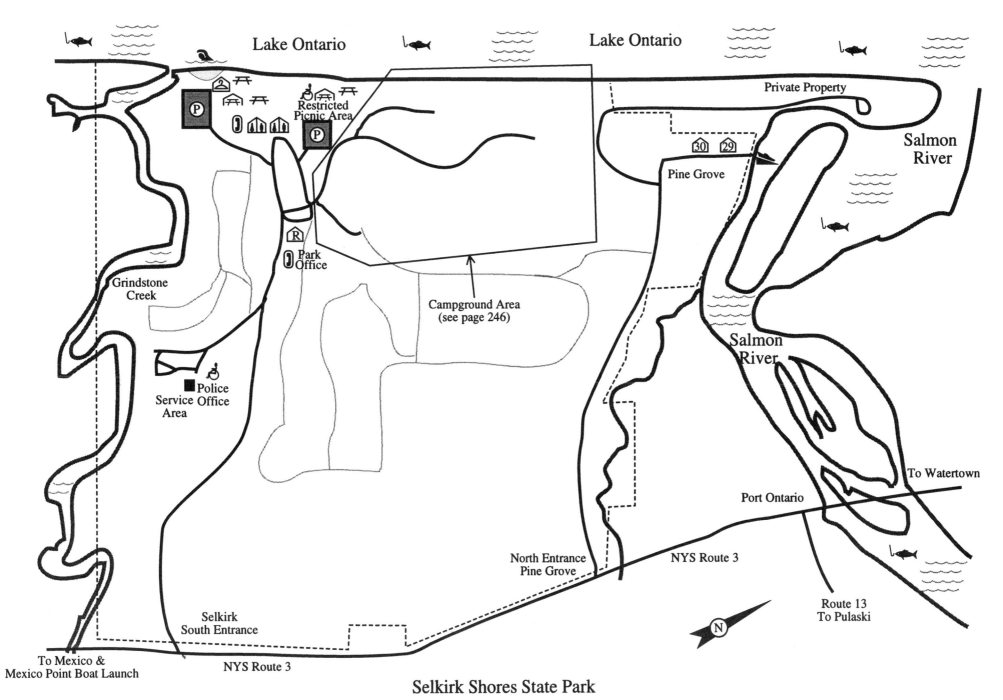

Lake Ontario

Lake Ontario

Private Property

Salmon River

Restricted Picnic Area

Pine Grove

30 29

Grindstone Creek

Park Office

Campground Area (see page 246)

Salmon River

Police Service Office Area

To Watertown

Port Ontario

North Entrance Pine Grove

NYS Route 3

Selkirk South Entrance

Route 13 To Pulaski

N

To Mexico & Mexico Point Boat Launch

NYS Route 3

Selkirk Shores State Park

Selkirk Shores State Park

(see page 243 for campground information and main park map)

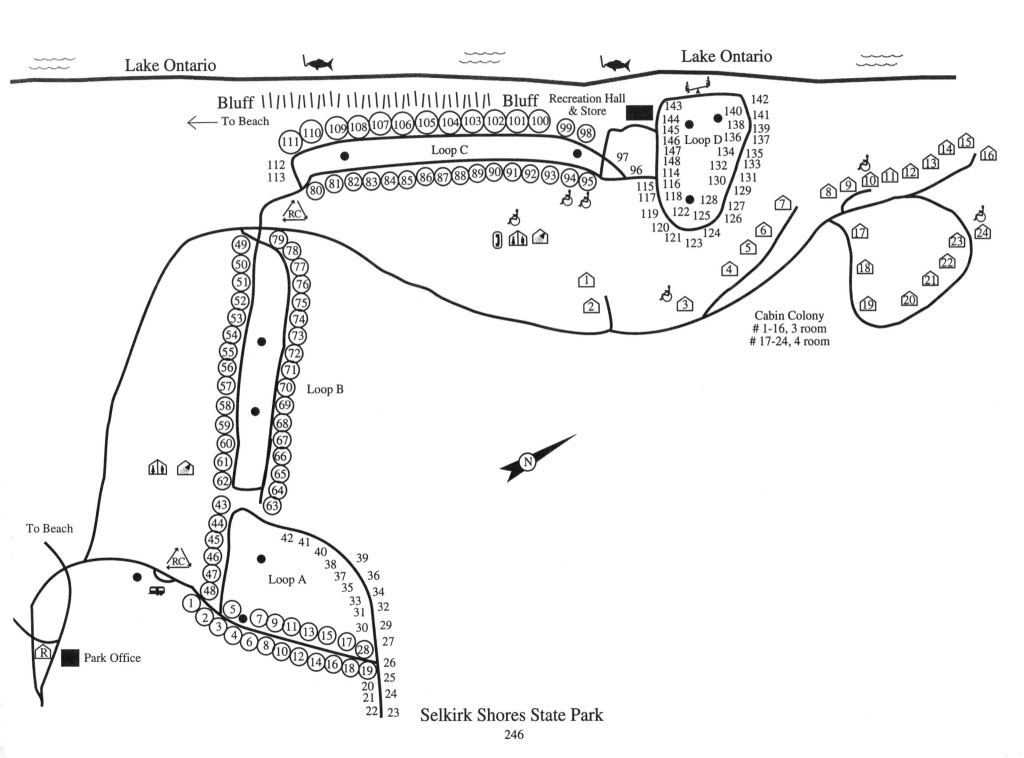

Lake Ontario

Lake Ontario

Bluff | | | | | | | | | | | | | | | | | | | | | Bluff

← To Beach

Recreation Hall
& Store

Loop C

Loop D

Cabin Colony
1-16, 3 room
17-24, 4 room

RC

Loop B

N

To Beach

RC

Loop A

R   Park Office

Selkirk Shores State Park

246

Sharp Bridge Public Campground

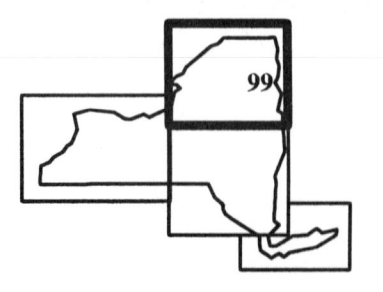

P.O. Box 296, NYS DEC, Ray Brook, NY 12977

(518) 532–7538

- Located 15 miles north of Schroon Lake or 13 miles south of Elizabethtown off US 9
- Open mid–May through Labor Day for camping
- 40 Tent & Trailer Sites (no electric sites, trailer dump, max 20 foot RV)
- 17 Acres
- Comfort Station & Pit Toilets, and Showers
- Potable Water
- Pets Allowed
- Handicapped Accessible
- Picnic Area
- Picnic Pavilion (reservable)
- Hiking Trails (within approximately 1/2 mile)
- Fishing in Schroon River
- Playground

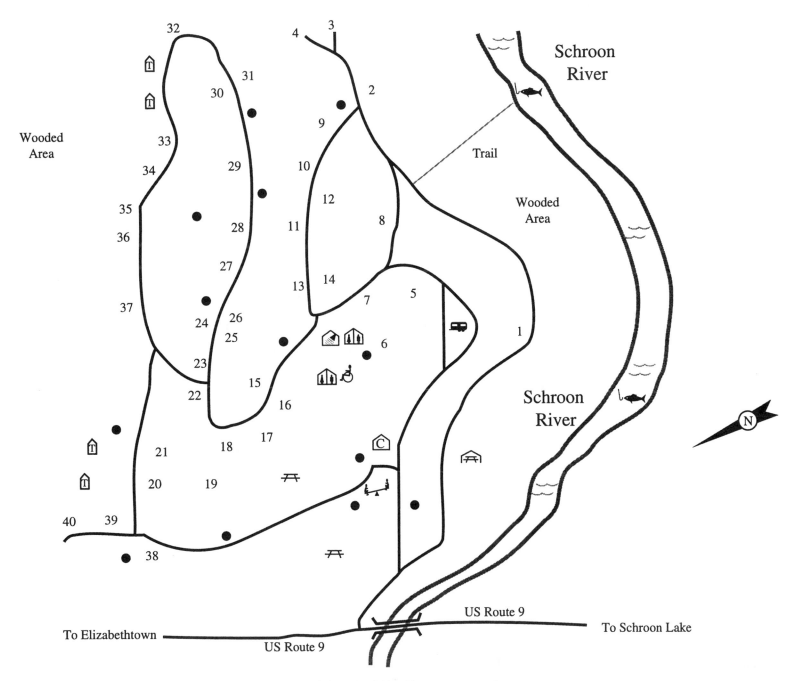

Schroon River

Wooded Area

Trail

Wooded Area

Schroon River

Wooded Area

N

US Route 9

To Elizabethtown

US Route 9

To Schroon Lake

Sharp Bridge Public Campground

Southwick Beach State Park

8119 Southwicks Place, Woodville, NY 13650

(315) 846–5338

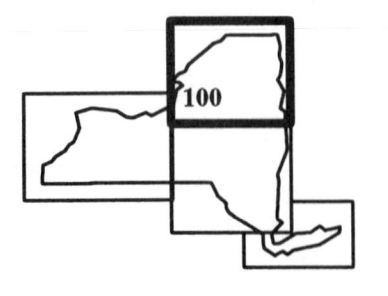

- Located 7 miles south of Henderson Harbor off State Route 3
- Open mid–May through mid–October for camping
- State Park is Open All Year
- 110 Tent & Trailer Sites (44 trailer electric sites, trailer dump)
- 500 Acres
- Comfort Station (flush toilets & sink) and Showers
- Potable Water
- Pets Allowed
- Handicapped Accessible
- Picnic Area
- Recreation Program and Building
- Nature Trails (trails start at the park and go into Lakeview Wildlife Area)
- Exercise Course
- Swimming with Sand Beach and Bath House (bath house is in recreation building)
- Fishing in Lake Ontario (not allowed on beach)
- Bicycling on Campground Roads
- Playground
- Boat Launch (cartop launch, public launch at Stony Creek – 6 miles)
- Cross Country Skiing and Snowshoeing
- Concessions

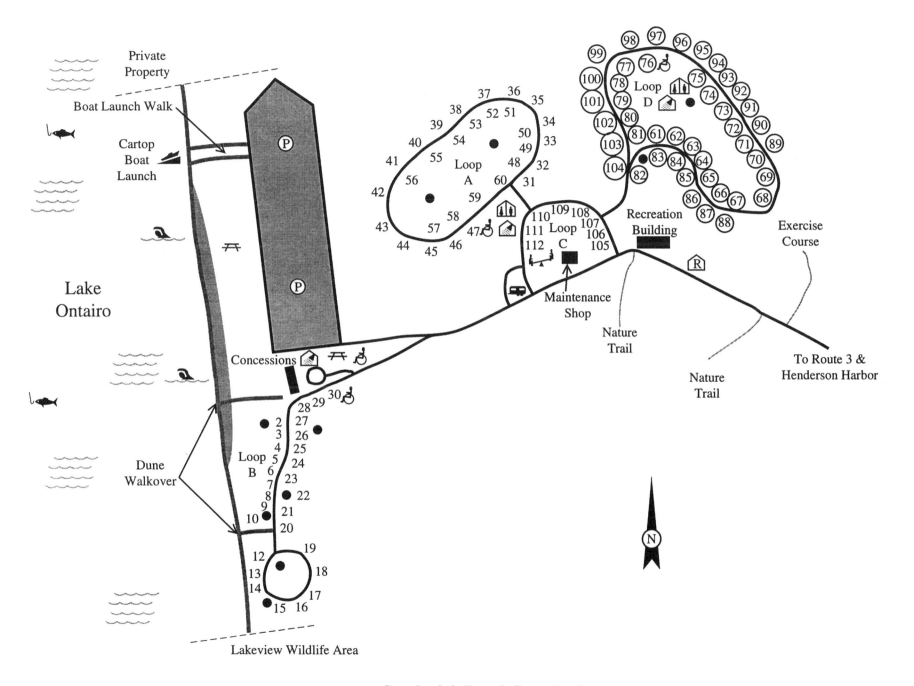

Southwick Beach State Park

Stony Brook State Park

10820 Route 36 South, Dansville, NY 14437

(716) 335–8111

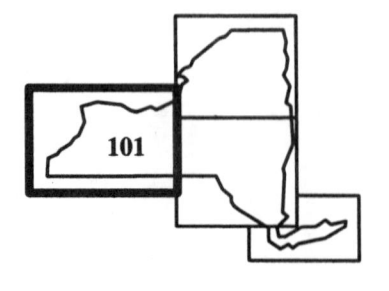

- Located 3 miles south of Dansville or 14 miles north of Hornell off State Route 36
- Open May through mid–October for camping
- State Park is Open All Year
- 125 Tent & Trailer Sites (no electric sites, trailer dump, max 30 foot RV)
- 577 Acres
- Comfort Station (flush toilets & sink) and Showers
- Potable Water
- Public Telephone
- Pets Allowed
- Handicapped Accessible
- Picnic Areas
- Picnic Pavilion (2 reservable)
- Hiking and Gorge Trails
- Swimming in Two Stream–fed Gorge Pools and Bath House (one in the camping area and one in the lower park)
- Hunting
- Baseball Field (lower park area), 2 Tennis Courts, and Playground
- Cross Country Skiing and Snowshoeing
- Concessions (in bath house in lower park)

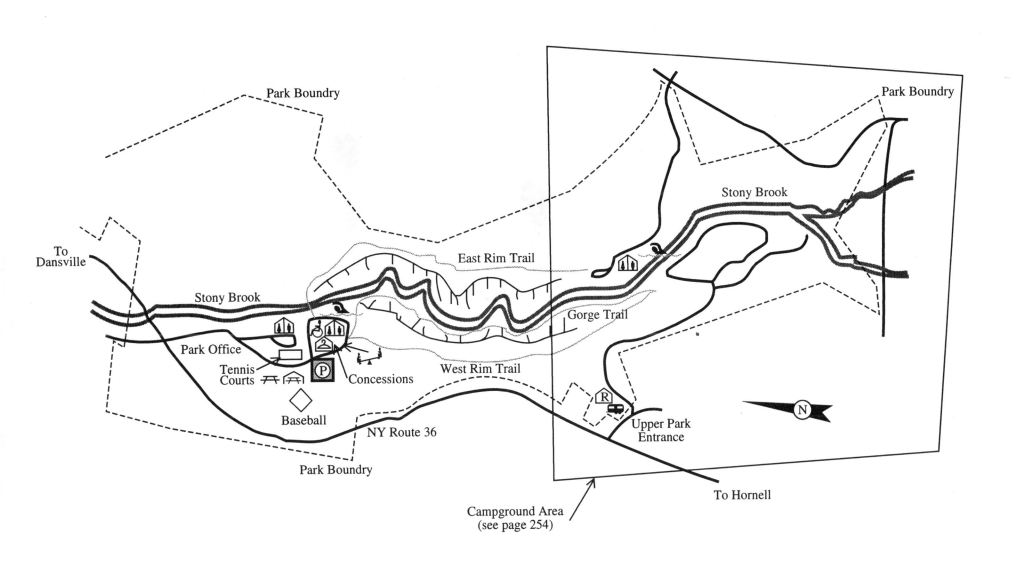

Park Boundry

Park Boundry

Stony Brook

To
Dansville

East Rim Trail

Stony Brook

Gorge Trail

Park Office

West Rim Trail

Tennis
Courts

P

Concessions

Baseball

NY Route 36

Upper Park
Entrance

N

To Hornell

Park Boundry

Campground Area
(see page 254)

Stony Brook State Park

Stony Brook State Park

(see page 251 for campground information and main park map)

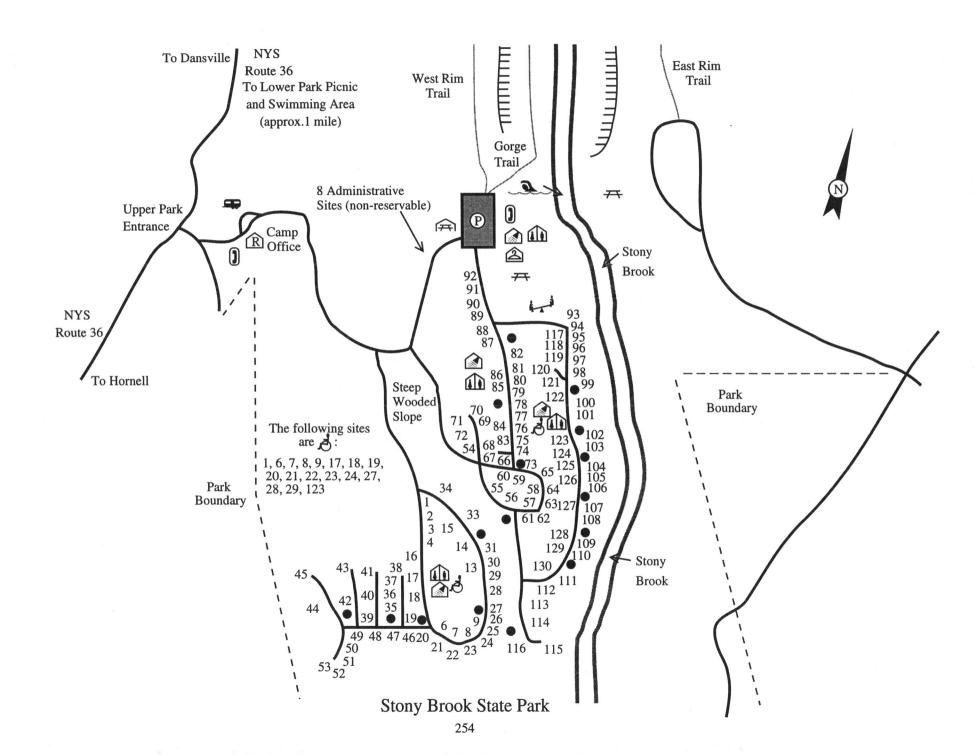

Stony Brook State Park

254

Taconic State Park – Copake Falls Area

Box 100, Copake Falls, NY 12517

(518) 329–3993

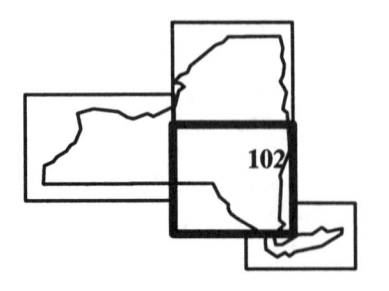

- Located 1/2 mile east of Copake Falls off State Route 344
- Open mid–May through mid–December for camping
- 112 Tent & Trailer Sites (no electric sites, trailer dump)
- 14 Cabins
- 4,485 Acres
- Comfort Station (flush toilets & sink) and Showers
- Potable Water
- Picnic Area
- Picnic Pavilion
- Recreation Program
- Nature Program and Center
- Hiking Trails (within approximately 2 miles)
- Swimming with Sand Beach and Bath House (wading pond for non–swimmers)
- Fishing in Ore Pit Pond and Bash Bish Brook
- Hunting
- Bicycling on Campground Roads
- Playground
- Cross Country Skiing, Snowmobiling, and Sledding Hills
- Day Use Area

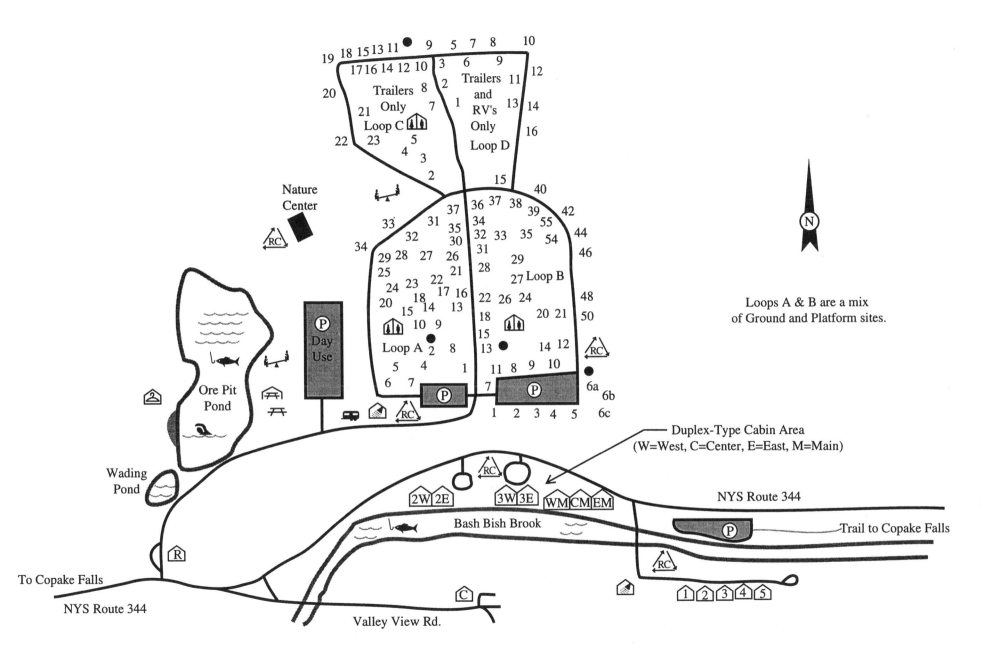

Loops A & B are a mix
of Ground and Platform sites.

Nature Center

Duplex-Type Cabin Area
(W=West, C=Center, E=East, M=Main)

NYS Route 344

Trail to Copake Falls

Ore Pit Pond

Wading Pond

Day Use

Loop C
Trailers Only

Loop D
Trailers and RV's Only

Loop A

Loop B

Bash Bish Brook

To Copake Falls

NYS Route 344

Valley View Rd.

2W 2E   3W 3E   WM CM EM

1 2 3 4 5

Taconic State Park - Copake Falls Area

256

Taconic State Park – Rudd Pond Area

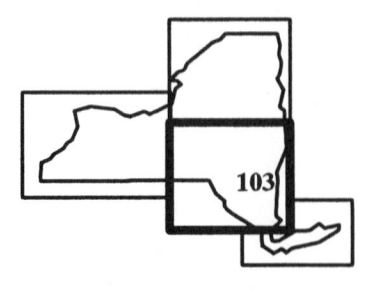

Dutchess County 62, Millerton, NY 12546

(518) 789–3059

- Located 3 miles north of Millerton off County Road 62
- Open mid–May through Labor Day for camping
- State Park is Open All Year
- 41 Tent & Trailer Sites (no electric sites, max 20 ft trailer)
- 210 Acres
- Comfort Station (flush toilets & sink) and Showers
- Potable Water
- Public Telephone
- Picnic Area
- Recreation Program
- Hiking Trails (within approximately 6 miles)
- Swimming with Sand Beach and Bath House
- Fishing in Rudd Pond
- Hunting (no small game)
- Bicycling on Campground Roads
- Playground
- Boat Launch (no motor boats)
- Rowboat Rental (at park office)
- Cross Country Skiing and Ice Skating
- Recreation Hall
- Day Use Area

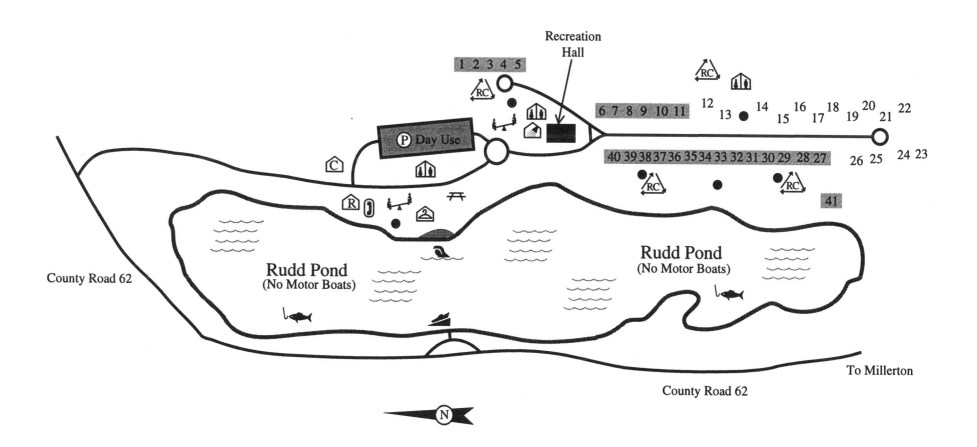

Sites 1-11 and 27-41 are platform tent sites (14ft x 16ft)

Recreation Hall

1 2 3 4 5

RC

6 7 8 9 10 11

12
13   14
15   16
17   18
19   20   22
21

RC

P Day Use

C

40 39 38 37 36 35 34 33 32 31 30 29 28 27   26 25   24 23

RC   RC

41

R

Rudd Pond
(No Motor Boats)

Rudd Pond
(No Motor Boats)

County Road 62

To Millerton

County Road 62

N

Taconic State Park - Rudd Pond Area

Taughannock Falls State Park

Box 1055, Trumansburg, NY 14886

(607) 387–6739

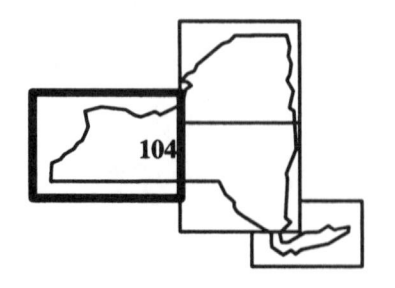

- Located 8 miles north of Ithaca or 3 miles east of Trumansburg off State Route 89
- Open April through mid–October for camping
- State Park is Open All Year
- 74 Tent & Trailer Sites (16 electric sites, trailer dump)
- 16 Cabins
- 783 Acres
- Comfort Station (flush toilets & sink) and Showers
- Potable Water (throughout campground)
- Pets Allowed
- Handicapped Accessible
- Picnic Areas and Pavilion (reservable)
- Recreation Program and Shelter
- Hiking and Gorge Trails
- Swimming with Gravel Beach and Bath House
- Fishing in Cayuga Lake and Taughannock Creek
- Hunting (archery for deer only)
- Rollerblading on Campground Roads
- Playground
- Boat Launch (seasonal dock berths at marina)
- Rowboat Rental (at marina)
- Cross Country Skiing, Ice Skating Pond and Sledding Hills
- Concession

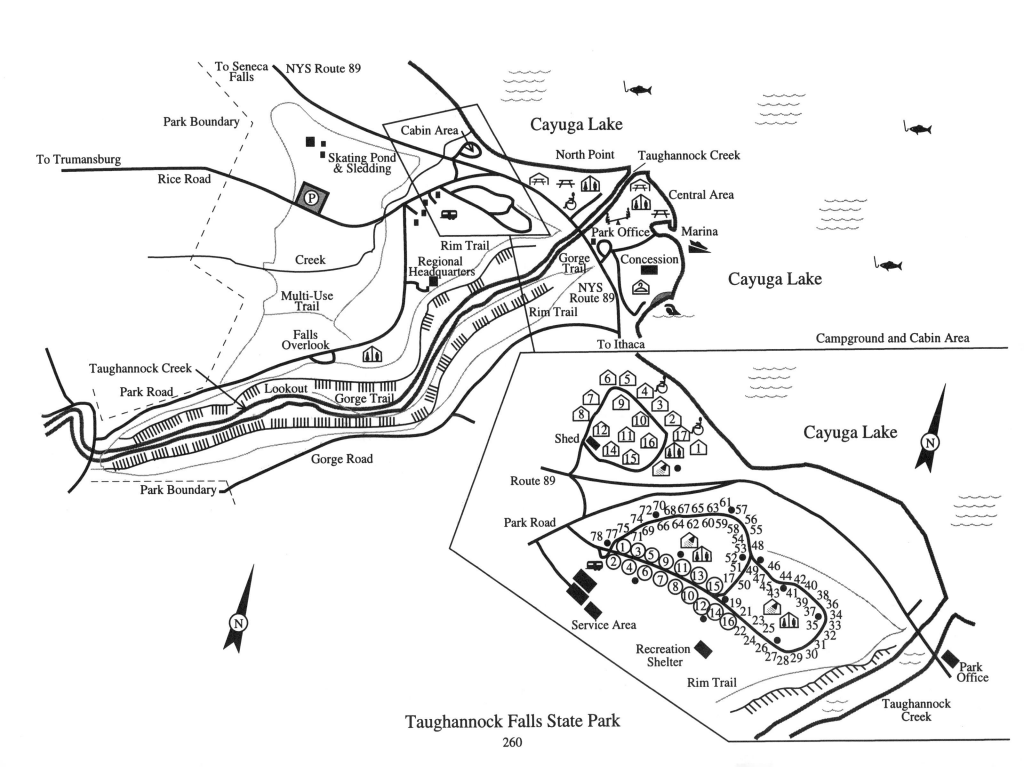

Taughannock Falls State Park

Taylor Pond Public Campground

Star Route 1, Box 144, Au Sable Forks, NY 12912

(518) 647–5250

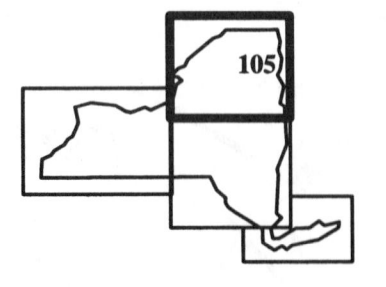

- Located 9 miles northwest of Au Sable Forks off State Route 9N
- Open mid–May through Labor Day for camping
- 30 Tent & Trailer Sites (no electric sites)
- 5 Interior sites in remote areas and do not have potable water or comfort stations
  (boat access only)
- 10 Acres
- Pit Toilets
- Potable Water
- Pets Allowed
- Handicapped Accessible
- Picnic Areas
- Hiking Trail
- Fishing in Taylor Pond
- Bicycling on Campground Roads
- Boat Launch
- Rowboat and Canoe Rental (at park office)

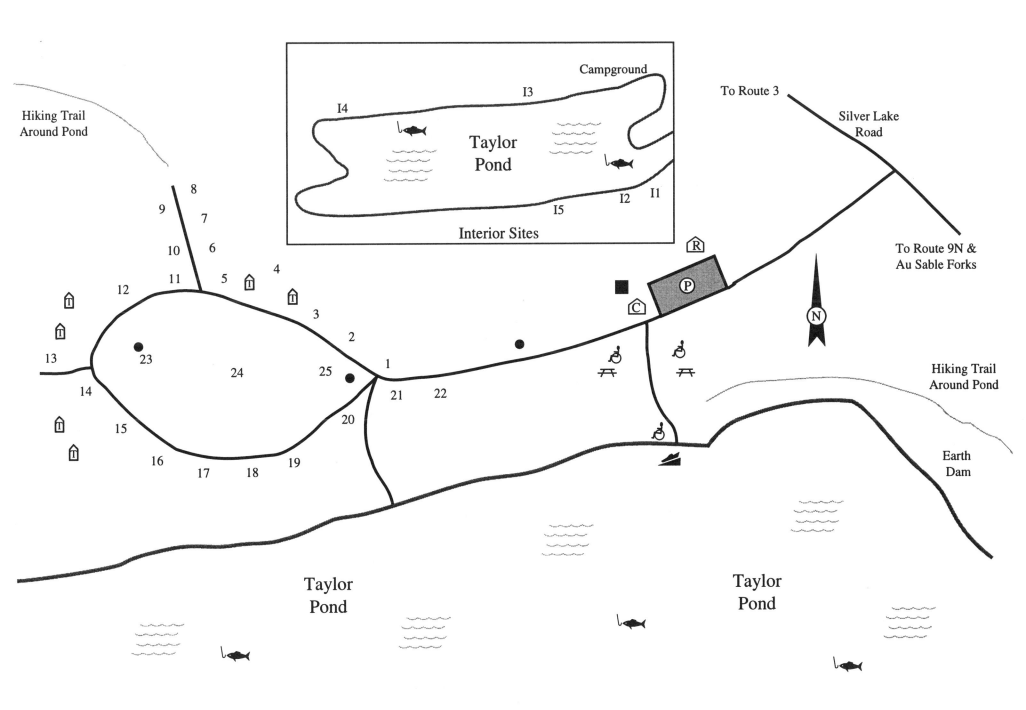

Hiking Trail
Around Pond

Campground

I4

I3

Taylor
Pond

I5

I2

I1

Interior Sites

To Route 3

Silver Lake
Road

To Route 9N &
Au Sable Forks

8

9

7

10

6

11

5

4

12

3

2

13

23

24

25

1

21

22

14

20

15

16

17

18

19

N

Hiking Trail
Around Pond

Earth
Dam

R

P

C

Taylor
Pond

Taylor
Pond

Taylor Pond Public Campground

262

Thompson's Lake State Park

68 Thompson's Lake Road, East Berne, NY 12059

(518) 872–1674

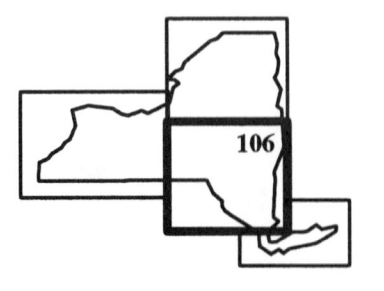

- Located 4 miles north of East Berne on State Route 157
- Open mid–May through mid–October for camping
- State Park is Open All Year
- 140 Tent & Trailer Sites (no electric sites, trailer dump, max 40 foot RV)
- 125 Acres
- Comfort Station (flush toilets & sink) and Showers
- Potable Water
- Public Telephone
- Pets Allowed
- Handicapped Accessible
- Recreation Program
- Nature Trail
- Swimming with Sand Beach
- Fishing in Thompson's Lake
- Bicycling on Campground Roads
- Ball Field and Playground
- Boat Launch (cartop launch)
- Boat Rental (at park office)
- Cross Country Skiing and Ice Fishing

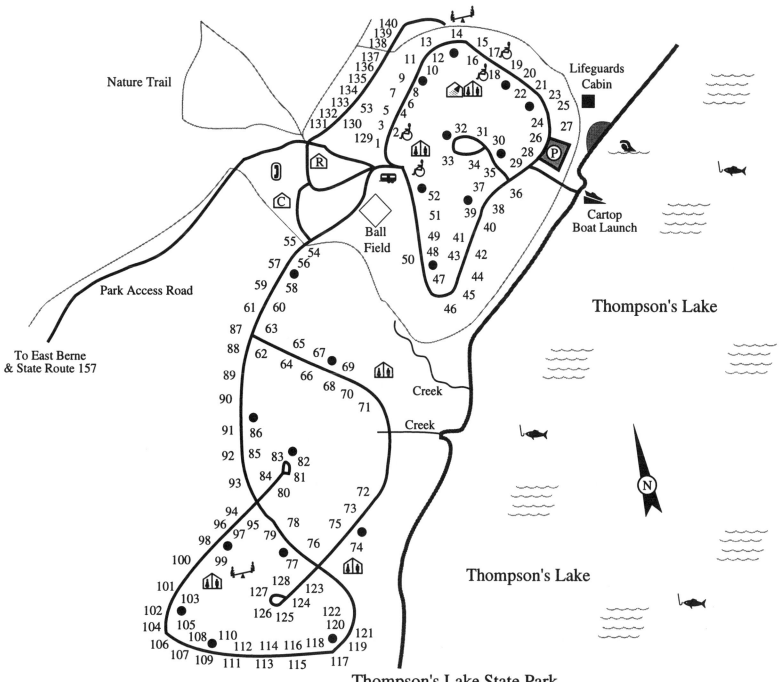

Nature Trail

Park Access Road

To East Berne
& State Route 157

Ball
Field

Lifeguards
Cabin

Cartop
Boat Launch

Thompson's Lake

Creek

Creek

Thompson's Lake

Thompson's Lake State Park

264

N

Tioga Point Public Campground

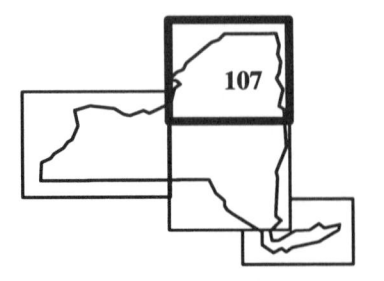

Route 28, Raquette Lake Village, NY 13436

(315) 354–4230

- Located 3 miles northeast of Raquette Lake Village or 4 miles north of Golden Beach Public Campground on Raquette Lake
- Open mid–May through Labor Day for camping
- **Boat Access Only**
- 25 Sites (15 Lean–To, 10 Tent Sites)
- Pit Toilets (throughout campground)
- No Potable Water
- Pets Allowed
- Picnic Area (throughout campground, no designated area)
- Hiking Trail
- Swimming (no designated area)
- Fishing in Raquette Lake
- Adirondack Canoe Route and Canoe Carry

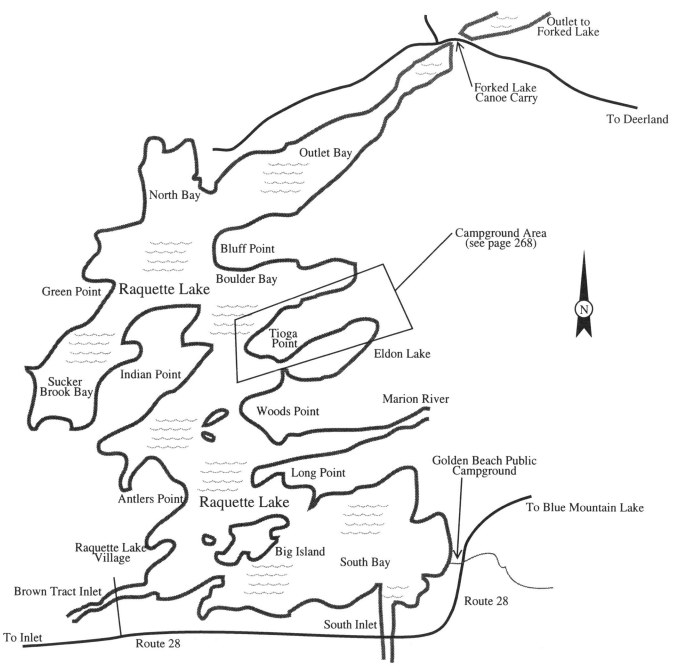

Outlet to
Forked Lake

Forked Lake
Canoe Carry

To Deerland

Outlet Bay

North Bay

Campground Area
(see page 268)

Bluff Point

Boulder Bay

N

Green Point

Raquette Lake

Tioga
Point

Eldon Lake

Sucker
Brook Bay

Indian Point

Woods Point

Marion River

Long Point

Golden Beach Public
Campground

Antlers Point

Raquette Lake

To Blue Mountain Lake

Raquette Lake
Village

Big Island

South Bay

Brown Tract Inlet

Route 28

To Inlet

Route 28

South Inlet

Tioga Point Public Campground

Tioga Point Public Campground

(see page 267 for campground information and main park map)

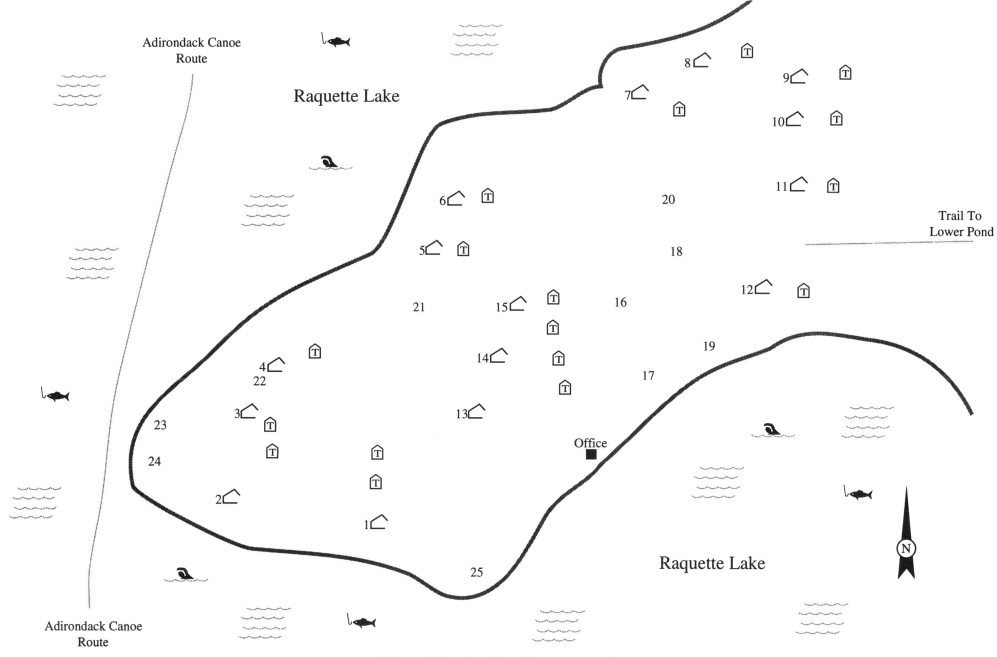

Adirondack Canoe
Route

Raquette Lake

8

9

7

10

11

Trail To
Lower Pond

6

20

5

18

12

21

15

16

4

22

14

19

3

17

23

13

24

Office

2

Raquette Lake

1

N

25

Adirondack Canoe
Route

Tioga Point Public Campground

Verona Beach State Park

P.O. Box 245, Verona Beach, NY 13162

(315) 762–4463

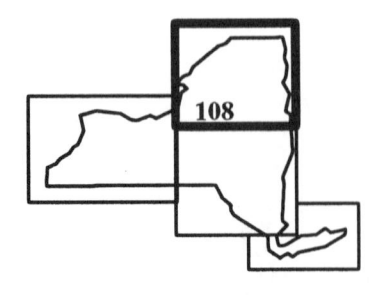

- Located 7 miles north of Canastota or 2 miles south of Sylvan Beach off State Route 13
- Open May through mid–October for camping
- State Park is Open All Year
- 45 Tent & Trailer Sites (no electric sites, trailer dump, max 55 foot RV)
- 1,735 Acres
- Comfort Station (flush toilets & sink) and Showers
- Potable Water
- Public Telephone
- Pets Allowed
- Handicapped Accessible
- Picnic Areas
- Picnic Pavilions (2 reservable)
- Recreation Program
- Hiking Trails (with approximately 1/2 mile)
- Swimming with Sand Beach and Bath House
- Fishing in Oneida Lake
- Hunting (bow and shotgun by permit only)
- Bicycling on Campground Roads
- Ball Fields, Volleyball Courts, Horseshoe Pits (near activity shelter), and Playground
- Horseback Riding Trails (trails are east of Route 13 and approximately 8 miles long)
- Cross Country Skiing, Ice Fishing, Snowmobiling, and Snowshoeing
- Activity Shelter and Concessions

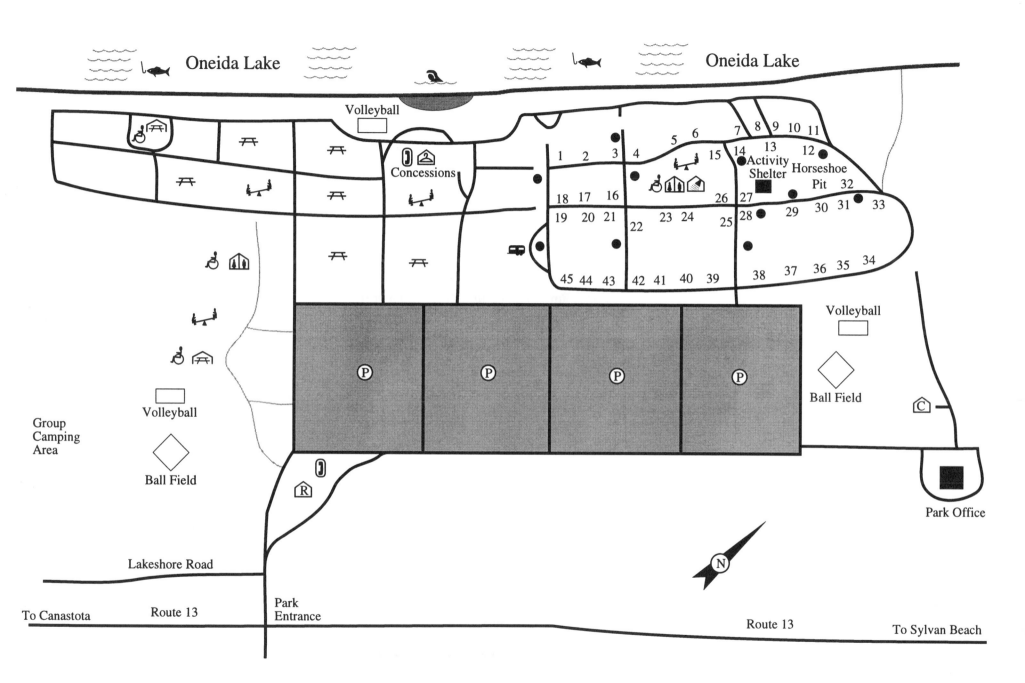

Oneida Lake

Oneida Lake

Volleyball

Concessions

1 2 3 4 5 6 7 8 9 10 11

15 14 13 12

Activity Shelter

Horseshoe Pit

18 17 16 26 27 32

19 20 21 22 23 24 25 28 29 30 31 33

45 44 43 42 41 40 39 38 37 36 35 34

P P P P

Volleyball

Ball Field

Group Camping Area

Volleyball

Ball Field

Park Office

Lakeshore Road

N

Route 13

Park Entrance

To Canastota

Route 13

To Sylvan Beach

Verona Beach State Park

Watkins Glen State Park

P. O. Box 304, Watkins Glen, NY 14891

(607) 535–4511

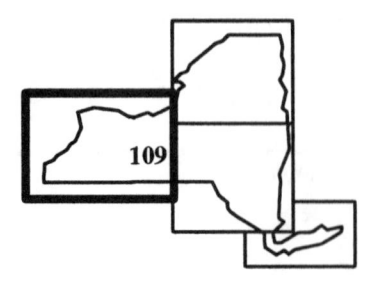

- Located in Watkins Glen off the junction of State Routes 14 and 414
- Open mid–May through October for camping
- State Park is Open All Year
- 303 Tent & Trailer Sites (56 electric sites, trailer dump)
- 763 Acres
- Comfort Station (flush toilets & sink) and Showers
- Potable Water (throughout campground)
- Pets Allowed
- Picnic Area
- Picnic Pavilion (1 reservable)
- Recreation Program and Building
- Hiking and Gorge Trails (gorge trail open mid–May thru mid–November)
- Finger Lakes Hiking Trail
- North Country National Scenic Trail
- Swimming Pool
- Fishing in Seneca Lake
- Hunting
- Bicycling on Campground Roads
- Baseball Field and Playground
- Boat Launch (in Watkins Glen)
- Cross Country Skiing, Snowshoeing, and Sledding Hills
- Concessions

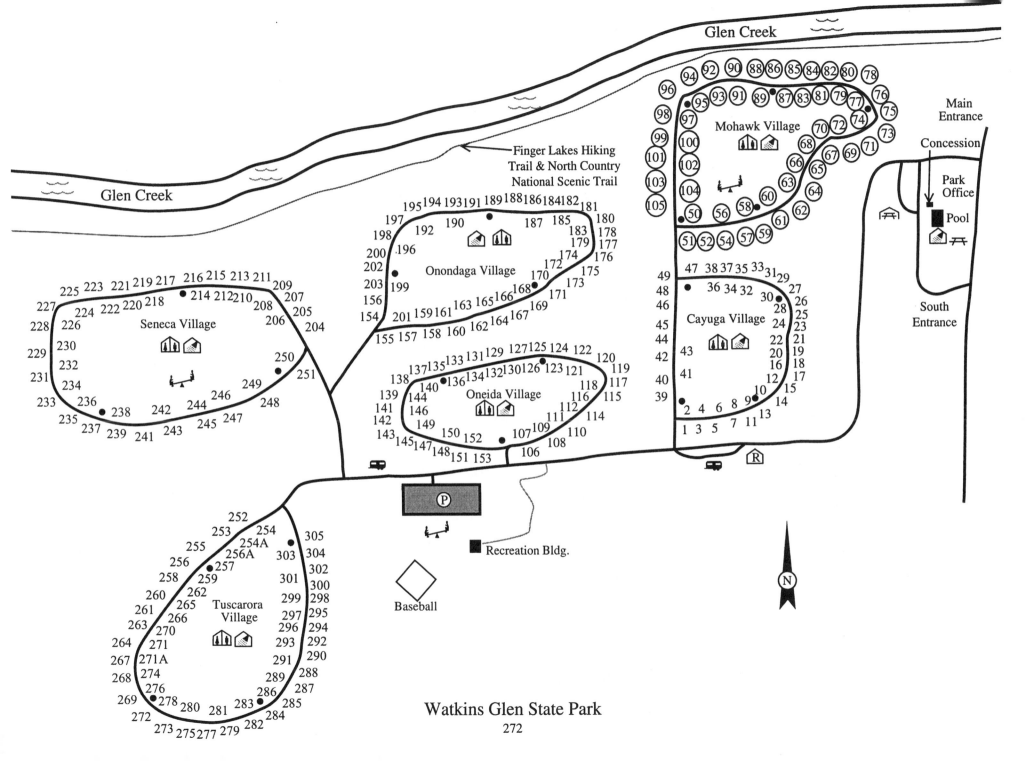

Watkins Glen State Park

272

Wellesley Island State Park

44927 Cross Island Road, Fineview, NY 13640

(315) 482– 2722

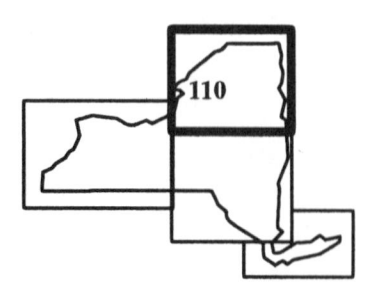

- Located on west end of Wellesley Island off Interstate 81 (Thousand Island Bridge)
- Open mid–April through mid–October for camping
- State Park is Open All Year
- 459 Tent & Trailer Sites (74 electric trailer sites, 57 full hookup, trailer dump)
- 10 Cabins (winterized) and 12 Cottages
- 2,636 Acres
- Comfort Station (flush toilets & sink) and Showers
- Potable Water (throughout campground)
- Public Telephone
- Pets Allowed
- Handicapped Accessible
- Picnic Area and Pavilion (a portion of the recreation building can be reserved)
- Recreation Program and Building
- Nature Trails (within the park at Minna Common Nature Center – 10 miles of trails)
- Swimming with Sand Beach
- Fishing in St. Lawrence River and Eel Bay
- Hunting
- Bicycling on Campground Roads
- 9–Hole Golf Course (approximately 3 miles), Mini–Golf Course, Store, and Playground
- Boat Launch (3 locations and cartop launch), Marina (open May through October), and Docks
- Boat/Motor and Canoe Rental (at marina)
- Cross Country Skiing, Ice Fishing, and Snowshoeing

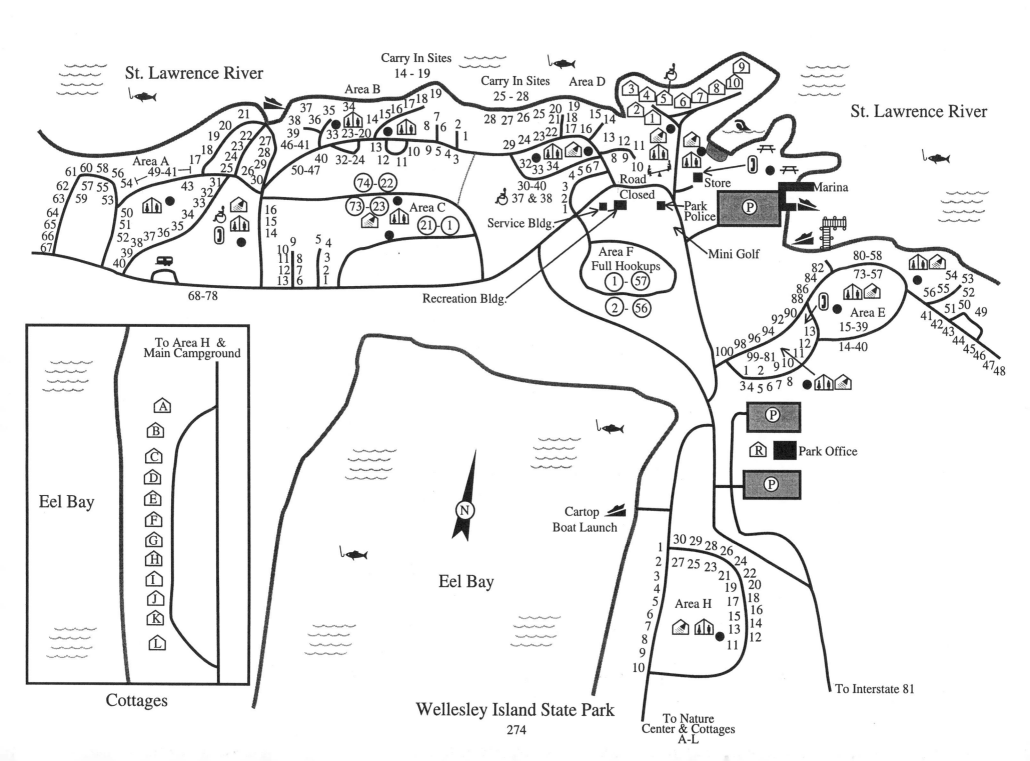

St. Lawrence River

Carry In Sites 14 - 19

Area B

Carry In Sites 25 - 28

Area D

St. Lawrence River

Area A

Area C

Service Bldg.

Area F
Full Hookups
①-㊾
②-㊻

Recreation Bldg.

Road
Closed

Store

Park Police

Mini Golf

Marina

Eel Bay

To Area H &
Main Campground

A
B
C
D
E
F
G
H
I
J
K
L

Cottages

N

Eel Bay

Cartop
Boat Launch

Area E

Park Office

Area H

To Interstate 81

To Nature
Center & Cottages
A-L

Wellesley Island State Park
274

Westcott Beach State Park

12224 NYS Route 3, Sackets Harbor, NY 13685

(315) 938–5083

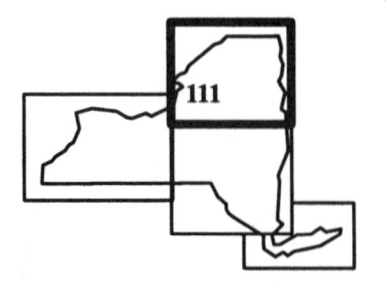

- Located 4 miles south of Sackets Harbor or 4 miles northeast of Henderson Harbor off State Route 3
- Open May through mid–October for camping
- State Park is Open All Year
- 166 Tent & Trailer Sites (83 electric sites, trailer dump)
- 319 Acres
- Comfort Station (flush toilets & sink) and Showers
- Potable Water
- Pets Allowed (only in sties 130 – 169)
- Handicapped Accessible
- Picnic Areas
- Picnic Pavilion (1 reservable)
- Recreation Program
- Hiking Trail
- Swimming with Sand Beach
- Fishing in Lake Ontario
- Bicycling on Campground Roads
- Baseball Field, Volleyball Court, Tetherball, Horseshoe Pit, and Playground
- Boat Launch and Marina
- Cross Country Skiing and Snowshoeing
- Concession, Observation Area, and Overlook

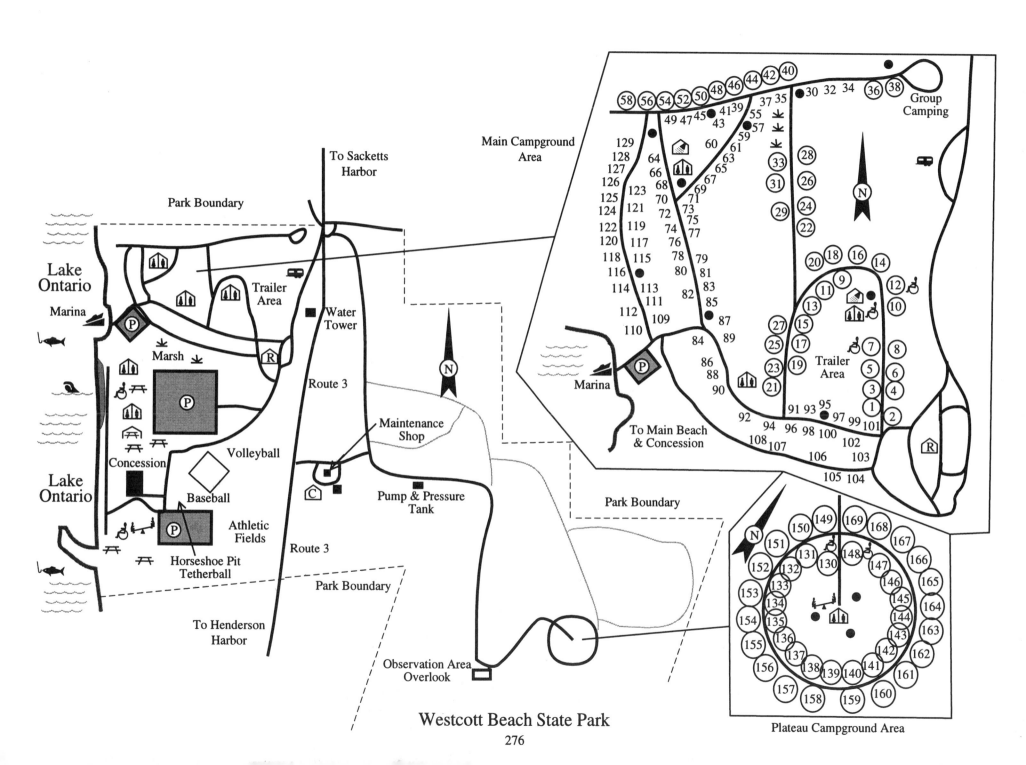

Westcott Beach State Park

276

Whetstone Gulf State Park

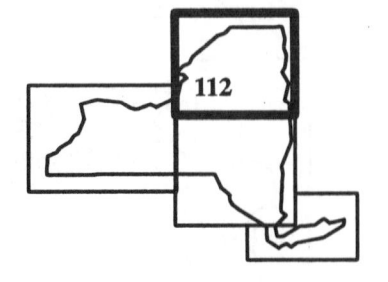

RD #2, Lowville, NY 13367

(315) 376-6630

- Located 6 miles south of Lowville or 15 miles north of Boonville off State Route 26
- Open mid–May through mid–September for camping
- State Park is Open All Year
- 62 Tent & Trailer Sites (12 electric sites, trailer dump)
- 2,100 Acres
- Comfort Station (flush toilets & sink) and Showers
- Potable Water (throughout campground)
- Public Telephone
- Pets Allowed
- Handicapped Accessible
- Picnic Areas
- Picnic Pavilion (reservable)
- Hiking Trails and Gorge Trail
- Exercise Course
- Swimming with Sand Beach and Bath House
- Fishing in Whetstone Gulf Reservoir (5 miles west)
- Hunting
- Bicycling and Rollerblading on Campground Roads
- Playground
- Boat Launch (cartop launch at Whetstone Gulf Reservoir – 5 miles west)
- Cross Country Skiing, Snowshoeing, and Snowmobiling

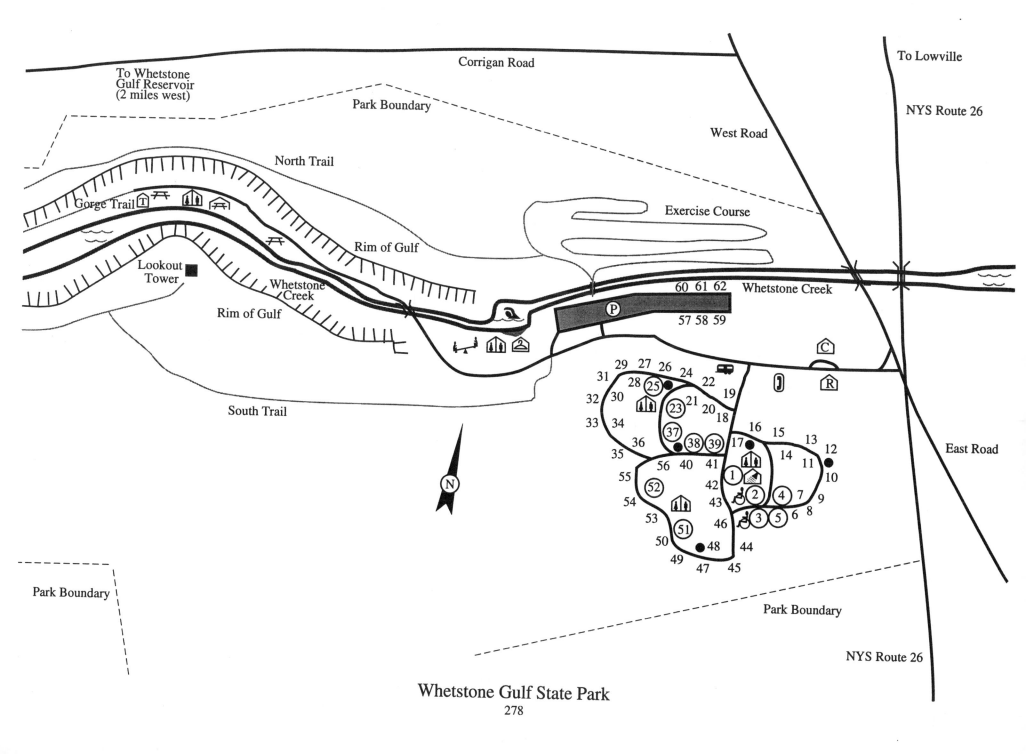

Whetstone Gulf State Park

278

Wildwood State Park

Hulse Landing Road, P.O. Box 518, Wading River, NY 11792

(631) 929–4314

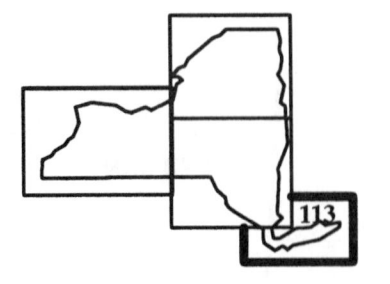

- Located 2 miles east of Wading River or 7 miles northwest of Riverhead off State Route 25A
- Open April through mid–October for camping
- 320 Tent & Trailer Sites (80 trailer sites located on non–loop sites # 1–80, trailer dump, and 69 platform sites)
- 767 Acres
- Comfort Station (flush toilets & sink) and Showers
- Potable Water
- Handicapped Accessible
- Picnic Area
- Recreation Program
- Hiking Trails
- Swimming with Sand Beach and Bath House
- Fishing in Long Island Sound
- Bicycling on Campground Roads
- Baseball Field, Basketball Court, Volleyball Court, and Playground
- First Aid, Refreshment Stand, Camp Store, and Playfield
- Cross Country Skiing

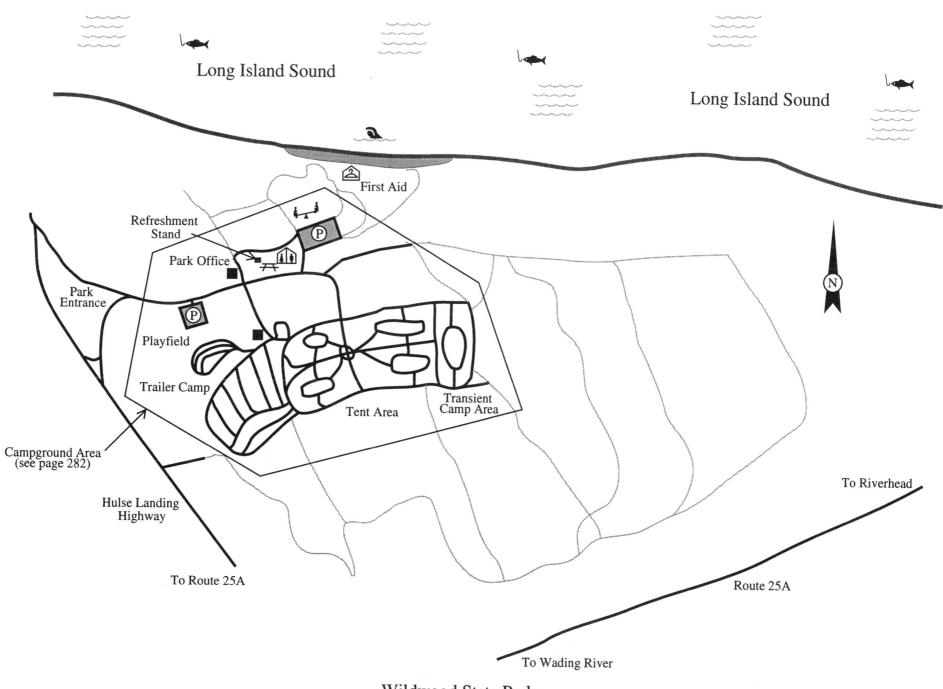

Long Island Sound

Long Island Sound

First Aid

Refreshment
Stand

Park Office

Park
Entrance

Playfield

Trailer Camp

Campground Area
(see page 282)

Hulse Landing
Highway

To Route 25A

Tent Area

Transient
Camp Area

N

To Riverhead

Route 25A

To Wading River

Wildwood State Park

Wildwood State Park

(see page 279 for campground information and main park map)

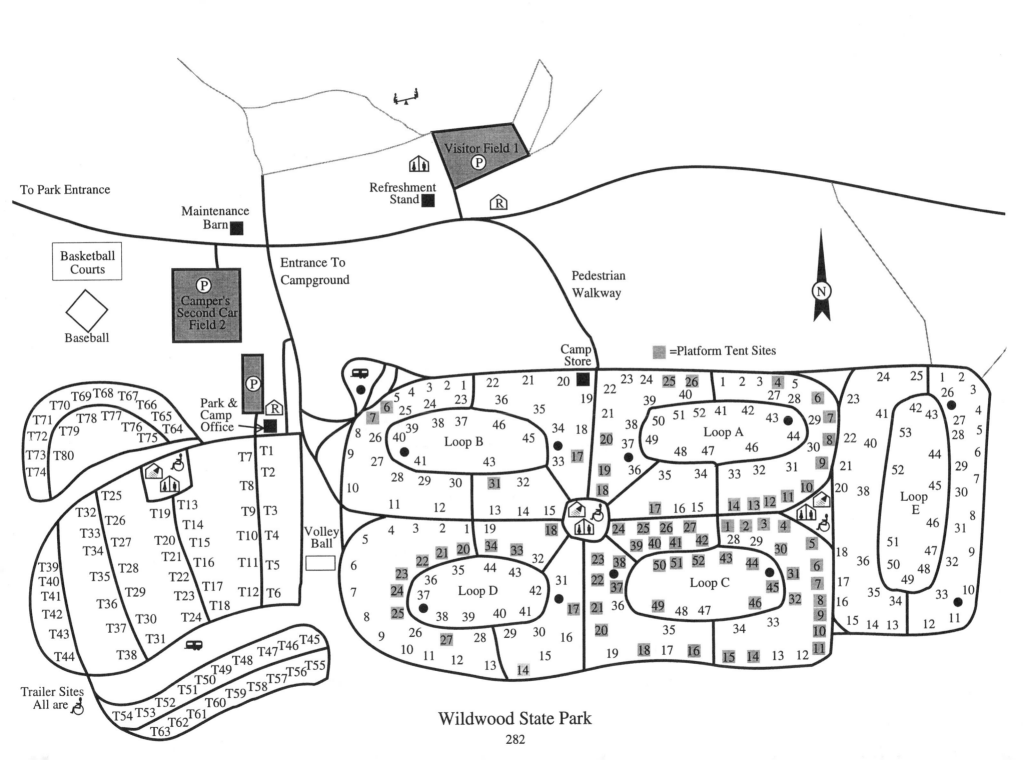

Wildwood State Park

282

Wilmington Notch Public Campground

State Route 86, P. O. Box 176, Wilmington, NY 12997

(518) 946–7172

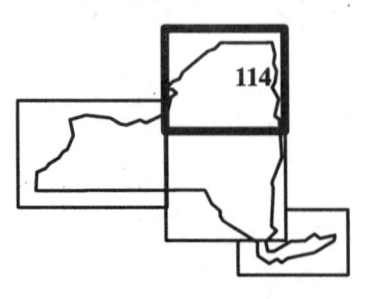

- Located 4 miles south of Wilmington or 8 miles northeast of Lake Placid off State Route 86
- Open May through mid–October for camping
- 54 Tent & Trailer Sites (no electric sites, trailer dump)
- 9 Acres
- Comfort Station (flush toilets & sink) and Showers
- Potable Water
- Pets Allowed
- Handicapped Accessible
- Picnic Area
- Hiking Trails (within approximately 5 miles)
- Fishing in Ausable River

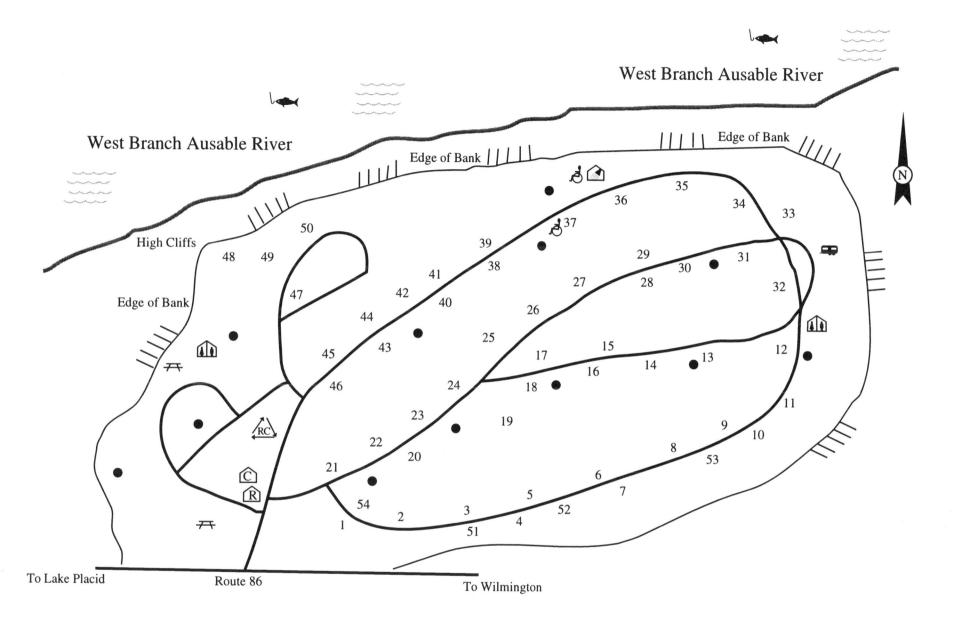

West Branch Ausable River

West Branch Ausable River

Edge of Bank

Edge of Bank

High Cliffs

Edge of Bank

N

To Lake Placid

Route 86

To Wilmington

Wilmington Notch Public Campground

284

Woodland Valley Public Campground

1319 Woodland Valley Road, Phoenicia, NY 12464

(845) 688–7647

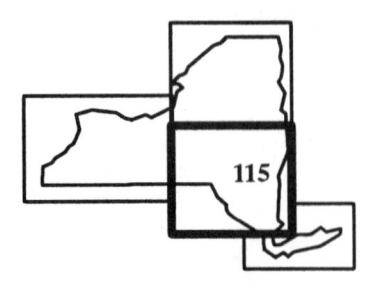

- Located 4 miles southwest of Phoenicia off State Route 28
- Open mid–May through mid–October for camping
- 60 Tent & Trailer Sites (no electric sites, trailer dump)
- 15 Acres
- Comfort Station (flush toilets & sink) and Showers
- Potable Water
- Public Telephone
- Pets Allowed
- Handicapped Accessible
- Picnic Area
- Hiking Trails
- Fishing in Woodland Stream

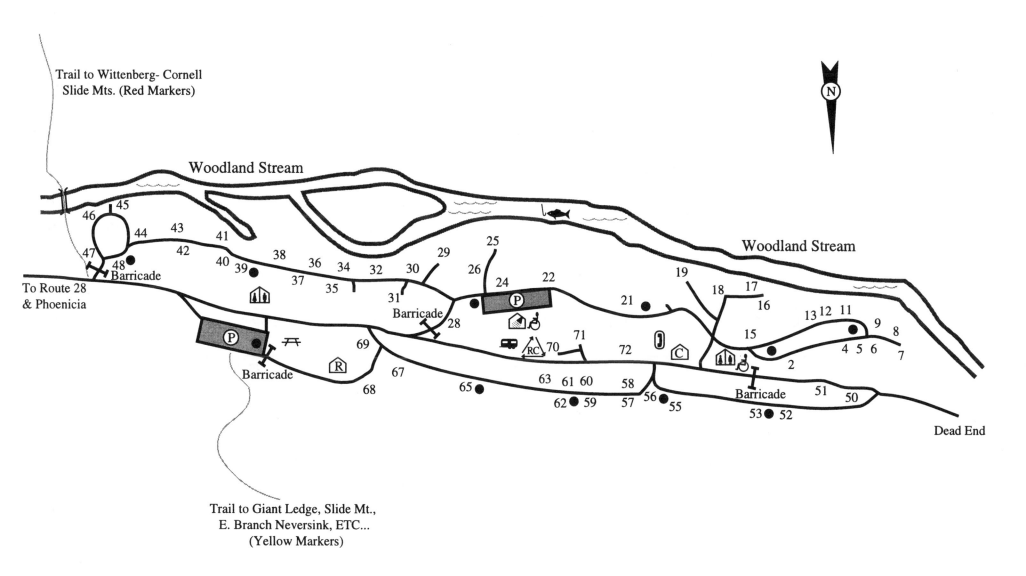

Trail to Wittenberg- Cornell
Slide Mts. (Red Markers)

N

Woodland Stream

45
46
44   43   41
47   38
42
48   40 39   36   34   32   29   25
Barricade   37   35   31   26   24   22
To Route 28   Barricade 28
& Phoenicia

Woodland Stream

19
18   17
16
21   13 12 11
15   9 8
2   4 5 6 7

P
R
Barricade
69
68   67
65
63 61 60   58   51 50
62 59   57   56 55
53 52

71
72
70
RC   C
Barricade

Dead End

Trail to Giant Ledge, Slide Mt.,
E. Branch Neversink, ETC...
(Yellow Markers)

Woodland Valley Public Campground

New York State Parks

Western New York

(without camping sites)

Allen Treman Marine	Ithaca	(607) 272-1460	Picnic Tables, Fishing, Boat Launch & Marina
Battle Island	Fulton	(315) 593-3408	Picnic Tables & Cross Country Skiing
Beaver Island	Grand Island	(716) 773-3271	Picnic Tables & Pavilion, Recreation Program, Nature Trail, Bicycling, Fishing, Hunting, Marina, Cross Country Skiing, Snowmobiling & Snowshoeing
Big Six Marina	Grand Island	(716) 773-3271	Fishing, Hand Boat Launch & Marina
Bonavista	Willard	(607) 869-5482	Picnic Tables & Golf Course
Buckhorn Island	Grand Island	(716) 773-3721	Hiking, Nature Trail, Bicycling, Fishing & Cross Country Skiing
Canandaigua Lake Marine	Canandaigua	(585) 394-9420	Fishing & Boat Launch
Conesus Lake	Livonia	(585) 493-3600	Picnic Tables, Fishing & Boat Launch
Dean's Cove Boat Launch	Cayuga Lake	(315) 586-5163	Fishing & Boat Launch
Devil's Hole	Niagara Falls	(716) 278-1762	Picnic Tables, Hiking, Nature Trail, Fishing & Cross Country Skiing
Earl Brydges Artpark	Lewiston	(716) 754-9000	Picnic Tables & Pavilion, Recreation Program, Hiking, Nature Trail, Fishing & Cross Country Skiing
Fort Niagara	Youngstown	(716) 745-7273	Picnic Tables & Pavilion, Swimming Pool, Recreation Program, Hiking, Nature Trail, Fishing, Hunting, Hand Boat Launch, Cross Country Skiing, Snowmobiling & Sledding
Harriet Hollister Spencer	Honeoye	(585) 335-8111	Picnic Tables & Pavilion, Hiking, Bicycling, Hunting & Cross Country Skiing

Honeoye Lake Boat Launch	Honeoye	(585) 335-8111	Fishing & Boat Launch
Irondequoit Bay Marine Park	Irondequoit	(585) 964-2462	Fishing & Boat Launch
Joseph Davies	Lewiston	(716) 754-4596	Picnic Tables & Pavilion, Frisbee Golf, Hiking, Fishing, Hunting, Cross Country Skiing & Snowmobiling
Lodi Point	Lodi	(315) 582-6392	Picnic Tables & Pavilion, Fishing, Boat Launch & Marina
Long Point	Aurora	(315) 364-8864	Picnic Tables, Swimming, Fishing, Hunting & Boat Launch
Long Point on Lake Chautauqua	Bemus Point	(716) 386-2722	Picnic Tables & Pavilion, Swimming, Recreation Program, Hiking, Nature Trail, Bicycling, Fishing, Boat Launch, Marina, Cross Country Skiing & Snowmobiling
Mark Twain	Horseheads	(607) 739-0034	Hunting
Niagara Reservation	Niagara Falls	(716) 278-1796	Picnic Tables, Recreation Program, Hiking, Nature Trail, Bicycling, Fishing, Cross Country Skiing & Museum
Oak Orchard Marine	Oak Orchard	(716) 682-4888	Picnic Tables, Fishing & Boat Launch
Pinnacle	Addison	(607) 359-2767	Picnic Tables & Pavilion, Hiking, Fishing, Hunting & Cross Country Skiing
Reservoir	Lewiston	(716) 285-3891	Picnic Tables & Pavilion, Recreation Program, Hiking, Nature Trail, Bicycling, Fishing, Cross Country Skiing, Snowmobiling, Sledding & Playing Fields
Seneca Lake	Geneva	(315) 789-2331	Picnic Tables & Pavilion, Swimming, Bicycling, Fishing, Boat Launch, Marina & Playing Fields
Silver Lake	Silver Springs	(585) 493-3600	Picnic Tables, Hiking, Fishing, Hunting & Boat Launch
Whirlpool	Niagara Falls	(716) 278-1762	Picnic Tables & Pavilion, Recreation Program, Hiking, Nature Trail, Fishing & Cross Country Skiing

Western New York

Wilson-Tuscarora	Wilson	(716) 751-6361	Picnic Tables & Pavilion, Hiking, Nature Trail, Fishing, Hunting, Hand Boat Launch, Cross Country Skiing, Snowmobiling and Snowshoeing
Woodlawn Beach	Hamburg	(716) 826-1930	Swimming & Hiking

Northern New York

Fourth Lake Picnic Area	Hinckley	(315) 369-3224	Picnic Tables, Fishing & Boat Launch
Hinckley Reservoir Picnic Area	Hinckley	(315) 826-3800	Picnic Tables, Swimming & Fishing
Lake George Battlefield Picnic Area	Lake George Village	(518) 623-3671	Picnic Tables
Lake George Beach	Lake George Village	(518) 668-3352	Picnic Tables & Swimming
Point Au Roche	Plattsburgh	(518) 563-0369	Picnic Tables & Pavilion, Swimming, Recreation Program, Hiking, Nature Trail, Bicycling, Fishing, Boat Launch & Cross Country Skiing
Prospect Mountain	Lake George Village	(518) 668-5198	Picnic Tables & Hiking
St. Lawrence Golf Course	Odgensburg	(315) 393-1977	Hiking & Cross Country Skiing
Waterson Point	Wellesley Island	(518) 482-2722	Picnic Tables & Pavilion, & Fishing (access by boat only)

Southern New York

Bear Mountain	Bear Mountain	(845) 786-2701	Picnic Tables, Swimming Pool, Recreation Program, Hiking, Nature Trail, Bicycling, Fishing, Boat Rental, Cross Country Skiing & Museum
Belleayre Mountain	Pine Hill Village	(845) 254-5600	Picnic Tables & Swimming
Blauvelt	Nyack	(845) 359-0544	Hiking
Cherry Plain	Stephentown	.(518) 733-5400	Picnic Tables & Pavilion, Swimming, Recreation Program, Hiking, Nature Trail, Bicycling, Fishing, Hunting, Hand Boat Launch, Boat Rental, Cross Country Skiing & Snowmobiling
Clark Reservation	Syracuse	(315) 492-1590	Picnic Tables & Pavilion, Recreation Program, Hiking, Nature Trail & Fishing
Franklin D. Roosevelt	Yorktown	(914) 245-4434	Picnic Tables & Pavilion, Swimming Pool, Recreation Program, Hiking, Nature Trail, Bicycling, Fishing, Boat Launch, Boat Rental, Cross Country Skiing & Snowmobiling
Goosepond Mountain	Monroe	(845) 786-2701	Hiking & Bridle Path
Grafton Lakes	Troy	(518) 279-1155	Picnic Tables & Pavilion, Swimming, Recreation Program, Hiking, Nature Trail, Bridle Path, Bicycling, Fishing, Hunting, Hand Boat Launch, Boat Rental, Cross Country Skiing & Snowmobiling
Harriman	Bear Mountain	(845) 786-2701	Picnic Trails, Hiking, Bridle Path, Fishing, and Cross Country Skiing
Harriman-Anthony Wayne	Bear Mountain	(845) 942-2560	Picnic Tables, Hiking, Biking, Cross Country Skiing & Playing Fields
Harriman-Lake Sebago Beach	Sloatsburg	(845) 351-2583	Picnic Tables, Swimming, Hiking, Fishing, Hand Boat Launch, Boat Rental & Playing Fields
Harriman-Lake Tiorati Beach	Sloatsburg	(845) 351-2568	Picnic Tables, Swimming, Hiking, Fishing, Hand Boat Launch & Boat Rental
Harriman-Lake Welch Beach	Stony Point	(845) 947-2444	Picnic Tables, Swimming, Hiking, Fishing, Hand Boat Launch, Boat Rental & Snowmobiling

Harriman-Silver Mine	Bear Mountain	(845) 351-2568	Picnic Tables, Hiking, Fishing & Boat Launch
High Tor	Haverstraw	(845) 634-8074	Picnic Tables, Swimming Pool, Hiking & Playing Fields
Highland Lakes	Middletown	(845) 786-2701	Bridle Path, Hiking & Fishing
Hudson Highlands	Beacon	(845) 225-7207	Hiking, Fishing & Hunting
Hudson River Islands	Coxsackie	(518) 872-1237	Picnic Tables & Pavilion, Hiking, Fishing & Hunting, 16 primitive campsites (no designated area, no charge to camp) available on first come first serve basis at Gays Point & Stockport (access by boat only)
Hunts Pond	New Berlin	(607) 859-2249	Picnic Tables, Hiking, Fishing, Hunting, & Hand Boat Launch, 18 primitive campsites (reservable only through the park and available on first come first serve basis)
John Boyd Thacher	Albany	(518) 872-1237	Picnic Tables & Pavilion, Swimming Pool, Recreation Program, Hiking, Nature Trail, Bicycling, Cross Country Skiing & Snowmobiling
Lake Superior	Monticello	(845) 794-3000	Picnic Tables, Swimming, Fishing, Hunting, Boat Launch & Boat Rental
Mine Kill	Middleburgh	(518) 827-6111	Picnic Tables & Pavilion, Swimming Pool, Recreation Program, Hiking, Nature Trail, Fishing, Hunting, Boat Launch, Cross Country Skiing & Snowmobiling
Minnewaska	New Paltz	(845) 255-0752	Picnic Tables, Swimming, Hiking, Bridle Path, Bicycling, Hunting, Hand Boat Launch & Cross Country Skiing
Nyack Beach	Nyack	(845) 286-3020	Picnic Tables, Hiking, Bicycling, Fishing, Boat Launch & Cross Country Skiing
Odgen Mills	Hyde Park	(845) 889-4646	Picnic Tables, Recreation Program, Hiking, Bridle Path, Bicycling, Fishing, Cross Country Skiing & Sledding
Old Croton Trailway	Croton Reservoir	(914) 245-4434	Hiking, Bicycling & Cross Country Skiing
Old Erie Canal	Fayetteville, Oneida, Rome	(315) 687-7821	Picnic Tables & Pavilion, Hiking, Nature Trail, Bridle Path, Bicycling, Fishing, Hand Boat Launch & Snowmobiling
Pebbles Island	Cohoes	(518) 237-8643	Picnic Tables & Pavilion, Hiking, Fishing & Cross Country Skiing

Southern New York

Rockefeller	Tarrytown	(914) 631-1470	Hiking, Bridle Path, Nature Trail, Fishing & Cross Country Skiing
Rockland Lake	Congers	(845) 286-3020	Picnic Tables, Swimming Pool, Recreation Program, Hiking, Nature Trail, Bicycling, Fishing, Hand Boat Launch & Cross Country Skiing
Saratoga Boat Launch	Saratoga Springs	(518) 584-2535	Boat Launch
Saratoga Spa	Saratoga Springs	(518) 584-2535	Picnic Tables & Pavilion, Swimming Pool, Recreation Program, Hiking, Nature Trail, Bicycling, Fishing, Cross Country Skiing & Museum
Storm King	Cornwall	(845) 786-2701	Hiking & Hunting
Tallman Mountain	Piermont	(845) 359-0544	Picnic Tables, Swimming Pool, Hiking, Bicycling & Fishing

New York City and Long Island

Bayard Cutting Arboretum	Great River	(631) 581-1002	Recreation Program & Nature Trails
Bayswater Point State Park	Jamaica Bay, Queens	(212) 694-3722	Hiking, Fishing & Nature Trail
Belmont Lake	North Babylon	(631) 667-5055	Picnic Tables & Pavilion, Recreation Program, Hiking, Nature Trail, Bridle Path, Bicycling, Fishing, Boat Rental & Cross Country Skiing
Bethpage	Farmingdale	(516) 249-0701	Picnic Tables, Recreation Program, Hiking, Nature Trail, Bridle Path, Bicycling, Cross Country Skiing, Sledding & Playing Fields
Caleb Smith Preserve	Smithtown	(631) 265-1054	Recreation Program, Hiking, Nature Trail, Fishing & Cross Country Skiing
Captree	Jones Beach	(631) 669-0449	Picnic Tables, Recreation Program, Fishing, Hand Boat Launch & Marina

Caumsett	Lloyd Neck	(631) 423-1770	Recreation Program, Hiking, Nature Trail, Bridle Path, Bicycling, Fishing & Cross Country Skiing
Clay Pit Ponds Preserve	Staten Island	(718) 967-1976	Picnic Tables & Pavilion, Recreation Program, Hiking, Nature Trails & Bridle Path
Connetquot River Preserve	Oakdale/Bohemia	(631) 581-1005	Recreation Program, Hiking, Nature Trail, Bridle Path, Fishing, Cross Country Skiing, Snowshoeing & Museum
Empire - Fulton Ferry	Brooklyn	(718) 858-4708	Picnic Tables
Gov. Alfred Smith/Sunken Meadow	Kings Park	(631) 269-4333	Picnic Tables, Swimming, Recreation Program, Hiking, Nature Trail, Bridle Path, Bicycling, Fishing & Cross Country Skiing
Hempstead Lake	West Hempstead	(516) 766-1029	Picnic Tables & Pavilion, Recreation Program, Hiking, Bridle Path, Bicycling, Fishing, Boat Launch & Cross Country Skiing
Jones Beach	Wantagh	(516) 785-1600	Picnic Tables, Swimming Pool, Recreation Program, Hiking, Bicycling, Fishing, Marina & Museum
Montauk Downs	Montauk	(631) 668-3781	Swimming Pool & Recreation Program
Montauk Point	Montauk	(631) 668-3781	Picnic Tables, Hiking, Nature Trail, Bridle Path, Fishing, Hunting & Cross Country Skiing
Orient Beach	Orient	(631) 323-2440	Picnic Tables & Pavilion, Swimming, Recreation Program, Hiking, Nature Trails, Bicycling & Fishing
Riverbank	Manhatten	(212) 694-3600	Picnic Tables, Swimming Pool, Recreation Program, Hiking, Playing Fields & Performing Arts Center
Robert Moses	Fire Island	(631) 669-0470	Picnic Tables, Swimming, Recreation Program, Fishing & Marina
Roberto Clemente	Bronx	(718) 299-8750	Picnic Tables, Swimming Pool, Recreation Program, Bicycling & Playing Fields
Valley Stream	Valley Stream	(516) 825-4128	Picnic Tables & Pavilion, Recreation Program, Nature Trail, Bicycling, Cross Country Skiing & Playing Fields

New York State Park Golf Courses

	Map Location	Nearest City	Telephone	Yards	Par
Battle Island	Western	Fulton	(315) 593-3408	5973	72
Beaver Island	Western	Grand Island	(716) 773-3271	6779	72
Bethpage	Long Island	Farmingdale	(516) 249-0700	7295	71
Bonavista	Western	Ovid	(607) 869-5482	3332	36
Chenango Valley	Southern	Chenango Falls	(607) 648-5251	6271	72
Dinsmore	Southern	Staatsburg	(845) 889-4071	5719	70
Gov. Alfred Smith/Sunken Meadow	Long Island	Kings Park	(631) 269-5351	3125	36
Green Lakes	Southern	Fayetteville	(315) 637-0258	6212	71
James Baird (pitch and putt)	Southern	Pleasant Valley	(845) 452-1489	6616	71
Jones Beach	Long Island	Wantagh	(516) 785-1600	1039	54
Montauk Downs	Long Island	Montauk	(631) 668-5000	6762	72
Pinnacle	Western	Addison	(607) 359-2767	3234	36
Robert Moses (pitch and putt)	Long Island	Babylon	(631) 669-0449	1425	55
Rockland Lake	Southern	Congers	(845) 268-7275	6864	72
Sag Harbor	Long Island	Sag Harbor	(631) 725-2503	2661	35
Saratoga Spa	Northern	Saratoga Springs	(518) 584-3137	7098	72
Soaring Eagles / Mark Twain	Western	Horseheads	(607) 739-0034	6625	72
St. Lawrence	Northern	Ogdensburg	(315) 393-2286	5719	70
Wellesley Island	Northern	Fineview	(315) 482-9622	2730	35

Camping Packing List

___ Air Mattress/Cot	___ Extension Cord	___ Paper Towels
___ Axe	___ Drying Towel	___ Pans
___ BBQ Utensils	___ Firewood	___ Playing Cards
___ Beach Blanket	___ First Aid Kit	___ Pots and Lids
___ Beach Towels	___ Flashlight and Batteries	___ Radio
___ Bug Spray	___ Garbage Bags	___ Raincoat
___ Can Opener	___ Ground Cloth / Tarp	___ Rain Fly
___ Candles / Citronella	___ Hammer	___ Rope
___ Chairs	___ Hand Soap	___ Saw
___ Charcoal and Lighter Fluid	___ Hiking Boots	___ Screen Room
___ Coffee	___ Hot Mitt	___ Shovel
___ Coffee Cups	___ Hot Pad / Trivet	___ Silverware
___ Coffee Pot	___ Ice	___ Sleeping Bags
___ Compass	___ Ice Cooler	___ Sponge
___ Cook Kit	___ Kindling Wood	___ Suntan Lotion
___ Cooking Grate	___ Knife - Swiss Army	___ Tablecloth and Clamps
___ Cooking Griddle	___ Lantern and Fuel	___ Tent
___ Cooking Utensils	___ Light	___ Tent Stakes
___ Cutting Board	___ Matches	___ Toasting Forks
___ Day / Fanny Pack	___ Measuring Cup	___ Toilet Paper
___ Dining Fly	___ Mirror	___ Wash Basin
___ Dish Detergent	___ Napkins	___ Wash Towel
___ Drink Cups	___ Newspaper (for fire)	___ Water Container

State Park and Campground Summary

Park / Campground Visited	Date	Preferred Campsites	General Notes and Comments

State Park and Campground Summary

Park / Campground Visited	Date	Preferred Campsites	General Notes and Comments

State Park and Campground Summary

Park / Campground Visited	Date	Preferred Campsites	General Notes and Comments